U.S.S.R.

MANCHURIA
(MANCHUKUO)
Japanese Occupation

Harbin

Vladivostok

Chahar

Mukden

Mongolia

JAPANESE

EMPIRE

Suiyuan

THE GREAT WALL

SEA OF JAPAN

Pehtaiho

PEKING

Tsinghai

Dairen

Inchon

JAPAN

Hopei   Tientsin   Port Arthur

Chefoo   Weihaiwei

KOREA
(CHOSEN)

Tsinan

Yenan   Shansi   Shantung

Pusan

Tsingtao   YELLOW SEA

Lienyunkang

Yellow River   Kaifeng   Haichow

Sian   Honan   Kiangsu

Shensi   Anhwei

Three   Nanking   Shanghai

Gorges   Soochow   EAST CHINA SEA

wan Wanhsien   Hupei   Wuhu

Ichang   Anking

Hankow   Ningpo

Chungking   Yochow   Kukiang   Chekiang

Changsha   Nanchang

Hunan   Kiangsi

eichow   Foochow   Matsu

Fukien   Taipei

Kweilin

Kwangsi   Amoy

Yungnan   Quemoy   FORMOSA
(Jap. Occ.)

Kwangtung   Swatow

Si River   Canton

Pakhoi   Hong Kong

Macau
(Port.)   (Brit.)

Kwang-chow-wan
(Fr.)

Hoichow   Pratas Islands

PHILIPPINES
(U.S.)

Hainan   SOUTH CHINA SEA

Meters
6000
4000
2000
1000
500
50
0
-100
-1000

Hainan

Paracel Islands

SOUTH CHINA SEA

INDOCHINA

PHILIPPINES
(U.S. Territory)

Spratly Islands

NORTH BORNEO
(Brit.)

MW01491111

AN AMERICAN IN CHINA

1936-1939

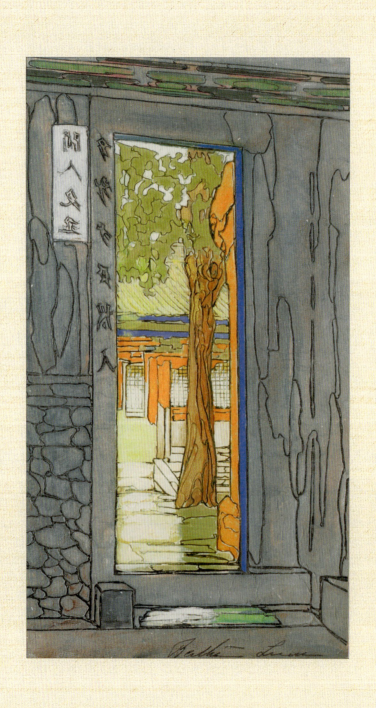

AN AMERICAN
IN CHINA

1936-1939

A MEMOIR
by
Gould H. Thomas

Published in the United States by Greatrix Press,
an imprint of Thomas & Sons Books,
New York, N.Y.

Text set in Times Roman
Printed in China
by C&C Offset

Library of Congress Control Number: 2004093983
ISBN 0-9758800-0-4

10 9 8 7 6 5 4 3 2 1
FIRST EDITION

To friends in far-off places
and to Marge and Merlin Fisk,
who did so much to help us settle
in Connecticut

Unless indicated otherwise

all black and white photographs are

by G.H. Thomas

CONTENTS

APPENDIX

ACKNOWLEDGMENTS

It has taken many years to edit the author's letters and put his book together. It had always been his ambition to publish the record of his China years but unfortunately he did not have the time or perhaps inclination to pursue what has proved to be a formidable task. This book could not have been accomplished without Mary Maki and Andrea Zimmerman, who helped with the word processing, setting up and proofing the manuscript. The New York offices of the National Tourist Office of the People's Republic of China; the Chinese Information and Culture Center of Taiwan; the Hong Kong Tourist Association; and the Japan National Tourist Organization have kindly supplied brochures, maps, photographs or information. Cheng Bede of the Hong Kong Film Archive has provided a great deal of background on Lily Lee, a film actress and close friend of the author's. The New York Times, the New York Public Library, the National Geographic Society, the Encyclopaedia Brittanica and the Internet have been vital research sources. Tess Johnston, author of several books on Western architecture in old China, has helped in determining the exact address of the Texas Company in Shanghai in the 1930's and verifying information about Shanghai and Canton. Thanks of course to Neil and Bill for all their careful work.

Beverley M. Thomas
BROOKFIELD, CONN. 2004

USE OF WADE-GILES

As the subject matter of the book is China in the 1930's, the old Wade-Giles system of romanizing Chinese and the conventional Post Office forms for place names have been used instead of the current system, Pinyin, which is now the international standard.

LIST OF MAPS

PREFACE

GOULD HUNTER THOMAS, born in New York City in 1912, was brought up in Hempstead, Long Island. Although named after a favorite uncle, he was always called Jim by his parents and Tommy by his friends.

After graduating from Yale University in 1934 he worked for Cargill Grain Company in Minneapolis, Minn., and Lincoln, Neb., and then Doubleday Doran Publishers in New York. In 1936 he thought he had saved enough money to go around the world and sailed to the Orient via the Panama Canal and San Francisco. He particularly wanted to see Peking.

He stayed a month in Peking, a charming, exotic city much loved by foreigners of all nationalities. When a segment of his trip, from Shanghai to Hong Kong via Manila on the *General Sherman*, was delayed by a strike in California, he became worried about having enough money to continue on to Europe. In Shanghai, however, he was fortunate to find a job with the Texas Company, later called Texaco. A new company, Caltex, was formed that year, owned jointly by the Texas Company and the Standard Oil Company of California. Jim was sent to Tsingtao as a marketing assistant.

Working for the oil company, he was able to see a part of Chinese life that few tourists saw. Apart from the missionaries, Westerners were scarce in the interior of Shantung Province. He visited agents in small towns and villages outside Tsingtao, sometimes staying several weeks at a time. An experienced Chinese employee always accompanied him to places where little had changed in hundreds of years and where everyone was always kind and courteous to him. Travel was slow and lodging uncomfortable unless he stayed at a missionary hostel. He found his travels to remote areas the most interesting of his trips. In Tsingtao, on the other hand, he enjoyed the cosmopolitan treaty- port life but knew this colonial lifestyle could not last much longer.

After the Japanese occupied the port city in January 1938, he was sent west to Chungking, the wartime capital of China, way up the Yangtze. It was full of refugees, there was much sickness, and conditions were miserable. He was surprised, however, to find himself looking after a large company house with several servants. In spite of the war and air raids, there were still things to enjoy. Instead of commuting on the Long Island Railway into New York, he crossed the Yangtze by launch or sampan every day when he went to the office. Then he was carried up the many stone steps by chair coolies. There were tennis games, picnics and always mosquitoes.

But the war situation in China became worse and World War II was about to break out in Europe. When he was transferred to Canton, which had been badly bombed, he began to worry about being interned by the Japanese if he stayed in China. He decided to resign and go back to the States. His romance with Lily Lee, a Chinese film actress, may also have influenced his decision.

During World War II, Jim served in Naval Intelligence, mostly in India, Ceylon and China. After the war's end he became assistant naval attaché in Nanking and left the Navy with the rank of commander. He married Beverley M. Poulton of Wraysbury, England, in December 1945.

In March 1947 he went back to work for Caltex in Tientsin and Canton until the Communists took over in 1949. His subsequent tours of duty included Okinawa in the Ryuku Islands; Wellington, New Zealand; Sydney, Australia; Bangkok and Tokyo. At the end of his career he worked briefly in Manhattan and then worked for Chevron, Caltex's parent company, in The Hague, Holland, and Brussels, Belgium.

In addition to taking many photographs he kept a detailed diary while he was in China, which he periodically sent as letters to his parents. These excerpts have been taken from his letters home.

Gould Hunter Thomas died in Connecticut in 1975 after a long struggle with cancer.

The author with Beverley M. Poulton, formerly of the Women's Royal Navy Service (WRNS), at the U.S. Navy Officers Mess in Shanghai in 1946, not long after their marriage in December 1945 in Colombo, Ceylon.

I

THE VOYAGE OUT

1

New York to San Francisco
Via the Panama Canal

July 1936

O N THE MORNING of the twenty-eighth of July, I was dressed and out on the deck of the SS *California* at quarter to five. The sun was not due up for half an hour, but it was light enough to make out the long, low line of Cuba stretching along several miles off port side. Almost straight ahead was a cluster of lights where the land extended out a bit—that was my first sight of Havana. When the sun rose, the land we were sailing by proved to be all green jungle with just a few scattered houses.

The famous landmark Morro Castle could be seen now just ahead. Right at the point where we started swinging in, we passed the Cunarder SS *Carinthia* on her way out. Another minute and we were right in the narrow passage leading to the wider harbor with its huge docks. At the narrowest point stands the castle, just a hundred feet or so from a ship passing through. It is on the left, and on the right, at no greater distance, are the streets and buildings of the city. The sun was shining brightly by that time. It was a wonderful sight, no matter which way I looked.

As we warped into position alongside the dock, the usual native boys rowed about in little boats on the off side and dived for coins. Father Hunkele, a fellow passenger watching them with me, said that the clipped English they used while begging for money to be thrown was not really part of their speech at all. They speak only Spanish he said and have learned such expressions as "Please, boss, money" not as real words but as cries or exclamations to attract attention.

As soon as the ship had docked, we had to have our landing cards stamped by the Cuban officials in the lounge and could then pass down the gangplank.

Postcard of the SS California *arriving in Havana Harbor.*

Father Hunkele had told me that he would be visiting friends all day, otherwise I would have had the luck of seeing the town with an old hand as a guide. Practically all the other passengers had made reservations for sightseeing cars, most of them paying five dollars a person to be driven around with the English-speaking driver. Some of them had asked me to join their parties, but I refused, as I wanted to get around by myself.

I went down the gangway with Father Hunkele, who said that as he had a little time before seeing his friends, he would walk about a bit with me. We went along through the docks and out into a large square where the cars were waiting for the tourists who had not already signed up for a drive while still on the ship. The drivers hound you, follow you and pester you incessantly. But as soon as Father Hunkele opened up on them in Spanish, they dropped off like flies and went after other bait. He wanted to buy some stamps, and I had a couple of letters to mail, so we walked over to the post office, a converted old church with high domed ceilings and surprisingly cool.

When we left there we walked over to the famous old cathedral. It occupies one side of a stone-covered public square. On two sides of the square are beautiful old buildings used for housing some of the municipal offices, and on the side opposite the cathedral is the Havana Club. All the buildings, including the church, rise right from the edge of the square, and the stones are all the same color, rather darkish gray-brown. There are balconies all around on the second and third floors.

Entering the cathedral I was struck again by the wonderful coolness of big stone buildings, even on such a hot day. Several people were sitting on low benches scattered around the huge main nave, at the end of which was the altar. We walked down one side and into a much smaller chamber at the left in back of the altar. There was a crucifix on the wall, and three old women in lace shawls were kneeling on the floor muttering prayers. In this area, as well as in the main part of the church, there were large religious paintings, most of them in dim colors that fitted in with the atmosphere. But there were some newer ones in bright cheap colors that clashed terribly.

We went into other rooms or chapels, one of which was crowded with dark-skinned altar boys with long gray cloaks and white collars. In another was a larger-than-life statue of St. Christopher carrying a child across the stream.

When we came into the square again, the sun was still out but it was raining slightly; the cool drops felt good coming down on my head. The beauty of the square lies in its not having a single marring note. Everything you see is old and Spanish.

Postcard of Cathedral of Havana in the 1930's.

While walking down St. Ignatius Street, I gave a little girl a nickel for a rose to put in my buttonhole. A moment or so later, I remembered the stain I got on my Palm Beach suit from bougainvillea in Nassau, so I gave the rose to another little girl.

On St. Ignatius Street, as in most streets that I saw in Havana, two persons cannot walk abreast on the sidewalks for they are only a foot and a half or so wide. In most places where you pass people walking either way, someone has to step down into the street. To complicate things, every so often you come to a dog sound asleep on the sidewalk, and you must either step over him or take to the street. The cars keep their horns blowing almost steadily to warn people who are forced to leave the sidewalks.

Many of the buildings are apartment houses, each with an open passageway leading back to an open court. They are colored light blue or pink and always with potted flowers around. The people are dark, light and every shade in between. Kids swarm all over the place, especially in the courtyards. Some of them wear nothing but a little shirt coming down to the waist. A few small ones were running about bare.

I left Father Hunkele about nine o'clock and set out on my own to find the Capitol, which is just as impressive as ours in Washington. Since the sun was almost killing me by this time, I sat down for a half-hour or so on a bench in the palm-filled park beside the Capitol. It was interesting just sitting there watching, being alone the whole day and not in one of the cars with their guides.

From the Capitol down to the harbor is a magnificent wide boulevard called the Prado. One walks not beside the buildings but on the boulevard part between two rows of giant palms. When you reach the harbor you are almost directly across from Morro Castle again. From there, I walked along back to a streetcar station right near the dock. Father Hunkele had told me that if I got on at that spot, I would get a good ride out to the other side of Havana and return. The tracks were elevated there at the station. I trotted up the steps and leaned against the rail on the platform until a car came along. Several Cubans and I got on. The conductor, a nice-looking young fellow, came up to me and held out his hand. I gave him an American half-dollar, which he took readily. For change, I got nine Cuban nickels. I asked him if the car went over and then returned to the ship. He stared at me and shaking his head answered me in Spanish in a friendly but naturally wholly unintelligible fashion. I gave up for the time being, but in a moment he was back jabbering at me and holding out a Cuban quarter. I finally realized he was out of nickels and needed some of mine to make change for a passenger who had just boarded. I gave him five nickels and took the quarter. He was all smiles and said, "Muchas gracias, señor," several times.

Pretty soon I was the only passenger. When the conductor came up beside me, I tried to figure out a way of getting where I wanted to go. I pulled out my landing card, on which there was some Spanish, found the word for port and tried it on him. He understood but pointing to the car we were in, shook his head, meaning that it didn't go there. He made motions saying that he would show me when we got to the end of the line. We laughed a lot together; at one point he offered me a Cuban cigarette, which I took, giving him a Chesterfield in return. It was quite an experience. I think he enjoyed it as much as I. At the end of the line he pointed out a car and indicated that I should show the conductor my landing card. We waved good-bye and I boarded the other car. Luckily for the sake of sightseeing, we came a different route, just as novel and interesting as the other. I was planning to go back to the ship and change my clothes, drenched with perspiration not rain.

Suddenly I was absolutely befuddled as to directions and couldn't see any familiar landmarks. But then around a turn appeared the famous Sloppy Joe's. I walked in and there at the bar were Sheelagh and David Arnold. Although it doesn't look like an internationally known place, Sloppy Joe's is a lot of fun, with a hot rumba band and a lively, informal atmosphere. A couple of Cuba Libres later, I felt much refreshed. When we had danced a bit, we hired a little kid to lead us back through the streets to the ship for a late lunch or early tea. It was still so hot. The air felt soaking wet and the sun came down on my head like a steam hammer.

I met some other young people on the ship after dinner, and we all went back on shore and sauntered about for a while. I would have loved to have stayed at least a week in Havana, a beautiful and colorful place. One thing that amused me was an advertising card on one of the streetcars. All were in Spanish but this one, which read: DINE AND DANCE ON THE ASTOR ROOF. NO COVER CHARGE. TIMES SQUARE.

On a little dinky side street behind the Capitol there is a Woolworth five-and-ten, and on practically every corner there is combination coffee shop and bar. All over one meets skinny rag-and-bone women selling chances of public

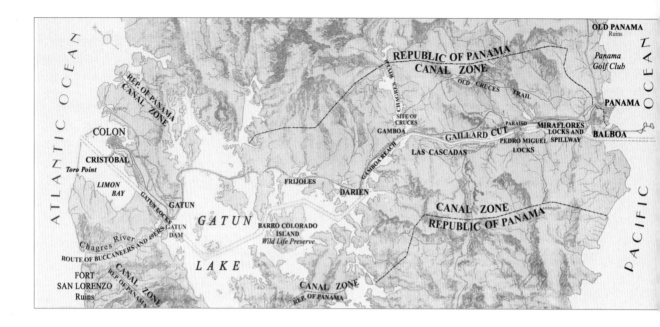

A 1930's map of the Canal Zone for Panama Pacific passengers. The rather unorthodox positioning, initially confusing, is correct. See North on compass.

lottery or numbers game. *Show Boat,* called *Magnolia* here, was playing at one of the theaters. All in all, I had a wonderful time and felt I did some good sight-seeing.

Sailing from Havana was only a little less exciting than entering the port. I got a big kick, in fact, at all our stops in watching the nautical details of docking and leaving. I never cease to wonder at the ease with which those big ships are handled. In Havana particularly, where the harbor is narrow at the docks, I was surprised to see how we managed to back around without the aid of tugs.

The next two days were hot and lazy but full of fun. We went swimming in the pool and I got a darker tan than I ever had. Bingo in the smoking room at 11 A.M. was a regular feature all the way and exciting to play, although I never won. In the evening there was dancing under the stars, "horse racing" in the lounge and movies in the air-conditioned first-class dining room. The films were pretty awful for the most part, but it was a good chance to cool off, so we all went.

Along this part of the trip we could see small flying fish and an occasional school of porpoises. At night there were wonderful electric displays in the sky, heat lightning really, but of a sort I have never seen.

Thursday night I went to bed right after the dancing and the movies so I could get up early for our arrival at Cristobal, in the Canal Zone. As Father Hunkele was leaving us there, he was up at 4:15 A.M., nervous, double-checking on his packing and looking out the porthole every other minute although it was pitch dark and nothing could be seen. I got up a little after four, took a shower, dressed and went up on deck to find a hot, humid drizzle of rain. Up

ahead I could see a cluster of lights, which I discovered later, when we passed through the breakwater, were ships in the harbor and not coming from the city. The rain stopped just before the sun appeared, but the sky remained cloudy and overcast.

Locks at Panama Canal in 2000.

It was 5:15 when we tied up at Cristobal, and I wasn't the only one on deck. A group of chorus girl entertainers left us there, along with Father Hunkele and a few other people. I was sorry to see Father go; he reminded me of Billy Phelps[1] in his innate happiness and enthusiasm for life. I made a real friend. During our long discussions on Catholicism and the history of the Roman Church, I found him a great combination of rigid dogma and broadness of mind. His address is: The Palace of the Archbishop, Guatemala.

Although we were tied up at Cristobal for only two hours, some of the through passengers were allowed to land. At 7:30 we sailed and half an hour later entered the first of the locks, Gatun. The water level of the two oceans is practically the same, but ships are raised eighty-five feet to the level of Gatun Lake and then lowered the same distance the other side. It is a marvelous process and can't fail to give one the proper thrill.

The skies remained overcast, a tremendous break for us as the temperature on deck was usually intolerable. It wasn't cool but it was bearable and without glare. The most surprising feature of the whole thing was that instead of an artificial-looking concrete canal, the passage in many parts resembles a narrow river winding through jungle.

---

1. William Lyon Phelps, 1865-1943, was a popular Yale professor, critic and scholar.

It took from eight in the morning until three in the afternoon to make the passage of the canal, and at the latter hour, we tied up at Balboa. There are two cities on the Pacific side, Balboa and Panama. Balboa is the modern, clean city that arose as the result of the construction of the canal, while Panama is the old native city, mostly Spanish and black. There is nothing to see in Balboa except the Army and Navy posts. Sheelagh, David and I took a bus over to Panama, where we walked about and Sheelagh bought some perfume at a good price. The city is somewhat like Havana in its atmosphere, but I much prefer the latter. The public buildings are far inferior to those in Cuba's capital, and the layout of the streets is poor. The main part of town reminded me of a small city in the Midwest, only not so clean.

The sun was out by this time, and the whole place was hot, sticky and muggy. Some of the passengers professed to like the climate in the Zone, but it's far too humid for me. It would take a long time to get used to it.

The three of us dropped in at Kelley's for a beer and to get out of the sun. A bit later, an old fellow sitting at the bar started talking to us. A soldier of fortune, he has apparently been mixed up in every revolution in those parts for the past forty years, sometimes losing, sometimes winning but always ready for the next one. He even has an office and a phone number in Panama so plotting generals can get hold of him quickly. We learned from the Japanese bartender that his story was mostly the truth.

While at Kelley's we made arrangements to be driven to Old Panama, about twelve or thirteen miles away. Here lie the ruins of a city founded about 1508 and destroyed in a single night in 1671 during a raid by the buccaneer Henry Morgan and his men. It is one of the few things really worth seeing at that end of the Canal.

The drive to get there was interesting. Upon leaving the Canal Zone, you enter the Republic of Panama, where the countryside is wholly tropical in aspect. Making the setting complete was a characteristically tropical downpour on the way out. It came down in torrents.

On arrival the rain had just about stopped, allowing us to get out of the car and look around on foot. The most arresting building was the old ruined church built in 1530, the oldest structure, in my record. I walked through the ruins, up on a small bluff, and there lying before me was the Pacific Ocean. I don't believe there's a better spot from which to view the Pacific for the first time. It was an experience I shall always remember. One could imagine that awful night over two and a half centuries ago when Morgan and his pirates wiped out a prosperous town.

Ruins of Old Panama, from 1930's brochure.

Back in Panama we climbed on a bus for the ship and retraced our way back to and through Balboa. Cars use the left side of the street, and the driving is reckless. I was expecting an accident any minute in the bus.

Dinner on the ship and then back to Panama for another look around at night and a few dances at beautiful El Rancho, which was wonderfully cool and had a swell dance floor and orchestra. I could have stayed there for hours. Eventually, it got so late, we thought we were going to miss the boat, due to sail at eleven. As it turned out, we didn't cast off until 12:30, but we had a hectic half-hour rushing back.

Although everyone said what a long stretch it was, the trip from Balboa to San Diego was idyllic: nobody wanted it to end. The tournaments started at this point, as well as the masquerade, the ship's concert and the captain's dinner. The first couple of days we were skimming the coast of Central America and often were near enough to get some startling views of the mountains. Then we were up along Mexico, where the marvelous scenery continued.

Arriving at San Diego between eight and nine in the morning, we weren't able to land until about ten because the U.S. Customs officials kept us standing in long lines while they stamped our cards. While we stood in the lounge waiting to disembark, we could hear a band playing on the dock and joked about which one of us was being honored.

Tommy and Helen and some of the others hired cars and went to Mexico, but Don, Ted, Gladys, Mae and I boarded a streetcar and went to the international exposition in Balboa Park. I was disappointed. In its second year, the fair, dowdy and commercial, gave the impression of having run down somewhat. Still, the buildings were beautiful, and in the evening when the lights went on, the place was a real fairyland. After we walked our legs off, we could honestly say we hadn't missed a thing. It was all Dutch so not expensive. We didn't see much else in San Diego and weren't willing to drive down to Mexico.

That was Friday, and we sailed at 11 P.M. At eight the next morning, we arrived at San Pedro, which unfortunately is almost thirty miles from Los Angeles. But the Arnolds had some friends coming down to meet them in a car and invited me to go along with them. That had been planned a week or so before, so I kept to it and arranged to meet Mae at the Ambassador Hotel later in the day. First we drove around Long Beach, where one of the men had to stop at his office. From there we drove over to Los Angeles and then on to Hollywood, where the Arnolds are settling. An American Legation convention was in town, so we had a difficult time finding room at any of the hotels for the Arnolds to stay.

I didn't see any movie stars, although I did get to see some of their homes as well as the famous Chinese Theater where the first showings are held and the footprints of the various stars are in the cement. We didn't get out to Beverly Hills, beautiful by all accounts. I saw enough, however, to convince me not to pay much attention to those zealous Southern California boosters. There's nothing sound or substantial about the place. Flat land and row after row of little bungalows in pseudo-Spanish architecture: that was my impression of most of Los Angeles. There are some beautiful things, of course, but on the whole I wouldn't want to live there. It looks like the result of a gigantic real estate boom.

I got on board about 4:30, dead tired. When I awoke, we were out at sea again; I never heard the ship leave when we sailed at eight on Sunday morning. So many friends had left us at Los Angeles that we seemed like a floating morgue. On top of the gloom, it drizzled all day long.

Early the next day we were standing off the Golden Gate, circling around in the fog and waiting for it to lift so we could get in. Our ship seemed to be all alone, but when the fog disappeared for just a minute, we could see a whole crowd of ships around us. After about an hour we started in, the fog still so dense that when we passed under the Golden Gate we could barely see the cables over us, not to mention the shore on either side. As we came into the bay, we passed right by Alcatraz Island prison, where Capone is. And then the fog lifted, allowing us to spot the huge Oakland Bridge across the bay.

At the dock we had a tough time getting through customs. I had nothing to declare, but it took me an hour all the same. As soon as I was through and had made arrangements to get my baggage over to the *General Pershing,* I walked over to look at her. She seemed terribly small at the time, but I like her now. After returning to the other dock and meeting one of the fellows, Eddie Meener, we went uptown and installed him in the Y.

On the way up we passed through Chinatown, where there's not much to see in the daytime. From the Y we got on a Gray Line sightseeing bus and had a three-hour drive all around the city with an announcer, the first time I've done anything like that. I found it worthwhile, except that with the fog many scenes upon the hills were wasted. The itinerary included Golden Gate Park, Twin Peaks, the Army post over the Gate and also a quaint old mission. San Francisco has character and made a strong impression on me. I liked it a lot, especially after Los Angeles.

After our ride we went up to the St. Francis and met the others, although I had to go down to the ship to make sure the luggage was on board then return to the hotel for dinner with the crowd. Later, they all came down to see me off. They are a swell bunch and I shall miss them.

Gaillard Cut, from a Panama Pacific Line brochure.

2

San Francisco to Yokohama

On board the SS General Pershing
August 14, 1936

HERE I AM on the next ship and liking it a lot. It's hard to tell about the passengers, since on this trip up the coast everything is a bit mixed up. There are some who are just returning from the Orient, some who are merely going from Frisco to Portland, and some, like myself, who are going on over. The *Pershing* seems small after the *California,* but it's clubby and comfortable.

I enjoyed my whole trip on the *California.* I was a little afraid the first couple of days out from New York that I wasn't going to like it too well, but I was pleasantly surprised. The crowd (quite a few changes at each port) seemed to get better, and one gets to feel so much at home on a ship during a two-week trip. I joined in all the deck sports tournaments, which started when we left Panama. A runner-up in the deck tennis, I also won first prize in Ping-Pong. At the handing out of prizes, I received a nice memento: a pearl-handled knife with a picture of the ship on it. A good bunch of young people were on board, almost a dozen of whom I feel I know as lifelong friends. Many left the ship at Los Angeles, but seven of them, including the first mate, were down here to see me off. They gave me a farewell party on board.

The atmosphere is different on the *Pershing*, mainly, I think, because almost all the staff is Chinese. They seem a good lot too. There is an excellent library on board—a number of classics as well as new books, many on travel and the Orient. I had a temporary cabin on the way up from Frisco, with Liner, a peach of a roommate.

The sea was quite choppy this morning with a strong head wind; I have an idea that we will roll and rock plenty. Even in a storm we had off Mexico, however, I have never felt the slightest bit of sickness, so it can get as rough as it wants to.

Unless it warms up when we get out farther on the Pacific, I'm afraid I'm through with white suits for a while. I needed a topcoat out on the deck today. What a change from the tropics.

Portland, Sunday, August 16

Liner and I are now installed in a nice double room with twin beds and bath in the Imperial Hotel in Portland. Rooms and meals are on the States Steamship Lines for the five days the company put us up here while the ship is being cleaned and loaded. This is a comfortable hotel right in the heart of town— much better than being on the ship way down in the docks. We are going to try to make changes on the ship so that we can room together going across.

On this beautiful warm day, Liner and I were up early. After breakfast we walked up to Council Crest for a view of the whole Columbia Valley. It was about a four-mile hike, mostly straight up, and great exercise. From the summit can be seen Mount Hood, a suspicion of Mount Rainier and a glorious view of the Columbia and Willamette Rivers. We came down through an attractive residential district where some late roses in the lovely gardens were still in bloom.

Liner, who is well educated, well read and plays classical music on his banjo like a professional, has tales of travel all over the world. For the last year he has been a wireless man and chief mate on a government fishing boat (biological experimentation) but is now on his way to Manila to take a job offered there in the advertising business. He worked in Manila for three years after graduating from the University of California in 1930. It will be fun and help-ful too to see him when I get to Manila. Travel is a good way of meeting peo-ple and making friends, although leaving them is not so pleasant.

This afternoon we made an excursion out to Mount Tabor on the other side of the city from Council Crest. The view there was entirely different and even finer, I think, although not quite so high.

Except for Liner and a few others, I don't know much about my traveling companions on the *Pershing*. There is a young Presbyterian missionary and his wife and child going to the Philippines;[1] also a young man and his wife who are returning to Manila after a vacation in this country and two young women starting off on a round-the-world trip. Those and a Japanese woman are the only ones I know yet. There will be sixty-five of us when we sail—that is ten less than capacity. By the way, we take a northerly route and skirt the Aleutian Islands, stretching out from Alaska.

I am back on the ship again, up in the lounge after dinner and a short time standing out on the deck with one eye on the sunset and the other on the gulls flying around. I feel strange, realizing that this is my last day in the United States for a long while.

We had quite a sailing—a great crowd of people on the dock and colored streamers and confetti. It seemed a shame not to have someone to wave to. The hundred-mile trip down the Columbia to the sea is very scenic. Just at dark, we dropped the pilot off at Astoria, our last contact, and headed westward. My roommate, Lloyd Millegan, eighteen years old, is going over to the University of Shanghai as an exchange student for a year. We get along first-rate.

As soon as the *Pershing* left the protection of the river, it started to toss around. The next day was so rough that the crew boarded up our windows on B deck and the spray was dashing against the windows on the promenade deck. It was hard to stand up. The chairs in the dining room were chained to the floor, and storm edges were put around the tables to prevent the food from sliding off. I felt queerly by afternoon but went down to dinner to try it. I lasted through the soup and then gave up and went on deck. I didn't actually get sick, but I felt awful. The next day was fairly smooth. Our windows were unboard-ed, only to be closed again for a bad day Friday. I haven't felt at all sick since the first day, however.

1. The Philippines at this time was a United States possession.

With the weather turning cold and unpleasant, one needs a coat to sit in the deck chairs; white suits, of course, are not even thought of. The ship is bobbing up and down, with canvas covers all around the open deck to keep out the wind and spray.

Tomorrow morning we are hoping to see some of the Aleutian Islands. Yesterday we spotted a whale spouting about a mile from the ship, also a school of porpoises.

August 18–25

Just a month ago today my parents and I were on board the *California* looking her over and saying good-bye. Today is Tuesday, and tomorrow will be Thursday as we cross the International Date Line.

I have enjoyed the ship's routine. When my table boy comes and awakens me at 8:15 on the dot, I dress and go down one deck to the dining saloon. I am at a table for four with Liner; Betty Zimmer, a girl from Minneapolis who knows a lot of people I knew when I was working there and is on her way to Manila to be married; and Joyce Helm, a girl just my age who was born in Japan and lives there. After breakfast I go up on deck and walk around with various people, usually about eighteen laps of the deck. Then I play games until about eleven o'clock, when bouillon and crackers are served. From then to luncheon I generally read or just sit around on the deck and talk.

Luncheon is at 1 P.M. After lunch almost everyone takes a siesta for about two hours, a habit that I have taken up. Then more games or reading until tea at 4:30, and then almost anything until six when my room boy comes to tell me it's my bath time. He looks all over till he finds me if I have forgotten the time. Dinner is at seven—not dress. After dinner every other night, we have movies in the lounge. Other nights we either dance to the phonograph or have horse races in the lounge, which I have won often enough to keep even on them. At ten o'clock the ship is just about ready to call it a day, and eleven o'clock always finds me in bed. I am getting a lot of good exercise, plenty of swell food and more sleep than I have ever had. I feel as fit as a fiddle and imagine I am putting on a lot of weight. The service on the ship is fine. I like the Chinese and the whole atmosphere of the ship.

As is rather natural, the people on board are sort of divided into groups. I am fortunate in being in three different sets. On the way up from Frisco, I became quite friendly with a Mr. and Mrs. Miller, who now sit at the captain's table with seven or eight others. A number of them and the captain have had several cocktail parties and a couple of private luncheons, all of which I have attended. I have enjoyed knowing them; they are a nice crowd.

Then too I have become friendly with several people who live in Manila, particularly with a young couple about my age, Dick and Blanca McGrath. Dick, who is in the shoe-manufacturing business, and his Spanish wife are returning from a trip around the world. Having been in Japan about a dozen times and knowing quite a bit about the place, he is going to join me if possible, saying he wants to do it on an absolute minimum of money. Blanca will go on to Manila alone if Dick gets off at Yokohama with me. Although Dick has been just about everywhere in the world, he thinks two weeks or so in the interior of Japan should be one of the best travel experiences possible. He has invited me to stay with them when I get to Manila.

I have been studying Japanese under the direction of Joyce Helm, the girl who has always lived in Japan. Never in my life have I been in such a cosmopolitan crowd. You can hear about any country on earth just by listening in to the conversation. It's a good introduction to the East, which I feel well acquainted with already just from the talk of the passengers. We have all sorts with us. Mr. Benninghoff, who is the American consul at Harbin in Manchuria, has his wife and baby girl with him; the little girl, about three and a half, talks in a combination of Chinese and Russian, which is weird. There is also an animal buyer on his way to Singapore, several round-the-world travelers and many businessmen from the Philippines.

The author with Blanca on the General Pershing.

Someone just shouted "Land!" So we all rushed out and caught a glimpse of the islands way off to the north.

August 30

There was a change in the weather this morning. It is now almost warm on deck, which makes such a difference. The sea is calm today but we are all sort of waiting for something to happen. It seems there is nearly always a bad blow when the ship is almost three days off Japan. We go about 320 knots every twenty-four hours and have to set our watches back about half an hour each night. Tokyo could be heard on the radio last night, so I can believe we are almost there. The ship is supposed to dock about five in the morning on Wednesday. I intend to be on deck before then to see the harbor and try to catch a view of Mount Fuji as we enter.

After talking with Martha Hecke and Katherine Clarke, who are going on to Peking, I have gained some valuable information. The College of Chinese Studies there has fine buildings on a nice campus right in town, and at the College Hostel, which accommodates strangers "of character," one can get a single room for $4 Mex.[2] a day or $100 Mex. per month. That rate includes room and board. In other words, I can stay a full month for about U.S. $33. I understand that people staying at the college have special advantages in the way of trips to the country, use of libraries, etc. I think it's a fine idea so I am planning to stay a month in Peking and become acquainted with the place. I have decided to let my trunk go to Kobe, leave it there in bond (no customs inspection necessary) and take it on the ship with me later on when I go to Tientsin and then up to Peking. Staying there a full month, I will want it, but I hope there won't be too much extra expense.

Although Dick has not yet had his radio message settling his trip to Japan he is counting on a favorable answer. Because we have done a lot of talking and planning, I am sure we will have a swell time and a worthwhile trip. Here is the way it shapes up at present: go up to Tokyo, staying perhaps three or four days; buy or rent immediately two bicycles and break ourselves in by fairly short trips, such as down to Kamakura and Yokohama; then check our bags some place and set out for Nikko. It should take us three days to get there, three days spent there, and three days back to Tokyo by a different route. Then set out again from Tokyo and take about six days for an around-Fuji trip seeing Miyanoshita, etc. Then back to Tokyo, and by train to Nara and a day or so in Kyoto, and travel to Kobe for a day before sailing. It should be great.

I have become friendly with a nice elderly lady on board who teaches Latin

---

2. In the 1930's the unit of Chinese currency was the yuan, a silver dollar loosely called Mexican. (In the 19th century the Mexican silver dollar, widely circulated in China, was accepted as currency.) The dollar "Mex." was about 33 U.S. cents in 1936.

in the American School in Shanghai and has a son in the sophomore class at Yale. I will be glad to see her when I get to Shanghai, where I shall also look up my roommate, Lloyd, at the university and several other people now on the ship.

There are five Catholic missionaries on board and several Protestant ones. Three of the Catholics are Jesuits in their twenties who have never been out of the States, and are now headed to China for life!

What a strange, different life from ours is led by the white people who live in the East. There are people on the ship who work and live there, to whom crossing the Pacific is hardly more of an occasion than a trip to Philadelphia. Some have made as many as twenty-five crossings. We all talk travel three-quarters of the time; one can get information about any spot in the world. It's all so interesting, and I find it hard to recall a time when *my* bounds seemed so very much more limited.

We ran out of fresh milk this morning, and I can't say that I like the powdered variety. Otherwise the food is as good as when we started. The baths on board are a combination of salt and fresh water, not mixed though. The boy draws a tubful of salt water (hot, of course) and puts a shelf across the tub, on which is a big pan of hot fresh water. It is impossible to make any suds with the salt water, so you sit there with your legs stretched out under the board and splash fresh water on and soap up. Then you rinse as best you can, trying to save enough fresh water to the end to get a real rinse.

I feel at home on the ship; it doesn't seem possible I have known all these people such a short time. The service provided by the Chinese boys is terrific. When I think of the trouble it is in the States to get good help and how expensive it is. Because the Chinese boys do not know English, one has to speak in certain accepted phrases and Pidgin English. "Topside" is up on the deck. Downstairs is "bottom side." The word *catch* means everything along the line of get, bring, receive, obtain, find. At six o'clock when the bath boy comes, he says, "Catch bath now."

Last night a group of us came up to the music room after dinner and turned on the radio to see what we could get. There was English from Hong Kong, Japanese from Tokyo, Spanish from Manila and Russian from Harbin, in Manchuria. Since tonight is a farewell dinner, we are going to wear tuxedos.

This morning we saw a fleet of Japanese fishing sampans off in the distance. Right now the ship is about 670 miles out of Yokohama. Yesterday there was a shore smell in the air. There is lot of stuff to fill out for the Japanese customs authorities. We even have to list books that we brought on a separate sheet by title and author; I am definitely going to put *Tinder Box of Asia* safely away in my trunk.

II

IN JAPAN

3

Tokyo, Atami and Nikko

September 2, 1936

A S ARRANGED the night before, my cabin boy called me at quarter of five in the morning, and within ten minutes I was up on the boat deck in the dim predawn light. The *General Pershing* was just sliding into the outer approaches of Yokohama harbor and making her way through the countless small fishing junks. Fujiyama looked particularly beautiful in the early morning. One is fortunate to see the mountain at all in Yokohama harbor, as the weather is often cloudy. It was supposed to be a good omen.

The ship was still underway while we were eating a hurried breakfast. Shortly afterward, we stopped just outside the breakwater to allow the port authorities and the medical examiner to come on board. The passengers had to line up on the promenade deck in single file while the doctor took a look at us. Then we had to go through passport inspection and answer a whole string of farfetched questions: Who were our grandparents, how long we expected to stay and exactly where we were going.

When the officials left we got underway again and proceeded to our dock.

While we tied up I was excited to see my first rickshaw, my first kimono and my first coolie. It is a shame that you have to attend to so many practical things like looking after your baggage when you would rather look around and enjoy the new scenery.

Martha, Katherine, Dick and I were all going to the Imperial Hotel in Tokyo, so we gathered our bags together. After a shore telephone had been connected and we made our room reservations, we located two Imperial porters and bargained the price for getting our twelve pieces of baggage off the ship, through customs and by truck to the hotel.

It was now 9 A.M. and getting unpleasantly warm. We saw our bags safely in the truck and decided to rent a car and see Kamakura. Yokohama itself, in most parts, is not particularly attractive, but we were soon out of the city and among the rice fields, which were remarkably fresh and green.

Our visit to the Daibutsu,[1] a monumental work that gives one a feeling of serenity and eternity, was worthwhile. It was so hot as we started leaving the grounds of the statue that I foolishly drank some water from a stone trough, after all the warnings about drinking unboiled water in the Far East. Fortunately, there were no unpleasant results. We visited several other shrines in Kamakura including Hachiman, but it was too warm to enjoy anything.

We decided to go on to Miyanoshita, a lovely drive up in the hills toward Fuji. The Fujiya, one of the world's most famous hotels, is itself a sight worth seeing. More luxurious appointments can hardly be imagined.

The hire of the car was making the day rather expensive so we decided not to splurge on lunch at the Fujiya and started down the mountain slowly, look- ing for an attractive inn we had noticed on the way up. We found what turned out to be the perfect spot. The delightful surroundings, the *neisans* in their bright colored kimonos, the elegance and spotless beauty of the place quite dazzled us. What a wonderful place to see on one's first day in Japan. It cer- tainly disturbs one's feelings of Western superiority. The food was a little too strange for real enjoyment, but we coped with the chopsticks, and the whole staff came to see us off, bowing and smiling.

It was a long ride back to Yokohama, where we arrived some time after dark. We drove through the suburbs where the people in the poorer parts live

1. The Daibutsu (great Buddha) in Kamakura is a bronze statue over forty-two feet high. Cast in 1252, it has an estimated weight of 90 tons.

close to the streets with a complete lack of privacy, undressing, dining and bathing for anyone to see.

On our arrival at Yokohama, we returned to the *Pershing* to say our farewells. Lloyd, Dick and I took a taxi to Sakuragicho Station and boarded a train for Tokyo. There are two lines running between Yokohama and Tokyo, one steam and one electric; we chose the latter.

Japanese trains are not very different from those at home. Second class is in every way comparable to our single class except that it is not as crowded and possibly a little better. The third-class carriages are usually jammed with people, while few people use first class. Second class costs twice as much as third and first class three times as much. It is all comparative because first class per mile is cheaper than trains in the States.

Tokyo, September 5

Dick and I have a beautiful large room on the second floor of the Imperial Hotel. We went down to breakfast shortly after eight o'clock, and while at the table, I spotted a stout man with a beard coming into the dining room. I thought he looked familiar and came to the conclusion it must be Dean Meeks of the Yale School of Fine Arts. I rarely saw him except as he sat in his robes on the platform on graduation day. When we were through I walked over to him and asked him. Sure enough, I was right. He is sailing soon to get back to open school. He gave me some helpful hints about Peking and was interested in my trip.

After breakfast I sauntered out of the hotel and strolled for almost an hour in Hibiya Park, right across the street. At the far end of the park one is practically at the moat of the Imperial Palace grounds, where the emperor lives. The park is not very unusual, but it is a pleasant place to stroll around and see the people. I felt this morning that it was almost worth the whole trip just to be right among these brightly dressed people in Tokyo. I don't think I would tire of watching them and studying them if I stayed three years instead of three weeks.

Dick and I had arranged to meet at Uyeno Park in the afternoon, so I went back to the hotel for luncheon and then took a cab there, a twenty-to-twenty-five-minute ride for the equivalent of about twelve cents. Uyeno Park, the largest and most famous of the Tokyo parks, is the location of the zoo, the art gallery, the Imperial Museum and a Shinto shrine known as the Toshogu. My guidebook spoke of a large bronze Buddha or Daibutsu out there, and that was where Dick and I planned to meet. It seems it was removed five years ago with the unexpected result of causing Dick and me to wander around separately for two hours without finding each other. I spent a considerable time at the zoo watching extremely serious Japanese schoolboys of twelve to sixteen years take notes on the different animals.

The Japanese are nothing if not thoroughgoing and serious when they consider it a time to be serious. They can laugh plenty too, and it seems that one of their biggest jokes is a foreigner trying to find someone to speak English.

The National Gallery was rather disappointing and the Toshogu Shrine not exceptional, but it was interesting to see the Japanese toss pennies in the receptacle and offer up a prayer. A dilapidated old pagoda of five stories on the right of the cryptomeria-lined avenue to the shrine was of some interest but pretty dowdy on the whole. Boy scouts, soldiers and uniformed students "do" the sights as if the future of Nippon depended on their close observance of the animals.

After returning to the hotel I went to the Kai-Kan[2] restaurant for an American-style meal: a pork chop with vegetables. Japanese meals are fine, but I need good solid food too. Japanese food is, as the guidebook says, "elusive at best." There are a lot of small dishes as big around as a small ashtray, half filled with things that are unknown to me.

Later, although it was terribly hot and I didn't feel like doing much of anything, I went out alone and tramped all over town from nine to eleven. In two hours of walking through the crowds down streets and alleys, I didn't see a single white person. The shops and bazaars, teahouses, dance halls, bars, restaurants, etc., were almost all open, teeming with colorful, gay crowds. Some of the buildings are really beautiful, especially at night when their use of lights is startling and effective. Two hours in the heart of Tokyo after dark—hundreds of thousands of people, thousands of signs and window displays, but hardly a word in our type of letter and practically none at all in English!

The crowd is well behaved and decorous. I saw few drunks and nothing at all objectionable or vulgar in any of the window displays or anywhere else. A

---

2. The Kai-Kan is a well-known restaurant near the Imperial Palace.

Hiroshige, Evening Scene, 1856.

lot of people stared at me, but everyone was polite; I wasn't bothered in any way. Most of the men were in European clothes, but the women were nearly all wearing kimonos and obis. It was a colorful scene.

I spent most of the time on the Ginza, the main street of the city. On one side of the Ginza the outer edge of the broad sidewalk is lined with movable booths as in the Lower East Side of New York. Here are all sorts of cheap little trinkets and toys, books, plumbing fixtures, cigarette cases, etc. Tokyo is not a tourist city where shops and markets cater to foreigners; everything is Japanese and for the Japanese.

September 6

Dick and I are leaving here tomorrow to spend a few days trying out life in a Japanese inn, or *ryokan*. There are two European hotels in Atami, so if we have difficulties we can always go there. If we invested our money in bicycles and travel equipment—knapsacks, shorts, bottled water, etc.—and started out for Nikko, we might find that we had done a very foolish thing. Along the way (at least three days) there would be no European places and no one at all speaking English. I am hoping that our experimentation in Atami will prove that the other trip is feasible, but I have seen enough to know that it would have been foolish to start out without that experiment.

Mr. Minamoto (the tourist guide at Chadsey's) was not very enthusiastic about the plan of starting out on such a trip with a meager knowledge of Japanese and no experience with the inns. We'll see how it works out and hope for the best. Getting to Atami, a sort of beach resort with hot springs and geysers, won't take long by rail, and train travel is very cheap. We will be able to get bottled water there. On the way to Nikko, we would have had to carry a full supply of water for at least three days, which would have been a difficult job on a bike.

Atami, September 7

I am writing this from the porch of our room at the Tamanoi Inn at Atami. Sitting sideways and looking to the left I can see into our very charming room, while on the right below the porch is a garden lit by lanterns. Still farther to the right, perhaps a hundred yards or so is the Pacific, which a while ago this afternoon was very blue. Now it is a dark expanse, dotted with lights of fishing boats far out from shore.

We decided to devote yesterday (Sunday) to one of the conventional sights of Tokyo—the Meiji Shrine[3] and surrounding parks. We took a *takushi* (cab) from the hotel and drove through well over a mile of shops (most of them open on Sunday) to the entrance beyond which cabs are not allowed. From that point, one must walk. Down the wide bluestone path a ways from the entrance stands the first torii, the gate that always comes before a shrine. Of beautiful wood from Formosa it stands immensely dignified to the height of almost seventy feet. A quarter of a mile farther along, the path turns to the left and goes under a similar torii before swinging to the right in the direct approach to the shrine. On all sides are stately pines; everything is majestic and solemn.

The shrine itself is the most striking example of simple grandeur I have seen, except perhaps for the Lincoln Memorial in Washington. There is not a touch of paint or stain—all is of natural gray wood. The Japanese, many of the men and all of the women in native dress, bow as they approach and then, going up the steps at the far end, toss coppers in the large chest and say a prayer.

The shrine itself is in honor of the Emperor Meiji, the first emperor after the restoration of imperial rule in 1868. He was well loved, and this shrine was made possible by the voluntary contributions of millions all over the country. When he died in 1912, the Japanese were thunderstruck, for they had come to

---

3. Meiji Shrine, built in 1920, is dedicated to the Emperor Meiji (1868-1912). His reign transformed Japan into one of the great powers of the world. The immense Meiji Park contains a sports center (used for the 1964 Tokyo games), museums and iris gardens.

ABOVE, LEFT: *Statue of warrior in Imperial Park, Tokyo.*

TOP: *The author, with fan, on balcony of Imperial Hotel, Tokyo, with Dick McGrath.*

ABOVE: *Imperial Palace.*

ABOVE: *The author, at left, with shipmates Katherine, Dick and Martha on the roof of the Tokyo Kai-Kan, a well-known restaurant.*

RIGHT: *The author, at far right, enjoying a beer with Dick at the bar of the Imperial Hotel in Tokyo.*

TOP: *The author with Blanca McGrath at Kamakura.*

ABOVE: *Visitors at the Imperial Palace, Tokyo.*

RIGHT, CENTER: *The Daibutsu or Great Buddha at Kamakura.*

RIGHT: *About to depart for Atami with Dick McGrath, left, at Tokyo Railway Station.*

LEFT: *The author asking for directions at the police station in Atami.*

BELOW: *In a kimono admiring the gardens at the Tamanoi Ryokan, an Atami inn.*

ABOVE: *With new friends at the Tamanoi Ryokan.*

LEFT, CENTER: *Geishas at the Tamanoi.*

LEFT: *Somewhere between Kamakura and Enoshima.*

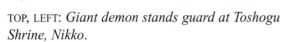

TOP, LEFT: *Giant demon stands guard at Toshogu Shrine, Nikko.*

TOP, RIGHT: *The author, at left, and Dick McGrath at Yomei-mon Gate, Toshogu Shrine.*

ABOVE: *At Toshogu Shrine.*

RIGHT: *The author gives a thumbs up at Kegon Falls, Nikko, with Dick McGrath.*

believe him eternal. Their initial shock of grief and amazement rapidly turned into a desire to have a beautiful memory of him. This shrine is the result—a truly impressive tribute.

From the shrine it is a ten-minute walk to Meiji Stadium, where the 1940 Olympics[4] will be held. They will have to make many changes and additions, I believe, to accommodate the crowd. Near the stadium is the National Art Gallery, another beautiful building, where, after putting coverings on our shoes, we saw eighty pictures representing the reign of the Emperor Meiji from birth to death. The only drawback to all this sightseeing is the heat.

After we went back to the hotel we wandered about the grounds and building and then talked and read till dinnertime. Just as we were about to go to the Kai-Kan to eat, Martha and Katherine from the *Pershing* who had been at the hotel returned from a short excursion to Nikko. They were full of the glories of the place and made me anxious to get up there. The four of us went out to dinner together, up on the roof of the Kai-Kan. We had a wonderful dinner for about 1 yen 40 sen. We walked for an hour or so and then went to bed.

This morning (September 7) we packed, took care of a lot of details and took some pictures, finally catching the 11:30 train for Atami. We came down third-class, which is not at all bad, practically the same as our coaches. It was a little less than fifty American cents for a seventy-mile ride. And what a beautiful ride it is! After the train leaves the Tokyo and Yokohama district, the scenery is marvelous: rice fields, mountains with their cultivated terraces, great stretches of ocean and above all, every now and then as the clouds shifted and changed, a thrilling scene of grand old Fujiyama.

Atami is nestled among the mountains, right on the sea. The Tamanoi Inn was recommended to us by the clerk at the Imperial, who was very doubtful, however, about our getting along without any real knowledge of Japanese. At Atami Station, we found an information man who was the proud possessor of some English. He telephoned down to the inn and made reservations for us, although they were not very willing to take foreigners who couldn't speak the language.

Upon our arrival by cab, the whole staff was out to meet us, fifteen or twenty giggling maids, the dark-kimonoed proprietors, the shoe boys and everyone, including quite a crowd of passers-by. We haven't seen a white person since

---

4. The 1940 Olympics were canceled because of the outbreak of World War II in Europe.

we left the hotel in Tokyo, and I'm sure there isn't a person who can speak English within miles, except at the European-type hotel two and a half miles on the other side of town.

First and always, off come your shoes to be replaced with light rush slippers. Everyone bows as you stand up after changing. Then one of the maids led us down clean polished corridors and up stairways to our room, with its sliding doors of paper windows. Directly inside the door was a small room separated by a transparent screen from the main room. In this small room was a rack for our clothes and a chest with a bowl of water and glasses. Beyond the screen in the main room, and beyond more sliding screens that could be kept open wide, was our porch, where there was a small wicker table with two chairs. In the main room, there was nothing but a six-inch-high red-lacquered table in the center of the floor, four cushions spread around, a writing table about a foot high and a little mirror on a stand. On one wall near the paneled ceiling was a large oblong painting of a mountain scene, and on the opposite side, a long wall hanging. The floor was of clean matting. You leave even your slippers before you enter any room. As soon as we arrived in our room, we were brought kimonos. We took off our clothes as soon as they left and put the kimonos on. In a minute or two a girl arrived with tea and some little sweets; a minute or two later, the manager came with cards for us to fill out. The instructions on the cards were in Japanese, so we had quite a time with them. Then a boy came and made the motions of a bath.

We were ushered downstairs and through more corridors to the hot-spring baths. We, being foreigners, were given private bathrooms, but right at the end of the hall was a room where quite a few persons were in a large tiled tank together. As this is a hot-spring resort, the baths are the specialty. My room was all tiled, with a drain in the floor, so I could do all the splashing and soaping I wanted before getting into the tub or tank in the corner. The tank is really a tiled-in hole in the floor, just like a swimming pool except much smaller. It was great and I felt a lot better afterward.

Tuesday afternoon, September 8

I am back again on our little porch. It's another scorching day but right now, for a change, I feel almost cool enough to be comfortable.

Yesterday afternoon, after my bath, feeling weak from lack of food, and and not too hopeful about our dinner here, I decided to go over to the Atami Hotel for something to eat. It was too late to rent a bicycle so I bargained with a man who owns a taxi that was out in front to take me to the hotel and back with a three-quarters-hour wait for 1 yen 50 sen. That was high by Tokyo rates but I was hungry.

When I arrived there I didn't see a soul except the Japanese proprietor and a serving maid, who subsequently brought me two chicken sandwiches and a glass of milk. The chicken sandwich was a mixture of white meat, skin and gristle, but I was so hungry, I ate it all. My worst meal was the one in the grill-room of the Imperial Hotel in Tokyo, when I ordered a sardine sandwich and a raw-fish sandwich arrived.

When I returned to our hotel, everyone was outside bowing again. They bowed when I left too. So often the Japanese girls giggle when they do not understand what we are saying. With a little ingenuity or imagination, a few signs for words such as eat or sleep could easily be used and understood.

I arranged to have dinner served at seven o'clock and we awaited the hour anxiously. Koko, our maid, brought in a large tray that had a bottle of beer, ice and slices of raw fish; there were also small dishes containing various vegetables and cooked bamboo shoots, which are very common. There was also a fish soup with something I didn't recognize floating on top. After we finished the soup, Koko went out and brought back two dishes of large fried shrimp with onions on toast. This seemed more American-style food. Before we were through with that, she went out again, and came back beaming, carrying dishes of *bif-stekki* and potato salad, and much to our surprise, knives and forks. It was a grand sight. We learned that we could have *cohee*, *toasto*, and *eggsu* for breakfast. The meal ended with fruit that tasted like a combination of pear and apple.

After dinner, we dressed in our own clothes, and went out to look at the town. The streets are very narrow, many on steep grades, many curves and twists, many lanterns, much laughing and singing and thousands of little shops. It was everything I had imagined the East to be.

We tramped up and down. There was a place where games are played; the object is to throw a ball at a row of figures. I tried it several times and won a bar of candy. There are countless inns here and many public bathhouses, all quite open on the street.

We came back to the inn after considerable walking. The bedding was spic-and-span clean, though the pillow a little high and hard. It was so hot I didn't use any covers. The mosquitoes were so bad I almost went crazy with them for about an hour. Then too I was terribly thirsty but didn't dare drink the water. I finally had a pretty fair night's rest and had two bottles of water sent to my room in the morning.

September 10

We are back at the Imperial Hotel in Tokyo for a night before starting up to Nikko. After bicycling for the last few days, we decided the weather was just too hot and the country too hilly. And then there's the difficulty with the drinking water. It seems a shame to give up the idea, but it is just not practical.

We will, of course, stay in a Japanese inn at Nikko and also at Lake Chuzenji, a side trip from Nikko.

We had a pleasant time at the Tamanoi Inn in Atami. Our maid, Koko, was worth going far to see. She was middle-aged and not very pretty but she was so much fun. She didn't know a word of English and still doesn't after three days' coaching. During mealtime, while she would be sitting there serving and fanning us, we would try to talk to her in English. She would laugh until tears came to her eyes, and when we tried our Japanese on her, that was even worse. Sometimes the other maids would stand right outside our door and talk and giggle with her. I left there with regret, feeling that the more I got to know the Japanese, the better I would like them. All the servants at the inn went out of their way to be helpful—their courtesy was amazing. The laughing outside our door was really not discourteous. They sensed that we didn't mind their entering into the fun of the thing.

Every once in a while I went down to one of the garden entrances and put on the high wooden clogs, or *geta,* for a walk around the place. These are not hard to use, although it is rather uncomfortable at first to have your big toe separated from the others. You must either go barefoot to wear them or have special socks.

On the morning of the eighth we walked around town till we found a bicycle store. It took us a long time to make a bargain. We rented two good bikes for two days at one yen forty sen apiece or seventy sen per bike per day. I think that was fairly high, but after all, twenty-one or twenty-two cents isn't much for a whole day.

We took a road leading south that follows the most interesting coast I have ever seen. High cliffs come right down to the ocean, with the road on the cliff—very much like the Storm King Highway above the Hudson. The sea has cut great caves and grottoes in the rock cliff all along. It is exceptional scenery, and exceptionally hard bicycling in the heat. After we rode to a town about nine miles south of Atami, we decided to turn back.

On the return trip, we saw a little path leading down the cliff to the ocean. We hid our bikes in the bushes and went down. When we finally reached the water, we found ourselves in a beautiful little cove with huge rocks all about. Off a little ways was a native boat, and scattered around were people diving. They were women pearl divers. They wore bulky white things like nightgowns and headpieces that looked like dusting caps. They each had a floating basket beside them, into which they put the oysters as they came to the surface. The person in the boat was a man. He sat there at ease while five or six women worked like Trojans. We stripped down to our shorts and had a swim. The water felt wonderful but we had an awful climb back to the road again.

In the evening, as we finished dinner, we could hear the sound of singing and a samisen from somewhere in the inn. From the balcony we could see a large open room with quite a few people in it. All of a sudden several men there were motioning us to come on over. We put on our kimonos and went through the corridors to where they were. In a large and beautiful but very simple room, there were about a dozen men sitting on cushions on three sides of a large square.

Opposite each man was a geisha serving him food and sake as well as fanning him. In front of the open side of the square, two geishas in wonderfully beautiful kimonos were dancing. Off to one side another geisha was singing and playing the samisen. When the dance was over, several of the men got up and beckoned us. Two of the maids brought in two chairs and a small table that was set up near the square. The party continued as if we were not there. Occasionally they spoke a few words of English to us. The dancing and singing were naturally different from our own. Geishas dance in a symbolic style, much like interpretive dancing. It was highly enjoyable, everyone so friendly and courteous. The group broke up about ten o'clock; we bowed and shook hands all around.

Yesterday morning, the ninth, we came downstairs and found someone had locked our bikes. Dick's lock came undone easily but mine had to be sawn off. It was even hotter than before and the roads were very dusty. Cycling was hard work and no fun. We had to walk uphill pushing the bikes most of the time, but coasting downhill was great. From the bicycles we saw a lot of people along the road and interesting sights that we would have missed otherwise.

When we left, all the records for bowing and smiling were broken. They seem such naturally pleasant people. Koko washed all our underwear, polo shirts and handkerchiefs without charge and without being asked.

It was almost like homecoming to get back to Tokyo, but I'm anxious to get up to Nikko tomorrow.

Konishi Inn, Nikko, September 11

We spent most of Friday morning in Tokyo at the Mitsukoshi department store shopping for presents. We had luncheon at the store in one of their beautiful dining rooms, an American luncheon. Then we went back to the hotel and packed. We caught the three o'clock train from Asakusa Station, one of the many stations in Tokyo, and again traveled third-class. We got a round-trip to Nikko from Tokyo for exactly one dollar American money! The inn where we are staying in Nikko gives us lodging, breakfast and dinner (mostly American style) for four yen or about $1.25 apiece. Luncheon is a problem as it usually costs about two yen fifty, which is out of proportion with the rest of it. Lunches we eat out, but they would cost the same in the inn.

On the way up here on the train the other evening, we got to talking with an English-speaking Japanese who turned out to be Kanaya Jr., whose father manages the Kanaya Hotel here in Nikko, and whose uncle manages the famous Fujiya Hotel in Miyanoshita, two of the best and most expensive hostelries in all Japan. I imagine that he was a little surprised to learn that we were staying at a Japanese inn here instead of his father's hotel, which is just behind us up on the hill, but he was very friendly. He spent a year in New York in 1927, working for the Electric Bond and Share Company and enjoyed talking about America, which stands high in his favor. He was not sure, however, as to the wisdom of the Japanese imitating us in all things. The movies, of course, have a great deal to do with that. He said that many Japanese girls had

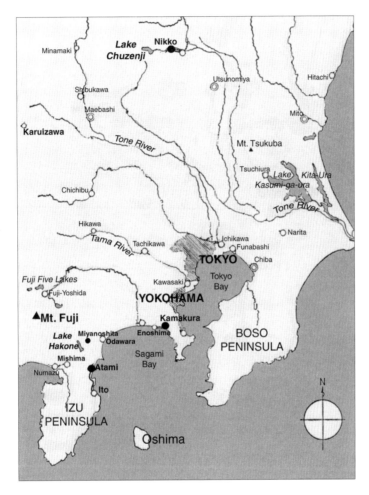

Map of Tokyo area showing major tourist destinations.

changed to American-style dress, but except for the strangely dressed girl conductors on the streetcars and buses, I have seen very few. Dick spoke about seeing geisha girls all over the streets in Tokyo when he was here five years ago, while now they seem rare. Kanaya Jr. replied that nowadays the geishas, by not wearing the traditional hairdress, are attempting to pass as girls of good family. Many stringent laws concerning them have been enacted recently, but Kanaya says that all Japan knows they are a permanent fixture in Japanese life.

Just before the train pulled into Nikko, we were right in the middle of an electrical storm. A group of Japanese schoolgirls had come on at the station before and were shrieking and laughing.

The inn here is not as nice as the Tamanoi at Atami, but the proprietor does speak a little English, which helps considerably. He has difficulty with the consonant endings in English and usually adds on a vowel—*soupu* and *lunchi*. They gave us four mattresses at night instead of the two for Japanese, and they folded up another one at the foot of the bed to increase the length. Fortunately, the mosquitoes did not bother us here.

On arriving at the inn, we had dinner and a bath and went right to bed. Early the next morning we went across the stream and up the hill to the mausoleums of the shoguns. There are two groups of temples, the most famous in Japan. The colors are strikingly vivid against a background of trees and mountains. Everything is so green with the reds and gold of the temples nestling into the hillsides. Last night we borrowed straw parasols from the innkeeper and strolled downtown. Many of the stores are junky but several are real treasure houses.

Today we spent most of the day in a trip to Lake Chuzenji, a mountain lake 2,500 feet higher than Nikko. First, one takes a bus to a point about halfway. From there, small cars go up to Kegon Falls, where the cars stop while you take an elevator down inside a cliff 350 feet for a view of the falls below. When we got to the top again, we walked to the lake. The ride up the mountain in the small autos was a hair-raiser! There was little to do at the lake but we walked miles and admired the exceptional beauty.

We had luncheon at a European hotel there, the Lakeside. Coming down to Nikko, you start out by bus to the upper terminal of a cable car railway. After a spectacular ride down in the cable car, we took another bus back to Nikko. Our transportation costs for the day were two yen, or sixty U.S. cents.

We arrived back in Nikko about three o'clock and went down to the shops again. We concentrated on one particular store called the Pawnbroker, which is supposed to be one of the best. The name has no bearing on the business. It is a large rambling place; the present owner, now quite old, is the third generation of his family to run it. There were many things, not very practical but fascinating to look at.

Tomorrow we plan to leave here in the morning and go to Kamakura, which we saw a little of on September 2, the day we landed. I am quite used to Japanese inns now. If you can get American-style food, they are perfectly all right in these larger places.

I am doing my bicycling and hiking a little at a time. It is much better to make the long trips by train, as the trains are fast and cheap.

4

Kamakura, Gifu and Kyoto

Kanko Hotel, Island of Oshima
Sept. 16, 1936

WE LEFT NIKKO Monday morning. On the whole, it is surprisingly easy to travel in Japan without a guide and without knowledge of the language. Trains are efficient and go just about everywhere. Passengers, a jolly crowd for the most part, slip off their wooden clogs and cross their legs on the seat as if they were sitting on the floor. At every big station, hawkers sell ice cream, sandwiches and neat little box lunches.

On arriving at Tokyo Station, we checked our bags and walked to the Kai-Kan for lunch. I left my purchases at the hotel and reserved a room for Thursday night. We decided to go to Kamakura[1] as we heard that a festival was being held there.

Needing to change some money, Dick and I started to walk to the bank. There were great crowds on the street with soldiers everywhere, and the main avenue from Tokyo Station to the Imperial Palace was entirely closed. We almost missed getting to the bank in time but we *did* see Emperor Hirohito, sitting in the backseat of a big Packard touring car upon his return from his summer palace at Hayama.

---

1. Kamakura is fifty miles south of Tokyo. A center of religion and culture with many temples and shrines, it was the seat of political power from 1192–1333.

I get news of the election campaign in the States from the *Japanese Advertiser*, a good English-language newspaper, but I don't have much idea what is going on or how Roosevelt is doing.

We arrived in Kamakura about four o'clock but found the hotel had Japanese accommodations for the summer only. The European rooms are expensive, so we went downtown and took a room at the Isomi Hotel. It is the poorest place we have struck so far but even so quite comfortable and clean. In the evening we went up to the famous Hachiman Shrine, which was celebrating the annual festival on Monday and Tuesday. A long boulevard leads from the center of the town straight to the shrine. Everyone, including the tots, had on an extra-bright kimono. Among the thousands of interesting sights on the street, lined with multicolored lanterns and huge banners and flags, were the ex-convicts with inverted wicker baskets covering their whole head right-down to the shoulders. Tiny slits in the baskets, which they wear as a sign of shame and to prevent recognition, allow them to see out a little, but it's a wonder how they get around.

The whole atmosphere was that of a fair; the shops, many of them temporary structures right in the shrine grounds, were doing a big business.

A little off to one side, but near the foot of the stairway leading up to the main shrine, hundreds of children were sitting on the ground waiting for an open-air movie show to start. We decided to see what was going on. For openers there was a Mickey Mouse movie, followed by a Japanese film that we didn't understand at all, a highly patriotic story dealing with the Japanese Navy Training School, their Annapolis. We didn't stop to watch it all but joined the throng plodding up the stone steps to the shrine. People came up by the thousands, tossed a coin in a big open chest, clapped their hands to get the attention of the god and said a short silent prayer. In the inner building, in sight of the people praying, the temple priests in white robes were going through their mysterious ceremonies.

Tuesday morning, we went to Enoshima, a little island connected to the mainland by a fragile bridge. It's more or less a temporary one because sooner or later all the bridges the Japanese put up are washed away by typhoons, so they don't bother much. This island is a beautiful spot, with a fine view of Fuji from the top of the hill if one is lucky. But we weren't.

On the trolley car to Enoshima from Kamakura and back, about five miles each way, the conductor got out a sprinkling can every other stop and watered the floor to keep us cool. They do that regularly on the trains too and even on buses. We arrived back in Kamakura shortly after noon, ate a snack at the Isomi and were up in the temple grounds by one o'clock, joined by crowds even larger than yesterday.

Where the movies had been shown the night before, there was now a large covered wooden platform on which contests of old swordplay were taking place. The contestants, appearing two at a time, wore old-style Japanese armor and protective masks, but in place of steel swords used strong rods or swords of bamboo. Their every step and shout seemed to be along well-prescribed lines.

At the foot of the shrine in a building open on all four sides sat a band composed of fife and five drums of varying size, playing loud and continuous music that was strange to Western ears. It was a picturesque sight, the musicians squatting there in the open pavilion, dressed in orange kimonos.

The main event, however, was the procession from the top shrine down the long flight of stairs to the middle of the town. Like all parades, it was a long time forming. Finally, white-robed priests started coming down the steps carrying the relics and treasures of the temple in several large closed chests of carved wood, supported on poles shouldered by four and sometimes eight priests. Then came black-robed archers with their bows encased in embroidered cloth. The main part of the procession was made up of three huge box-shaped objects, presumably the shrines themselves, which were manned by twenty-five priests. Trailing these was the high priest in brilliant orange and purple robes. As soon as the heavy shrines were down in the courtyard, the priests started running round with them in a crazy fashion. The purpose of all this turning and twisting was evidently to fool the evil spirits and throw them off the track. While all this was going on, the high priest mounted a fine chestnut horse, and then another horse, a beautiful white Arabian, perhaps to represent the Emperor's presence, came out last of all. The priests by now seemed completely mad, rushing around the shrines, no doubt affected by the heat—or maybe large amounts of sake.

Way down at the end of the street, a special place had been prepared for the carriers to place their burdens. After the high priest performed some rites, great quantities of food were placed before the shrines. By this time we were exhausted and sweltering, so we walked back to the hotel, collected our bags and went back to Tokyo by train.

Mount Fuji and Lake Shoji at dusk.

Moat of the Imperial Palace in Tokyo.

The Imperial Hotel in Tokyo, designed by Frank Lloyd Wright, was constructed between 1915 and 1922. It survived the violent quake of 1923 intact but was dismantled in 1967 to make way for a larger building.

Iris gardens at Heian-Jingu Shrine in Kyoto.

It is raining and has been raining ever since I left Tokyo yesterday morning, except by great luck, during the two hours I saw the cormorant fishing at Gifu last night. Today, on the train, I was sorely tempted to go right on through to Kobe and give up Kyoto because of the weather. A party of Spaniards on the train, however, informed me that Kobe is having an air-raid practice tonight and tomorrow night, which means that nothing is doing in the city and that all lights must be out.

So here I am, alone again, in a native inn. As usual the maid brought in my kimono and welcoming tea. The innkeeper will be here in a minute with the slip for me to fill out. Every place one stops there is a form to fill, requiring name, age, profession, nationality, where you have come from and where you are going. As the form is in Japanese, the result may be funny if I have filled in the wrong line.

This section of Japan is flooded with soldiers, probably having something to do with maneuvers at Kobe. The train was full of them today, the common soldiers traveling in third class and the officers in second. If it is fair tomorrow, I intend to see some of the temples Kyoto is famous for. I think, though, that I will get on to Kobe tomorrow night in spite of the war games because I have to arrange about my trunk, which is being held for me there, and check up on my tickets before I sail at noon on Wednesday.

I left Tokyo on the 10:30 train yesterday morning, the nineteenth, Dick seeing me off at the station. It is a seven-and-a-half-hour trip through mountains, along the coast and then inland past Nagoya to Gifu.

The dining car has good food at reasonable prices, even if the choice on the European menu is rather limited: they seem to think we eat nothing but eggs! By now I have acquired a taste for curry rice. From the dining car window I had a perfect view of the elusive Mount Fuji for a couple of minutes during a break in the clouds. I would like to see it with its mantle of snow, however, for beautiful as the mountain is, it doesn't look quite right without the snow.

The Japan Tourist Bureau at the Imperial Hotel gave me the name of a Japanese inn in Gifu and this one, the Seikoro, in Kyoto. Last evening at Gifu I took a cab from the station to the Sumiyoshi Inn. I was bowed in as usual but a man soon showed up and with many gestures made it known that there were no rooms to be had. After serving me tea, the staff called a *takushi* and gave

Map of Japan showing places visited by the author in large bold type.

the driver the name of a hotel in Gifu. This was in an excellent location for the fishing and quite reasonable too, with European accommodations and food. The charges were three yen for the room, with dinner and breakfast coming to another three—not bad for a European-style hotel.

The cormorant fishing started about seven o'clock last night. Since the Nagara River runs right in front of the hotel, I was able to get in a little boat at the dock there. The fishing season is every night from May 11 to October 13, except once a month at the full moon. The boats used for the fishing (usually twelve in number) go to a point upstream from town and then go down the river about two miles in single file. They are narrow and about twenty-five feet long. Hanging out from the bow of each to attract the fish is a basket containing burning pine fagots that make a tremendously bright light, accompanied by much sputtering and thousands of flying sparks. The master fisherman in medieval costume stands near the torch and controls twelve cormorants by strings. Beside the guide string, each bird has a cord around its neck quite far down that prevents it from completely swallowing the fish it catches.

It is amazing how the man manages to keep the twelve cords from getting tangled up, for the birds scurry about like mad catching the fish. When the fisherman sees that the neck of one of the birds is full, he pulls the bird in and forces it to disgorge the catch. The birds cooperate, seeming to know what it is all about. At the end of the run down the river, when the fishing is over, they all clamber up on the side of the boat and stand there according to rank. Each bird is rated according to its skill, and each knows its own position perfectly. If there is a mistake in the lineup, there is a lot of fighting and moving around until everyone is right!

Many boats such as the one I was in are for the benefit of people who wish to see the fishing at close hand. They all carry brightly colored lanterns, and the hundreds of these, together with the flaming pine baskets on the fishing boats, make a dazzling sight. The boats crowd around the fishers, each trying to get the best view. The result is jumble and confusion. As we kept getting tangled up with the other boats, I expected to be turned over any minute. The river has a lot of shallow spots, so all the boats kept going aground and getting stuck. Some of the sightseeing boats are like large barges; several of these contained regular dinner parties with geishas, music and all. I don't know how they found time to eat with so much confusion and so many mosquitoes.

I saw a couple of Germans at the hotel, but the rest of the guests were

Japanese. At the inn no one speaks English, but I managed to make the maid understand that I wanted a bath at six o'clock, dinner at seven with beefsteak and rice—I'll probably get sukiyaki which is always good—and that I'm going to Kobe to get a steamer for Tientsin. In answer to her question, I told her that I am twenty-three and found out that she is twenty-two. That is practically the limit of my Japanese. How I wish I knew more.

Oriental Hotel, Kobe, September 21

When I got up this morning at the Seikoro Inn (established in 1831) in Kyoto, I discovered to my disappointment it was raining even harder than the day before. I decided, however, that I would go out and see some of the temples, and with a map of the city, charted out a route, part walking and part taxi, that would cover the three most important shrines and a glance at the old Imperial Palace. Kyoto was the capital of Japan for more than a thousand years until 1868, when the Emperor Meiji moved the administration to Tokyo.

At any rate, I borrowed one of the yellow parasols made of heavy piled paper from the innkeeper and started off in the teeming rain. Japanese inns in cities are on bustling little narrow side streets. There are no sidewalks; the rickety buildings almost meet overhead in a jumble of shops, people, beasts of burden, and vehicles all over the unpaved street, thousands of signs in Japanese, a lot of noise and plenty of strange odors. When it rains the Japanese resort to umbrellas and shoes that are almost like stilts. Workmen, who can't hold an umbrella over them as they work, wear cumbersome coats of straw that are rough and crude. I saw Heian-Jingu, Chio-in and Kiyomizu and was greatly impressed. Needless to say, because it was pouring I was the only one around out there among the temples. At the Heian-Jingu, where there is a famous garden at the rear of the main shrine, the priest who collected the ten sen entrance fee for the garden looked at me as if I were crazy to be walking around with a parasol in the rain. Afterward I went back to the inn, changed my clothes and caught a train for Kobe.

Places visited: Tokyo, Atami, Nikko, Kamakura, Yokohama, Miyanoshita, Lake Chuzenji, Enoshima, Oshima,[2] Gifu, Kyoto, Kobe and Moji. I've trav-

---

2. No manuscript for trip to Oshima.

eled by train, bus, private car, local steamer, bicycle, and trolley about 1,200 miles in Japan, not counting the 250-to-300-mile trip through the Inland Sea.

On board MS Chojo Maru
September 24, 7:45 A.M.

We are entering the port of Moji,[3] and I have just had a thrill. I came up from breakfast five minutes ago, and right there alongside us was the *General Pershing!* It is on its way home now and will be in Kobe early tomorrow morning. No one was out on deck as it is still so early in the morning, but I believe I saw Bill Zeeb, the assistant purser. The *Pershing* was my home for three weeks. What a feeling it was to be so close to her out here at the end of the Inland Sea.

This ship is even smaller than the *Pershing* and not nearly as nice, especially in the line of food. It will do, though, for the four days I am on it. My roommate, an old gentleman by the name of Monsieur Léon de Hoyer, is a good person for me to know, having spent many years in Peking. He lives in Paris now and writes, but comes back now and then for a period of several months. Daniele Vare, the author of *The Last Empress*, is an old friend of his. Like all persons who have been in Peking, even for a short time, de Hoyer is a staunch believer in the city as the world's foremost for real living. He writes his articles in German, French, English and Russian, and can speak Japanese, Chinese and Spanish as well.

The French chargé d'affaires at Peking and his wife are also on board. Their daughter, who is only fourteen, speaks English as well as I do. Possessing an excellent vocabulary, she can converse on any subject that comes up, and her whole manner of speaking is superior to that of many college girls in the States. While France is her home, she was born in Chile and has lived all over the world. She talks about the election in the States and considers Roosevelt, like most people in Europe, as the savior of his country.

The day before yesterday at the hotel in Kobe, I got talking with a young Englishman in the lobby, and spent the whole day with him. A lieutenant (lef-

---

3. Moji today is now part of the modern metropolis of Kitakyushu, created in 1963.

tenant!) in the British Army in India, now on leave, he is going back to England via the States and Canada. Lieutenant J.I. Ballin, a graduate of Sandhurst, has been in India most of his life. We had a great afternoon going up by rope and cable car to one of the high peaks in the back of Kobe. In the evening we were joined by a chap named Booth, a Canadian Pacific agent going back and forth between Vancouver and the Orient.

The author, left, with Lieutenant Ballin near Kobe.

September 25

We are sailing along in the China Sea, directly south of Korea, and occasionally see some desolate-looking island off the coast. I have discovered more about Monsieur de Hoyer. I had felt sure he was French, and when he spoke about his life in Peking, I had taken it for granted that he had been at the French Legation. Yesterday afternoon, however, while I was playing bridge with three American women, one of them, a quite elderly lady, asked me if he was Russian. She then asked me if he had been in finance or banking, which was indeed the case, and then said she was almost positive that she and some other Americans had saved his life by smuggling him out of Russia during the revolutionary period. She had been with the American Red Cross there.

I went to de Hoyer after the bridge game and put the question to him. It was true, and he went to find the lady. My roommate is none other than the head minister of finance of Russia under the czar![4] He was general manager of the Russian Imperial Bank and vice president of the Russian Imperial Railroad. He had been staying in Moscow until the last minute, using every device he could find in shipping the imperial funds out of the country into China. Then came the days of terrorism, and a price was put on his head. On Christmas Eve 1918, his secretary came running in with the news that a crowd was on its way after

---

4. Research has turned up nothing on the mysterious Léon de Hoyer, most likely an alias.

him. The minister, his secretary and his secretary's family fled across the river to a spot where they had a car and chauffeur waiting. But they soon found that the Bolsheviks were in control of that side of the river as well. Then they saw not far off the trains of the foreign diplomats, whom the Reds were shooing out of the country. De Hoyer and his party ran over to the cars and were taken in by the Americans, who had a train with several cars. On board were some American soldiers, some Red Cross nurses (one of them my bridge partner) and the American chargé d'affaires. The American ambassador, David R. Francis, had left several months earlier, about which leave-taking de Hoyer had some caustic comments.

The train was stopped from time to time on its trip across Siberia, and de Hoyer was saved more than once by crouching down in a corner behind the dresses of the nurses. Finally they came to a place where the train cut through the estate of a White Russian count, a bitter enemy of de Hoyer's. Having somehow heard that de Hoyer might be on the train, he stopped it by simply taking away the engine. He hadn't quite the nerve to ransack an American diplomatic train; instead, his plan was to hold the engine until de Hoyer was handed over. De Hoyer told me that if he had been given up, the count would not have turned him over to the Reds but would have tortured him to death. After a long delay, during which, the American nurse later told me, he played bridge calmly with the American officers all day long, another engine was attached thanks to the Japanese ambassador's intervention, and the train was allowed to go through.

For several years de Hoyer had charge of the imperial finances (with offices in China, London and New York) and backed several movements to regain Russia from the Bolsheviks. Eventually, however, all was given up as hopeless, and he has lived in Paris, Japan, and Peking ever since. He married a Japanese woman who is spending several months in Tokyo now, but will join him later when they go to Paris. What a life he has led and what stories he can tell!

III

PEKING

5

Peking Language School
College of Chinese
Studies

Peking, September 28, 1936

H ERE I AM at my real goal, the capital of Kublai Khan, the eternal city of China, and it's more wonderful than I ever pictured it to be. Peking's famous charm has taken hold of me already, though it's scarcely more than twenty-four hours ago that I pulled into the station by the Ch'ien Men Gate.

Saturday afternoon, while the ship was coming into the Bay of Pechili, we ran into an electrical storm, followed by high winds. Half the people on board were sick and in their cabins by 5 P.M., but I stuck it out during a meager dinner. After the meal, M. de Hoyer, a Mr. Lamb (an English resident of Tientsin) and I were the only ones left. We sat in the smoking room and held ourselves in our chairs. To stand up was next to impossible, and things were sliding, falling and breaking all about us. I felt awful but just couldn't make myself go below. Finally, we made the effort and got downstairs. It was the first time I have ever felt seasick.

We had seen the coast of the Shantung Promontory Saturday morning, but my first real sight of China, of course, was at the entrance to Tangku. It seemed flat and drab except for the mud huts of the village of Taku. Upon docking at Tangku about noon we were immediately deluged under a swarm of shouting coolies fighting for our luggage. All was confusion, bustle and noise. Somehow we got taken care of and passed through the quite lenient Chinese

Maritime Customs and up to the dismal and dirty railroad. The town and every-thing about it seems to be openly under the control of the Japanese military. Their soldiers are everywhere, running things in general and marching up and down the streets.

We had to wait for two hours for the Peking Express, which came in at 2:55. The crowd at the station was certainly an odd mixture. There were all the white people from the *Chojo*, many Japanese in their kimonos, many Chinese in their gowns, which are different from the gowns the Japanese wear (single colors, coarser, no opening down the front, slits partly up each side); Japanese soldiers and officers by the dozen; a couple of French sailors; and even a geisha in a brilliant silk kimono—a motley crew to say the least.

We made a stop of several minutes at Tientsin, where we lost all our Japanese passengers and most of the others, then on to Peking. I was playing double solitaire with M. de Hoyer and looking out of the window from time to time. It is flat, not unlike our Middle West, even to the fields of corn. Off to the left and ahead of us in the distance, behind a glorious sunset, we could see the Western Hills. Soon we were speeding by the great outer wall of the city and suddenly plunging through the Chinese city. I was surprised to see stretch-es of ground and to learn that there is still room for expansion within the wall, whose current incarnation dates back to the early fifteenth century. It soon became congested, however, and just as it got dark, we came into the station.

I had a difficult time getting my bags and my trunk into one of the old Model-T Fords that serve as taxis. I left de Hoyer after being invited to lunch with him on Tuesday, and set out for the College of Chinese Studies. My trunk was tied to the running board, and I was sure that each jolt would throw it off. What a ride! I'll never forget it. I had no idea where I was going or what await-ed me at the other end. I didn't at all like the looks or the actions of the boys taking me, and when we got into one terrible quarter after the other—down narrow alleys farther and farther away—I began to worry. Then we turned into an alley that looked worse than any I had seen yet, and after following for a while, we stopped.

When I got out there was a fine-looking entrance. How relieved I was to be greeted by a polite Chinese who spoke very good English and supervised the unloading of my trunk and bags and led me through a charming, quiet cam-pus to the office. It had been such an awful day, on the ship the night before, followed by that terrible taxi ride, that I was overjoyed to be in this wonderful place. After a welcome bath and dinner at eight I saw some friends who had arrived last Wednesday. The college office informed me that a Mr. and Mrs. Miller, a nice couple I met on the *Pershing,* were at the Wagons-Lits Hotel and wanted to see me, so I spent the day with them. They had gone on to Manila and back to Shanghai on the ship and then up here by rail.

I have a pleasant room with lots of space, excellent food with fresh fruit from a private garden, and water for drinking that is always boiled. There is a library that I can use, and if I had a racquet, I could play tennis on the courts. The people here are mostly students, writers and serious-minded travelers who are staying in Peking awhile. It's ideal, and for all this, I pay thirty dollars a month. After a good night's sleep, I awoke at seven to find a perfect day, brisk and rather like the early fall at home.

The college helped me to engage a rickshaw coolie. For six dollars a month, he takes me any place I want to go and waits for me. It will take me a while to get used to being such an autocrat. For instance, I had a great stack of laundry that the room boy sent out to be washed and a linen suit to be cleaned: the charges came to about thirty cents. It doesn't seem possible.

Postcard of Chi'en Men, tower at left, and railway station in the 1930's. Chi'en Men today is one of the few remaining gates of the old wall of Peking.

Peking, October 2

I have been in the Orient now about four and a half weeks. One becomes quickly accustomed to the different life, to the wonderful service from the servants and the slow tempo. Time seems to mean nothing here and labor hardly more.

Today I have been up since 5:30 on an expedition to the Great Wall. What an experience it was to stand on the watchtower at the point where the wall cuts across Nankow Pass: there below me and extending out to the horizon in the west, was the old road to Mongolia, the road of the camel caravans. This is the road that the Mongol hordes under the Great Khan followed when they broke through the wall at that very spot in the early thirteenth century. I saw hundreds of camels returning to Peking after spending the summer five hundred miles away in Mongolia. It was as if nothing had changed. The watchtowers have crumbled somewhat and there are no sentries on the wall, but the road is just the same. The few farmers in the pass are having the same struggle with the terribly rocky soil they had hundreds of years ago and are using the same implements.

The other day, I visited the observatory on the wall of the Tartar City. Originally built by Khan at the end of the thirteenth century, it is supposedly

the oldest in the world. The instruments are amazing, great bronze affairs mounted on fierce dragons. This is history of a different kind, of advancement and knowledge.

I also went across the lake to the Winter Palace and saw the famous Dragon Screen, as bright in its colors as if it had been made last year, instead of in the eighteenth century. The marks of the last empress, Tz'u-hsi, are everywhere, at the Summer Palace, and out at the foot of the Western Hills she loved so well. One can see her sitting with her attendants along the shore of the lake or in one of her royal barges threading its way through the thousands of lotus pads.

It doesn't seem possible that in 1936, I am living in a city with strong high

Postcard of Legation Street in the Legation Quarter, Peking, in the 1930's.

walls guarded twenty-four hours a day by a patrol of several thousand soldiers. The gates are closed at night to keep out bandits and wolves. One cannot go out to the Eastern Tombs, where the Empress Dowager is buried, just forty miles from the city because of the bandits. Just last week the American Embassy issued a statement requesting Americans not to go even to the Ming Tombs.

The Legation Quarter is a wonderful place with many associations. One part of the wall of the British Embassy was left unrepaired after the Boxer Rebellion[1]; beside the holes is written "Lest We Forget." I ride through the quarter every day in my rickshaw. Although right in the heart of the city, it is a quiet, peaceful place. Lovely shade trees of all varieties line the streets. Every legation is surrounded by its walls—French, Belgian, Italian, English and Russian. Now everything is tranquil, but one is well aware that peace was won by many lives lost and that unrest could happen again. The quarter itself has walls, and its gates are closed at night.

Thursday night I was invited to dinner by Mrs. Picket of the *Chojo Maru* (the ex-Red Cross worker who knew M. de Hoyer). We had eight in the party

1. Boxer Rebellion 1900: The uprising started as an anti-Christian struggle and ended as an anti-foreign uprising. The siege lasted eight weeks until the city was finally relieved by an international force of nineteen thousand troops. Tz'u-Hsi and the young emperor fled to Sian.

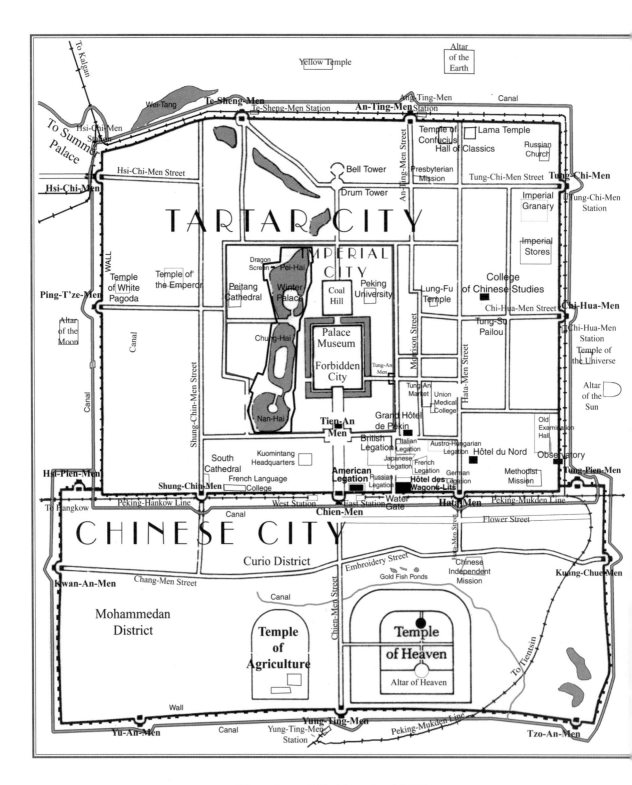

The city of Peking in 1936

and went to a Chinese restaurant. First of all, we sat at a table and had tea and delicious candied walnuts. Then we moved to the main table where we had duck livers, chicken and peppers, Peking duck in pancakes, pounded chicken breast, wine, lotus seeds, various vegetables and lastly fish in sweet-sour sauce and two soups. Finally we moved back to the other table for some more tea. The Chinese are incredible cooks: what a feast.

October 5

The college opened officially this morning and everyone, old and new students alike, went to the opening language class. The beginners' course is given by a popular Chinese teacher who didn't use a word of English but made himself understood by sign language, holding up objects and repeating the words over and over again. He had a good sense of humor and a pleasing personality. At the beginning of the class, as at all classes, the students rise and bow to the teacher when he comes and when he goes. There are about sixty students enrolled here, coming from all over the world, many of them missionaries and YMCA workers.

How Peking grows on one. Riding through the streets by rickshaw, I get views and impressions that I shall always remember. I was on my way back to the college after an afternoon looking around Flower Street in the Chinese City. It was beginning to get dark as I came to Hatamen Gate, and the lamps of the rickshaws were all lit up. These are hung low near the foot of the occupant, lighting up his face and the boy's back in an eerie fashion. The massive gate—ninety-nine feet high—was a great blotch against the darkening sky, while through the narrow tunnel-like passage below passed in steady but confused succession swarms of rickshaws, street vendors with squeaky carts, kimono-clad men and women on foot, numerous beggars cringing, donkey carts and even a string of camels. Those are the things, together with an occasional honking automobile, that make up many a street scene in Peking, but at nightfall, it looks more bizarre and Oriental than ever. Tonight, as always, I got a thrill going through the gate in that press of animals and humanity.

Halfway out of Hatamen Street in the Tartar City, a light rain began to fall. Shong (my boy) stopped, put up the hood on the rickshaw and threw the canvas over my legs and lap. Then with a waxed parasol over himself, we continued to the college, passing on our way the spot where Baron von Ketteler, the German minister, was killed in the street—a fatality of the Boxer Rebellion.

I have spent quite a bit of time with Gilbert and Fran Olson, a fairly young couple staying here at the college. Both teachers in Chicago schools, they are on their way around the world during their sabbatical year.

I took my Palm Beach suit to be copied at the Clock Store. When all made up to satisfaction it will cost me U.S. $3.63. If it comes out well I should really get another one, but as money is getting scarce, I have to be careful.

I called on a Mr. S.H. Shao (a friend of my cousin Jean Noling) from the Peking Union Medical College.[2] I asked him to dinner here at the college tomorrow night, but he said that according to Chinese etiquette I must first be his guest. So the night before last he called for me here and took me to an excellent Chinese restaurant. He had also invited a friend of his from the Medical College, a Mr. Wei, and the three of us had a grand time.

The other morning, I went to see M. de Hoyer at the Grand Hôtel de Pékin, where he has a large suite with a private balcony overlooking part of the Forbidden City and all of the Legation Quarter. His No. 2 boy sits in the hall of his suite and announces visitors and runs errands. M. de Pelotier, the editor of the French newspaper, was also there, and a little while later a Baron Somebody-or-Other called. They spoke in English most of the time in deference to the "dumb American" in their midst, but often lapsed into French. On one occasion, when de Hoyer brought out a copy of his newest book in Russian, they all switched to that language. A great deal of the talk was naturally on the tense situation between Japan and China, and as all three are friendly with the various ambassadors, I got a lot of information on the official slant. Last week it seemed as if war was inevitable, but this week, conditions are better, perhaps because of pressure on Tokyo from Great Britain and the United States. It is generally agreed that the first step in the Japanese plan would be the annexation of Peking and Tientsin to Manchukuo. I don't believe that the Chinese would try to defend the city since there are enough Japanese soldiers inside the walls right now to accomplish their purpose. There are so many rumors going around.

---

2. Founded in 1906 with joint support from the Chinese government and several foreign religious groups (thus the term Union). In 1917 it was reorganized with the support of the Rockefeller Foundation. P.U.M.C. is a top medical school today.

At the Great Wall, northwest of Peking, 1936.

RIGHT: *Gate at Temple of Confucius.*

ABOVE: *At Summer Palace.*

RIGHT: *In front of North Gate of Forbidden Palace with Katherine Clarke.*

LEFT: *Kunming Lake, at Summer Palace.*

BELOW: *From left, Martha Hecke and Katherine Clarke (former shipmates of the author) with Fran and Gilbert Olson at the Yellow Temple, north of Peking.*

CENTER, LEFT: *With friends at Nankow Pass, Great Wall.*

LEFT: *In front of the Dragon Screen at the Winter Palace, Peking.*

ABOVE: *Having lunch at Winter Palace on the North Lake with Mr. Wei, center, and Mr. Shao from Peking Union Medical College.*

LEFT: *At steps of Temple of Heaven, Peking.*

BOTTOM: *Funeral procession on Embroidery Street in the Chinese City, Peking.*

Today is the Silver Jubilee of the Chinese Republic, so all the flags are out and many soldiers have been marching up and down the streets.

I get my Chesterfields at the United States Marine Post attached to the American Legation. I had been paying forty cents but my rickshaw boy put me wise. Every time I go through the great gate of the embassy, the American soldier on guard clicks his heels and "presents arms." You would think I was carrying an important letter of state instead of saving twenty cents a package on my cigarettes. They cost me only six American cents a package, eight cents less than at home.

October 16

I went with the Olsons (my schoolteacher friends) to the Temple of Heaven, its white marble now spotless and gleaming after the restoration by the government. In the morning we went to the Western section of the Forbidden City, where the last of the Manchus lived until about twelve years ago. Some of the palaces and furnishings are fine, but the influence of the West brings out some ludicrous sights. One sees fine old tables covered with cheap oilcloth, cheap brass beds, terrible pictures and ugly bathtubs. A bottle of Listerine was standing on one dressing table.

I have enjoyed my time with Mr. Shao and his friend Mr. Wei, and have learned a lot from my talks with them. The night before last, they invited me to dinner at a famous Mohammedan restaurant down near the market. The main course was a Chinese version of the Japanese dish sukiyaki. After dinner we went back to Mr. Wei's house, quite a ways out from the center of the Tartar City—almost to the East Wall. His home is not splendid by any means but is comfortable. His cousin lives with him and had prepared some excellent coffee. We had some interesting talk and a look at his cousin's collection of curios and art. I took my leave at quarter of eleven and waking up Shong, my rickshaw boy, went home alone. I enjoyed picking out Orion and the Dipper on my ride home through the wall-lined streets in the starlight.

I have wanted all along to go up the gorges of the Yangtze to Chungking, but thought it would be far too expensive. If I left here on October 27, arrived in Hankow the twenty-ninth, sailed up the river on the thirtieth and got back to Hankow on the fourteenth, then I could take the train to Changsha (Yale-in-

China), bus to Nanchang, train to Hangchow, train to Shanghai, arriving about November 20. It would be about 3,400 miles of travel in inland China. Chungking is about 1,500 miles up the Yangtze from Shanghai.

It would be a worthwhile trip and cost a little more than living in Shanghai for the same length of time—three weeks. But, on the other hand, getting a job in Shanghai is so important that I need the time. If I don't get work, my trip is over in the middle of February, seven months after I left home. Conditions in the East are good for the moment, but Europe looks ready to blow up.

College of Chinese Studies
Tu Tiao Hutung, Tung Sze Pailou
October 25

When I wake up each morning there is a pleasant sound of soft, sweet whistles made by bamboo attached to pigeons. The birds circle over the college in a flock, giving us quite a concert. It is hard to imagine having a street address as the one above. *Hutung* means a little street or alley; *pailou* is an ornamental arch. The college has been ideal for me, with fine buildings, beautiful trees and green lawns. The blowing dust is the only drawback to life in Peking. If there is any wind it can be annoying and uncomfortable. March and April are the worst months.

Wednesday a bunch of us spent considerable time in the northern part of the city at a rug factory owned by an American named Fette. The rugs cost $2.50 Mex. per square foot and are exquisite. A nine-by-twelve can be had for only $302.40. Everything is done by hand, of course—even the spinning of the wool. The workers live right on the place and form their own community.

This morning the Olsons and I have been over at the Winter Palace in the Imperial City, just wandering around and enjoying the place. Last Sunday Mr. Shao, Mr. Wei and I spent the day there, having our noonday meal at a pavilion on the North Lake. Martha and Katherine, my friends from the *Pershing* who had been staying at the college, have moved to Mrs. Calhoun's, where they will stay another month. Mrs. Calhoun, the widow of a former American ambassador to China, runs an exclusive boarding house in her home, which is actually a converted temple. Her Wednesday afternoon teas are one of the highlights of Peking foreign society.

Much as it hurts, I have decided to give up the Yangtze trip. I can't let myself get so nearly broke before I have given a thorough try at the job situation in Shanghai. I will leave here by train Wednesday evening for Hankow, arriving there Friday morning. I have a man there to look up about a job. Then I will run down to Changsha to see Yale-in-China and then go to Shanghai and stay in the YMCA, which costs about the same as the college in Peking.

November 4, Nanchang

I was lucky enough to be in Peking for Navy Day, October 27, just before I left. All the Americans in Peking were invited to a celebration by the Marine Post at the Legation. We have a full battalion of six hundred men there, a wonderful bunch. They are handpicked, of course, and seem head and shoulders above the men of other legations. It was a grand occasion, the Marines in their dress uniforms, a really good band with soldiers marching, horses galloping and flags flying on the American parade ground against a background of the Tartar Wall and the Ch'ien Men Gate. There was a buffet lunch on the lawn. How good it was to hear Western music. In the evening we were again guests of the Marines at a dance in Johnson Hall. The whole thing was like an old high school dance, including the stampede when refreshments were announced. The Marines, evidently, had orders to keep everyone dancing. The female tourists had a great time.

I spent most of Wednesday, October 28, packing. I never expect to see another city like Peking.

6

Peking to Shanghai via Hankow and Nanchang

WHEN I BOARDED the train for Hankow, I found someone else was in my berth. The Japan Tourist Bureau, which arranged the trip, had made a mistake. No one could speak English, but then Mr. Shao and Mr. Wei came along to see me off and straightened out the confusion with the ticket master just in the nick of time before the train left.

The first-class coaches on the *Hankow Express* are the best in China. They were made at terrific expense by the Pullman Company of Chicago and used to be the regular *Shanghai Express*. In the revolution of 1927, they were seized by one of the generals and taken up to Manchuria. The Central Government got them back and put them on the Peking-Hankow run. There are two berths in a compartment and a washroom between each compartment. The chap in my compartment was Mr. Donaldson, a well-known tour director from California. He was taking a party of eight up the Yangtze to Chungking. They were going to fly most of the way through the gorges; the people who had never flown before were scared stiff.

I don't imagine I'll know the results of the American election until I reach Shanghai. It sounds as if there is a large Roosevelt plurality—the Republicans have botched it badly.

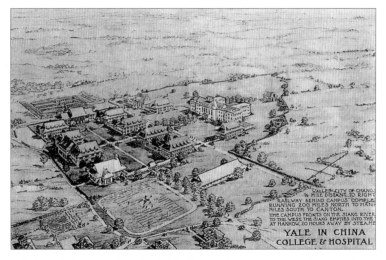

A 1916 design for the Yale-in-China campus, Changsha.

I left Peking Wednesday by train and arrived in Hankow Friday morning; left Hankow by train Sunday evening and arrived in Changsha (Yale-in-China) Monday morning; left Changsha by bus Tuesday morning; arrived Nanchang Tuesday night. I won't be able to get a train out of here until tomorrow morning. Then it's a thirty-hour run into Shanghai. When I get there, I will have spent four nights on a train—two of them in first class, one night in second class and one never-to-be-forgotten night in a third-class sleeper. Two nights in a Lutheran mission, and one night at Yale-in-China[1] just about complete the picture. Along with the third-class sleeper ride, I'll never forget the twelve-hour bus ride from Changsha over here to Nanchang. I don't know the exact mileage, but it's probably less than two hundred miles—not as much as the time makes you think.

The train pulled into Hankow about 9:30 A.M., and after showing my passport and giving the customs man my calling card (I have to use about five a day to give officials), I was allowed to get out onto the street.

At the suggestion of one of my fellow students at the language school, I had written ahead to the Lutheran Mission House. There was a boy to meet me, which was a great help. He got my bags and me into a drosky while he took care of my trunk. Hankow is the only place where I have seen droskies, which are Russian carriages. They have two men to a carriage, one to hold the reins and the other to help pull the horse around corners. This sounds silly but it's

---

1. Yale-in-China Association: The association was formed in 1901 to promote mutual understanding between the peoples of China and the United States. The Chinese University of Hong Kong and Yale-China, as it is now called, have created a consortium of environmental institutes in China, Taiwan and the United States to work on critical water management and pollution problems in the Pearl River Delta.

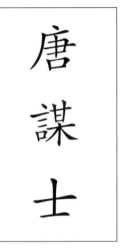

Chinese characters
for Thomas:
Tang Mo Shih.

the sort of thing you get used to in China. Mr. Hansen of the Lutheran mission, welcomed me cordially. I have a good room and meals for $4 Mex. per day.

In Hankow I went to the American Consulate down on the Bund on the corner of Rue du Président Wilson, where I had my passport translated into Chinese and was given a Chinese name—Tang Mo Shih. The first word is the name of a dynasty, the second means a well-organized plan, and the third means a scholar.

Then I had to go to the Bureau of Public Safety to get a visa for the trip to Changsha and Nanchang. I had to get another photograph taken, as they need to keep one in the bureau. This red tape sounds more like the Japanese officialdom than the Chinese.

China is so interesting. I love being here, but on the whole I think I get on better with the Japanese; they are polite, progressive and honest. Baggage is no problem in Japan; you just give it to a porter and forget it. In China you don't dare let it out of your sight.

I had tea with the missionaries in Hankow on Friday afternoon. The tea was a reception for a Mr. McGavan from Shanghai, who is the secretary of the National Bible Society of Scotland. After dinner at the mission house I went to see Mr. McGavan off on the ship to Shanghai. It was a Jardine[2] boat and impressive. I was almost tempted to go that way instead of the hard overland trip, but since going by train and bus is such a good opportunity to see the country, I stuck to my plans.

The Yangtze was a wonderful sight in the full moon with all the pictur-

Deke Erh

Present-day view of the old American
Consulate on the Bund, Hankow.

2. Jardine, Matheson & Co., the powerful British shipping, banking and entrepreneurial firm, in China since 1842. Its great rival was Butterfield & Swire, founded in 1866.

Early 20th-century postcard of the English Concession in Hankow,
with Yangtze visible upper left. The river is about a mile wide here.

esque junks and sampans. My trunk was a real problem. I had to send it down-river to Shanghai by ship. This was difficult, as there is an inter-province customs in China. I went back and forth between the shipping office (Jardine, Matheson) and the Customs House five times. It didn't cost very much but it took me all day.

Saturday evening I went out with Hardenbrook of Eastman Kodak and Bob Taylor of the American Consulate and drank some beer. Everyone knows everyone else in Hankow. There are quite a few Germans here—at one café there was always a group singing old German songs. I thoroughly enjoyed the whole evening, especially hearing the American sailors tell stories about the Upper Yangtze and going there on their ships.[3]

The Burlington Hotel in Nanchang is freezing cold. Although it is supposed to be the best inland hotel in China, it's pretty miserable and the food is wretched. I hate to spend two nights here, as it's expensive, but I have to wait till the train goes. When I walked into the dining room for lunch, I was surprised to see twelve foreigners, all in black shirts. They were Italian flyers China has borrowed from Mussolini to teach their men how to fly.

---

3. Hankow was a major base of the United States Yangtze River Patrol, which operated gunboats on the Yangtze from the middle of the 19th century to 1941.

7

Stranded in Shanghai

Foreign YMCA, Shanghai,
November 16, 1936

THIS FOREIGN YMCA, the highest-toned Y I've ever run across, is rather like a ritzy residential city club. It's at 150 Bubbling Well Road, opposite the racecourse and next to the Park Hotel. A short bus ride or twenty-minute walk on Nanking Road brings one to the Bund[1], passing through the shopping center of town on the way.

I've signed up for room and board at $4.25 per day, which is reasonable for what the place has to offer: swimming pool, gym, lounges, library, etc. And this special rate gives me three meals a day.

I'm really in a predicament about money and ships. I have a ticket on the *General Sherman* but have heard that she is stuck in San Francisco because of a strike. And when the strike does break, she will have to go up to Portland

---

1. Bund: Anglo-Indian word for a river embankment. Pronounced like fund.

Postcard of the Willow Tea House in Shanghai in the 1930's.

before starting across the Pacific. The steamship company is doing nothing whatsoever about putting ticket holders on ships of other lines. The man in the office told me that it might well be January when she arrives. If I turn in my ticket for a rebate, it would take months to collect it from the office.

By December 1, I won't have a cent over a hundred dollars. It would take practically seventy dollars to get a ticket to Manila and Hong Kong.[2] If I buy a ticket on another line, I would be almost flat broke. I would also have to go right on through, without getting off at Manila, and hope to make a good connection in Hong Kong. And then I would also have to stay on the ship to northern Europe instead of getting off at Naples. I think that plan is out.

What an evil deus ex machina that strike is. My chances for getting work

2. The author had booked a round-the-world-trip by ship, with return to New York via Europe, on several lines. The *General Sherman* of the States Steamship Lines was to have taken him from Shanghai to Hong Kong with a side trip to Manila.

SHANGHAI

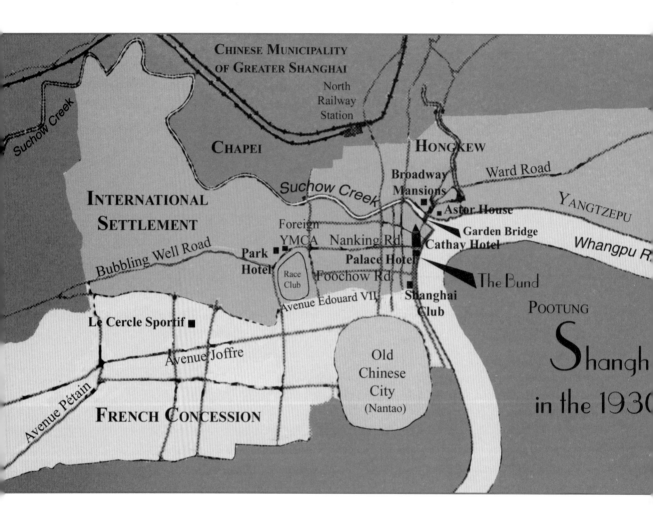

CHINESE MUNICIPALITY
OF GREATER SHANGHAI

North
Railway
Station

Suchow Creek

CHAPEI

HONGKEW

Broadway
Mansions

Ward Road

Suchow Creek

YANGTZEPU

INTERNATIONAL
SETTLEMENT

Foreign
YMCA   Nanking Rd.

Astor House

Garden Bridge
Cathay Hotel

Bubbling Well Road

Park
Hotel

Race
Club

Palace Hotel

Whangpu R.

Foochow Rd.

Avenue Edouard VII

Shanghai
Club

The Bund

Le Cercle Sportif

POOTUNG

Avenue Joffre

Old
Chinese
City
(Nantao)

Shangh

in the 1930

Avenue Pétain

FRENCH CONCESSION

*Shanghai in the 1930's was a booming international metropolis and the fifth largest port in the world.
Power in this city of over three million Chinese was essentially in the hands of a small number of foreigner*

Postcard of the Bund, Shanghai, 1936: Building with dome, center, is the Hong Kong and Shanghai Bank, where the Texas Company (Texaco) had its China headquarters; clock tower marks the Customs House; the Shanghai Club is at left, with white awnings.

RIGHT: *Postcard of the racecourse: tall building left of center is the Park Hotel; the Foreign YMCA is to its right; the building at far right is the China United Apartments Building, later the Pacific Hotel.*

LEFT: *Press photo of the USS Augusta, flagship of the Asiatic Fleet, moored in the Whangpu River. It remained off the Bund from August 1937 to January 1938 to protect American interests.*

BELOW: *Postcard of Nanking Road, the main shopping street.*

LEFT: *Postcard of view from top of Broadway Mansions: Whangpu River with Bund at right, Public Garden, at left, and Garden Bridge over Soochow Creek, foreground.*

BELOW: *The Cathay Hotel, where Noël Coward wrote* Private Lives *in 1929.*

CENTER: *View of Bund, taken by the author.*

ABOVE: *Postcard of junks on the Whangpu.*

Postcard of Soochow Creek, showing Szechuan Road Bridge, center, the main post office, left; Broadway Mansions Apartments, tall building, center; the Astor Hotel, to immediate right of Broadway Mansions. The Whangpu River is visible upper right.

seem pretty dim right now; they are remote enough so that I shouldn't count on them in facing the question of what to do. I think I'll trust to luck and lay my hopes on the strike breaking and getting a reservation on the *Sherman*. It's a gamble, but if I can get out of here by the middle of December, I'll still have seventy dollars or so. That will mean that with economy I'll be able to see more in the Far East and also have a little for Europe.

Golly, I'm bewildered and frankly a little scared. It is hard to do any sight-seeing when I am worried about money.

Shanghai[3] is a large modern city, notable mainly for the mad whirl in which it lives and its amazingly cosmopolitan population. It is a world unto itself. Many of the foreigners here seem to have lost their home ties. On the other hand they know less about China and the Chinese than the person who stays home and reads about it.

How I pity those "round the worlders" whose notions of China are derived from a two-day layover in Shanghai and an equal stay in Hong Kong. I can see though that it would be much easier to write articles about China with such a background (as many do) than after seeing more of it.

November 17

I have talked with the assistant commercial attaché of the American Consulate, the secretary of the American Chamber of Commerce, the secretary of the University Men's Club and Mr. Nottingham, editor of the *Shanghai Times*. I was given little or no encouragement from any of these sources, but from the talk around here, I might be able to land something with the Texas Company. I met a chap[4] last week who works for them, and I'll go down there this after-noon. The other night, I met a young fellow who took me to a banquet at the Shanghai Rowing Club. The Americans in the club are outnumbered consider-ably by the English and other northern Europeans. It is a rule, of course, at English banquets that no smoking is to be done until the toast to the King,

---

3. Shanghai was the first Chinese port to be opened to Western trade. In 1863, the Hongkew district, which was originally developed by American and Japanese concessionaires, was com-bined with the British concession to create the International Settlement.
4. Philip Le Fevre, who later became head of the Texas Company operations in China.

which is given about dessert time. When the toast came, it was "Gentlemen! To our respective rulers!"

On a forlorn hope, I walked into the office of the Texas Company, on the Bund, and twenty minutes later, I walked out with a job. I was so lucky finding it, and the opportunity came about so suddenly. There are hundreds of fellows in Shanghai walking the streets looking for work. Many of them have been looking for months, and many have had experience out here and are specialists in some line or know Chinese. I simply walked in cold and got the job! When they asked me how much I wanted, I screwed up my nerve and asked for $450 Mex. They gave me $520, or U.S. $155, which is very good for a newcomer.

On board the Hoten Maru, *November 18*

I have a marketing job with the Texas Company (China),[5] a large outfit with offices and branches all over Asia. I am to be stationed in Tsingtao and will probably see considerable traveling about Shantung Province. Tsingtao is, according to everyone I have spoken to, just about the best place to live in

5. The Texas Company, later Texaco and now Chevron-Texaco, was founded in Texas in 1902. About a decade later it had many offices overseas, including China, where it would compete with the Asiatic Petroleum Co. (Shell) and Standard Oil. In 1936, when the author was hired, the managing director of the China operation was W.H. Pinckard.

China. It is far and away the healthiest, with mountains, woods (rare in this country), seashore with fine bathing and also good mountain water, fresh milk, etc. The most popular summer resort in the Far East, Tsingtao is crowded with visitors during the warm season. During the winter, which is much quieter, the foreign population dwindles considerably.

How long I will keep the job, I don't know. It depends on the job and I intend to give it a good go. I'm well out of that mess about ships and money and don't have to worry about missing Europe.

IV

TSINGTAO

青島

8

Tsingtao

Tsingtao, November 28, 1936
Pension Victoria, 9 Kin Kou Road

I HAVE JUST MOVED over here from the hotel where I have been staying since my arrival. The Pension Victoria, run by a Russian woman, is comfortable and convenient. It's a relief not being a tourist any more. Now I'm a China resident, selling oil for the lamps of China, an integral part of the community, and what a fine community it is, with people of all nationalities.

Tsingtao[1] is a pretty red-roofed town passed down from the German occupation of the port and control of the surrounding region. It has a perfect bay with bright blue water, some picturesque little islands dotted here and there with junks and sampans, even a Chinese temple along the shore. The three Japanese destroyers anchored out in the middle of the bay give a realistic touch

---

1. Tsingtao was a quiet fishing village until it was transformed into a minor naval station at the turn of the 20th century. Germany, anxious not to be left out of the foreign powers' demands for concessions in China, seized the area in 1897 and built an efficient port city and popular summer resort. Tsingtao was taken over by the Japanese at the outset of World War I and returned to the Chinese in 1922. But Japan continued to maintain a strong presence there.

Tsingtao in 1936, showing City Hall, with flag, and Little Tsingtao Island, top left.

to the picture. Behind the bay, on all sides, rise immediately jagged hills. No wonder it is called the most beautiful spot in all China.

The foreign community is mostly British, as usual, but the American percentage is higher than in most places. There are quite a few Germans and Norwegians, and all together about three hundred foreigners, not counting the Russians. They are White Russians, refugees from the Revolution, and have a strange standing in China. These are people without a country, and their lot is a sad one. There are about forty thousand of them in Shanghai alone, mostly in the so-called French Concession, living a hand-to-mouth existence.

My boss, Frank Keefe, has been here with his wife and children for six years, except for their home leave. I had Thanksgiving dinner with them at their attractive home on top of a hill overlooking the bay. The other guests were a Chinese couple and our Chinese Texas agent here in Tsingtao (proper pronunciation: Ching-tow).

This past week I have been working outside of town at the Texas terminal where we have our oil tanks, godown[2] and factory. I have just been watching

---

2. Warehouse, from the Malay *godon*.

operations to get my feet on the ground a bit. The scene at the godown is just like a picture in a book—an endless line of coolies with two or sometimes four five-gallon tins hanging from the ends of the bamboo pole balanced across their shoulders. They swing along with a peculiar sort of gait but with a different chant from the Shanghai coolies. I've seen them making five-gallon cans, filling and sealing them, and helped direct the loading on the freight cars, trucks, steamers and junks. I also assisted in the inventory and in general learned all I could. After another day I am to go back to the office.

Tsingtao, however, is only my headquarters. I'm to be traveling up-country most of the time, starting about the first of the year. With a cot, some bedding and an interpreter, I will be gone on trips varying from three to six weeks in length. For weeks at a time I won't hear a word of English except by my interpreter, or see a white face. That is just the kind of job I had in mind when I came out here.

It hurt to pay my $100 initiation fee for the International Club, but it is well worth it. A fairly large place with great food and dancing every Saturday night, the club is much more of a home than the Victoria. As a rule I dine out. Chinese

Postcard of the International Club, meeting place for the foreign community.

TSINGTAO

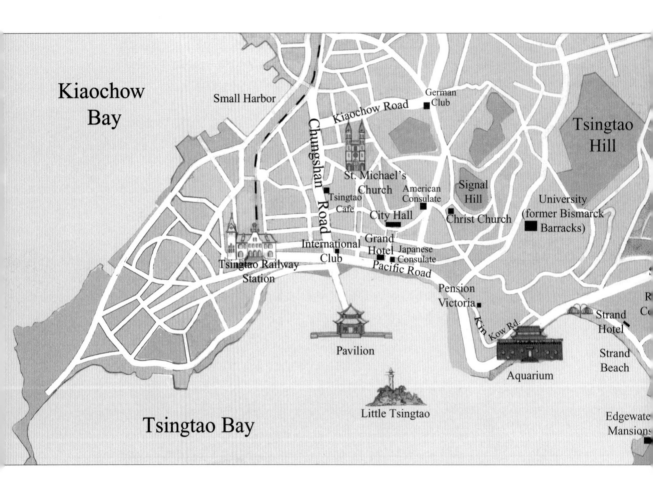

Kiaochow
Bay

Small Harbor

Kiaochow Road

German
Club

Tsingtao
Hill

Chungshan Road

St. Michael's
Church

American
Consulate

Signal
Hill

University
(former Bismarck
Barracks)

Tsingtao
Cafe

City Hall

Christ Church

Grand
Hotel

International
Club

Japanese
Consulate

Pacific Road

Tsingtao Railway
Station

Pension
Victoria

Kin Kow Rd.

Strand
Hotel

R
Co

Pavilion

Aquarium

Strand
Beach

Little Tsingtao

Edgewate
Mansions

Tsingtao Bay

Map showing Tsingtao in 1937 and principal sites mentioned by the author.

food is always good and the Tsingtao Café serves marvelous Russian food, especially borscht and beef stroganoff. Sunday night I had a real chili dinner at the home of some Americans who are originally from Texas.

The St. Andrew's Day Ball was a great affair. The Scots in town came in their kilts and danced Scottish reels. They even had haggis—everything but the bagpipes. Last night a mixed bunch of us had dinner at the club and bowled all evening. This Saturday night is the big German party at the Grand Hotel,[3] one of the biggest occasions of the winter season. And that's the way it goes all the time. I think that left to themselves, the Americans would be as quiet and settled as most of them are at home. It's the English influence I suppose, that makes them act differently. The Britishers are the controlling element in the society here. I have to hand it to them. They have this colonization of outposts down to a tee, after their many years of practice. It's said of the English that if there were just two of them living in an African jungle they would form a club. I believe it. Here I am in an outpost of China that I was only vaguely aware of, and I'm enjoying more social life than ever. What's more, I can live like a king on U.S. $155 a month.

I'd better enjoy it while I can for it will be a very different story before long. Mr. Keefe told me today that I would almost certainly spend four weeks at a stretch up-country without hearing a word of English, except from my interpreter. The Shanghai office notified me today that my camp cot is on its way up for me.

December 3

We are having a little excitement here just now. There has been some trouble at the Japanese cotton mills in town, and at three this morning the Japanese landed a thousand marines with ammunition and supplies. They are patrolling the mill district; such places as the wharf, the landing field and the station are all in their hands. "The marines have landed and the situation is well in hand!" It sounds like our own actions in Central America. The Japanese are wearing steel helmets and actually bristle with arms. I wonder if the New York

---

3. The Grand Hotel, formerly the Prinz Heinrich, on Pacific Road, the "Bund" of Tsingtao. It was under the same management as the Strand Hotel on the Strand Beach.

newspapers carried the stories about the Japanese marines landing. The situation looks better now but it is only a matter of time before there is real trouble. The Chinese are at last developing a national feeling and patriotism. There is a strong sense that they must and will fight Japan.

The longer the war holds off the better for China, for she is growing stronger all the time. The trouble is the country seems unable to supply law and order for her own people. The day I arrived in Tsingtao, one of our junks carrying oil to a port south of here was pirated. So often we hear daily reports of our travelers changing their itinerary in Shantung because bandits are holding the next town on their list. So it is all over China.

At this time wild rumors are thicker than bees in a hive, but I'm still of the opinion that nothing will happen. The foreigners are safe at any rate—it's only business that can be affected, and then only in case of Japan taking over, as they did in Manchuria. They set up a government monopoly on such products as oil so there is little the foreigners can do. Our office in Mukden is no more.

For these several weeks I'm in an office with a Chinese member of the staff who handles the kerosene end of the business. Every day we have some of our agents in from out of town. Naturally they don't speak or understand English. Lee Ding-fong tells me all about each one—how crooked or how honest he is.

Most of these Chinese businessmen cut imposing figures in their long gowns. They wear little round mandarin caps like black skullcaps and may have little silky goatees and curling mustaches. Here, in town, you see fewer facial adornments but no more than one or two in a thousand Chinese wear foreign clothes, less than that probably.

Many older women you see on the street hobble along on bound feet. Pigtails are rare although I have seen them occasionally. The street hawkers are more on the Peking style than the Shanghai type, but there must be more running water[4] here than in Peking as you don't see the noisy water carts that form one of the interesting pictures in the Peking scene.

The German bazaar on Saturday was a huge success, with dancing, rifle shooting, raffles, etc. It wasn't over until 5 in the morning. On Sunday I went riding with a crowd of young people on racing ponies that sure give you a ride for the money. Last Sunday I was out again on an even livelier pony and experienced a runaway and a fall. I never went so fast or was so scared in my

---

4. The Germans built an impressive water and sanitation system that still functions today.

Strollers on the shore at Tsingtao in 1937. Building at center is part of the Aquarium.

ABOVE: *The fleet's in.*
Chungshan Road in
Tsingtao, summer of 1937.

RIGHT: *Japanese women on*
Chungshan Road. Texaco
office is in modern building,
background center. Notice the
Texaco sign, center, and gas
price, near right, $1.07 Mex.,
or 32 U.S. cents, on the
Socony pump.

RIGHT: *Pedestrians on Chungshan Road, Tsingtao's Main Street.*

BELOW: *Entrance to Pension Victoria on Kinkou Road.*

ABOVE: *Main bathing beach.*

LEFT: *Lushun Park, near Pension Victoria, with Tsingtao Bay in background.*

Scenes in Tsingtao: TOP, *workers loading junks with Texaco kerosene in Little Harbor.* ABOVE, *St. Michael's Church in background with German colonial buildings. Tsingtao was under German control from 1897 to 1914.*

life. What a beautiful day it was though and what a fine place to ride—mountain trails that give you a view down on the town and for miles over other mountains and out to sea.

Sooner or later, all the Westerners here get considerable Pidgin English in their speech. Food is always *chow* even in a relatively polite conversation. The midday meal is always tiffin.[5] I don't think of it as lunch any more. Every foreigner in dealing with servants is either Master or Missy. And if one wants something quickly one says "Chop-chop." "Chow water" is boiled water for drinking or brushing one's teeth. I always use a glass of boiled water for brushing my teeth, and it is so difficult to remember not to use tap water.

It is going to be hard to leave this country. Life, for a foreigner with a decent job, certainly has many advantages. There's not just the material advantage in the way of service and more money to spend but also the indescribable feeling that binds the foreigners together. It makes for a community life that I like.

Besides, I rather enjoy "being somebody." At home, until one gains wealth or fame of some sort, a man is just one in a crowd of humanity. On the whole, I suppose, I wish that I could have secured work in Peking, but I think it's a stagnant city in a business sense. The royal court was all that supported it except for schools, missionaries and museums.

The abdication of Edward VIII has fallen like a ton of bricks on Tsingtao. More than half the foreigners are British, who are taking it hard. Besides loss of empire prestige, most of them seem to feel a real personal grief that such a thing could happen. No matter which way he decided, I think he was bound to feel that he had done the wrong thing. If he had decided to give Mrs. Simpson up, at least he would have had the feeling that he had done his duty. Now, he can't be sure, and theirs will have to be a powerful love to withstand his doubts as to the rightness of his action.

It has been a week since Chiang Kai-shek was "detained" in Shensi.[6] Just

---

5. Tiffin: Anglo-Indian term for light meal, usually lunch and often a curry.

6. Chiang Kai-shek was determined to defeat the Communists but many Chinese supported a united front against the Japanese. General Chang Hsueh-liang, under pressure, detained Chiang when he came to Sian until he agreed to call off the civil war with the Communists and unite the country against the invading Japanese. He was released on Christmas day, but General Chang was held for twenty-five years.

Old postcard from 1914 showing the Tsingtao railway station in background, center, with tower. In a short period of time the Germans laid out an orderly Bavarian town. The station and many of the colonial buildings are still standing.

when things seemed to be improving under Chiang's leadership, General Chang Hsueh-liang had to pull off a trick like that. Most of the factions in this country are supporting Nanking and are praying for Chiang's safety.

The Japanese marines are actually withdrawing from Tsingtao, which only means that they go to their permanent places on ships, several hundred yards off the Bund.

Mr. Keefe, my boss, follows the regular China-side custom of giving a party for the whole staff on Christmas morning—Chinese clerks and their families and all of us. For dinner I am going to Barden's, the No. 2 of Socony-Vacuum.[7] There is a big New Year's Ball at the club in fancy dress and probably other small parties.

It's getting pretty cold: 26 degrees yesterday. We had our first snowfall Thursday morning, and the mountains still have a white mantle. My overcoat

7. Standard Oil (now Exxon), which had been selling kerosene in China since the 1880's, and Socony-Vacuum (now Mobil) combined their Asia-Pacific holdings into a joint venture, Standard-Vacuum, in 1933. Its main China office, like the Texas Co.'s, was in Shanghai.

was finished just in time, and although good and warm, it weighs a ton. The rickshaws have their winter curtains up now to keep out the wind. You are completely enclosed in them with just a tiny patch of isinglass in the front through which you see the back of the coolie's head.

The night before Harold Dennis (No. 2 in the office) sailed, Li Yung-fu, our kerosene manager, had us all at his home for a Chinese dinner. The day before, one of our Chinese agents invited the office staff for tiffin at a Chinese restaurant. There were twenty-five different courses, brought on two or three at a time and of course each one in just one bowl for everyone to dive into. There were two famous dishes that I had up to then stayed clear of: bird's nest soup and shark-fin soup.

He had hired several singsong girls for the party to make it more impressive—that's about all they're there for. They sat there so bored as if they would die the next minute. The constant pastime at a Chinese feast is playing finger games for the small cups of wine—the loser having to *gambei* or finish it then hold the cup upside down to show it's empty. There are continual toasts, so the dinners are always gay affairs. The wine is served hot, like sake, in small cups.

Postcard of the three buildings, from left, of the Grand Hotel in the late 1930's.

Christmas morning

It was interesting to watch our Chinese staff, about twenty, at the Keefes' house. Some of them are pretty good mixers, but most of them stood around not speaking, even to each other, but eating lots of turkey and salad. They are a nice crowd though; I felt sorry for their evident embarrassment at being in the boss's house.

General Chiang was released on Christmas night and China is rejoicing. With firecrackers popping all over Tsingtao, the town seems in a gala mood, all except the Japanese of course. The foreigners are behind Chiang and are almost as glad as the Chinese that he is safe and free.

December 30

My birthday yesterday was a quiet one. Mrs. Haimovitch, my landlady, promised a long time ago to have a birthday cake for me, but she and her little daughter went to Shanghai a week ago to stay several weeks. So Harold Davis and I have been alone in the house except for servants until yesterday, when a young Russian girl from Shanghai moved in. A beauty, she has been the toast of the town since she arrived a week ago. Quite an addition to our little household.

9

The Shantung Peninsula and Dairen

December 31, 1936

I'M TO SET OUT on a journey with Mr. Li on Sunday that will take about a month. As this is my first trip, an itinerary was chosen that is a little easier than the others. We are to go northeast, circling around the promontory and return to Tsingtao from the west. There are places where I can be with foreigners and travel can be done by bus. The two towns are Weihaiwei (pronounced Way-hi-way), where I can put up at a hotel, and Chefoo, where there is a club. The former is the summer base for the British Asiatic fleet; the latter is the summer base for half of our own fleet—the other half summers in Tsingtao.

I'm going to take some George Washington coffee, canned fruit, crackers and chocolate. Mr. Li is going to help make sure that I get boiled water and no uncooked food on the way. I eat salad freely in Tsingtao but not up-country. When I hit the road, it will be just six weeks from my arrival in Tsingtao. I feel as if I had known the place all my life.

I have been in the Orient four months now—twenty more years and I could be eligible for the title of Old China Hand!

Chefoo, January 13, 1937

It was an exciting week, full of new experiences and sights. It was also one of the hardest, most uncomfortable weeks in my life. I often slept on mud kongs (beds) with a fire built underneath them for warmth at night. The opening to the fire pit is not in the room but outside the house. A coolie keeps the fire going with peanut shells and straw all night long.

The only place I was warm was in bed, for in general Chinese merely add more gowns in the winter instead of providing heat. It is wonderful to be at the Chefoo Club with real heat, lights, plumbing, good food and a proper bed. Weihaiwei was disappointing. Y.F. Li and I stayed at a huge barnlike summer hotel that was almost empty. It was cheerless, uncomfortable and morguelike.

I left Tsingtao about 7:45 A.M. and after an uneventful bus ride arrived in Tsimo an hour and a half later. Tsimo is a walled city with a wall within the wall. Women were sitting at a stream pounding clothes on rocks. It's a town of

The Bund at Weihaiwei, 1937. During the foreign "scramble for concessions" in 1898, the British had leased the port to counter Russian and German influence in the area. They gave up the lease in 1930 but continued to maintain a summer naval presence.

uphill-downhill mud streets at all angles with houses and dirt and filth of all sorts. There are no rickshaws, the only conveyance I saw were the Peking carts. We went directly to the agent and looked over his book and checked stock. After a great amount of *wallah-wallah*, tiffin was brought up from a restaurant. One expects a certain amount of spitting on floors, but it is disconcerting when someone blows his nose on the floor. We walked around the town, calling on candle makers, a match factory, the bus station and the chamber of commerce.

I stayed at the missionaries' house—very clean and comfortable but no electricity. Mr. and Mrs. Sell and one other woman connected with the Lutheran Mission are the only white people in Tsimo. They have lived here for five years. Mr. Sell was away visiting a place where there are two cases of bubonic plague. Their son was playing in the compound with a Chinese girl and talking Chinese as well and naturally as she. They also have a baby girl a year and a half old.

We had a long wait at the Tsimo bus station before the bus finally arrived. As the road was terrible, the trip was extremely uncomfortable; in most places it was like riding across a field in tracks made by a few predecessors. Streams crisscross this part of the country, and all have to be forded. I arrived at Kin Kow (pronounced Jin Ku) with my feet half frozen, body cramped and lungs filled with garlic odor. If it wasn't a pleasant ride, it certainly was unusual. Every so often the so-called road left the fields and hills to call on a little walled village. Shortly after 12:30 we clattered into Kin Kow. An armed officer came up to me and started asking questions. Mr. Li explained that I was a "Tezacu" man. My business cards, which are almost as important as tickets in traveling here, haven't arrived yet from Shanghai. We met our agent and were told that the road to Si Tsun is considered too rough for a mule cart and that we must travel by sedan chair the next day. We visited another agent and drank more tea. It is so cold everywhere: a cup of boiling tea is man's best friend. Sometimes there is a dish of glowing charcoal on the floor, but the heat is negligible; sometimes there is a little coal stove in a five-gallon kerosene tin on which they boil water for tea.

We met a Mr. Ma, who is head of the State Salt Gabelle[1] here, and were

---

1. A Chinese government agency that monopolized the production of salt in China. Gabelle was the term for the tax on salt imposed in France before 1790.

invited to spend the night at his office. A very clean but cold room is kept for visiting officials. Both Mr. Ma and his colleague spoke a little English. We were up at seven the next morning to start the day's travel to Si Tsun. After tackling three fried eggs with chopsticks (try it some time), I bundled up and went outside. The coolies had arrived and were stowing away our kit for the journey.

The "sedan chairs" were actually little thatched huts mounted on two long parallel poles. The traveler's baggage is placed in the under-slung bottom of the chair and covered with straw and blankets, after which the whole affair is hoisted up on two poles, one fore and one aft. The finished job looks as unstable and uncomfortable as it is. The custom is to start out on foot. It seems a lot of equipment to get a pair of travelers to a town just seventeen miles away.

Outside the walls spreads a large mountain-hemmed plain across which hundreds of people, carts and animals were making for Kin Kow, for this was market day. Some people carried bags and others were in charge of several carts; straw, charcoal, grain and livestock predominated. We walked about a mile and then climbed into the chairs. The motion is most unpleasant, sway-

The author's "chariot" outside Kin Kow.

Straw for fuel stacked outside a village in Shantung Province.

ing, bumping and jerking. There is not enough room to sit up properly or stretch out. It was much better to walk if possible, so I could take photographs. It was exciting crossing streams and small rivers with the coolies yelling at the mules to encourage them.

To one used to the rural sections of the United States, it is strange to pass through thousands and thousands of acres of land under cultivation without seeing a farmhouse. The farmers band together in villages for protection from bandits, and each morning go out to their own particular fields, in some cases many li[1] from their homes.

On entering one of these villages, you invariably pass through a section on the outer limits where straw for fuel is stacked in large, strangely shaped piles. Then you go through a gate in the usual stone wall to a community whose physical surroundings and way of living haven't changed in a thousand years.

Although each village resembles the other, there is always something different to be seen. The houses are built of dried mud, stones, straw and thatch, and face each other across narrow dirt streets (sometimes sparsely cobbled).

---

1. A li is about a third of a mile.

Jutting off from two or three streets are many little alleys scarcely wide enough for two unladen mules to pass. Half-wild dogs are all about, and they aren't very friendly to strangers. Children too are everywhere, and usually about as dirty.

China is a place where misery, filth, disease, cruelty and ugliness are often large parts of the daily scene. I've talked with old China residents in Peking who say they refuse to leave the Legation Quarter in the coldest part of winter because they couldn't face the misery that would meet their eyes. But this assessment, doesn't apply nearly as much to the country-side as it does to parts of Shanghai, Peking and Hankow I've seen.

Village scene at Haiyang, Shantung. Texaco star at left.

In the villages during the winter, the children romp around gaily, playing games in their heavy padding of scruffy but brightly colored clothes. Often a score would follow me clear through the village and out on the other side, the smallest of them being dragged by a curious older sister.

Another sight common to each community is the stone block and roller for grinding grain. The donkey that walks around in a circle to supply power for this primitive mill is blindfolded so it won't get dizzy. And in all the villages I passed through, somewhere along the main street in a sheltered spot would be a group of village elders. They sit wrapped in their gowns and dignity, smoke, chat and watch the children play. Some sit on little stools, but others sit or squat in the dirt of the road with their backs against the wall.

Everywhere I am treated with the greatest courtesy, getting the best place to sit down and being offered tea before anyone else.

Chefoo, January 19

It is snowing heavily today—everything I see from the window is white. We had an appointment with a shipping firm this morning, but they broke it because of the weather. Our agents from Pinglitien are in town and gave us a big dinner last night. At tiffin today we are to be guests of Mr. Li's uncle, who is manager of the large flour mill here. Our agents in Chefoo have been feting us considerably since our arrival, so I am getting a lot of Chinese social life.

I have been working hard though, and putting in long hours. I've called on approximately one hundred retail shops and small factories, from small hair-oil stores to the municipal power plant. I expect to stay about a week in Chefoo. Then we must take a long trip back southeast to Shihtao for a day or so, after which we'll proceed west to Weihsien and down the railroad from there to Tsingtao.

Saturday afternoon I decided on the spur of the moment to go to Dairen, partly on business, partly to see the place. I scurried around, checked up on my visa at the Japanese consulate, bought my steamship ticket and packed, all within an hour, and only just made the boat.

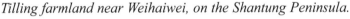
Tilling farmland near Weihaiwei, on the Shantung Peninsula.

Postcard of ships in Dairen, Kanto Peninsula, in Japanese-controlled Manchukuo.

The SS *Kwanglee* was the worst ship I have been on. I traveled so-called first class, but it meant nothing. I had to share the cabin with one of the stewards who brought me tea and coffee. The cabin was alive with roaches and the bedding was filthy. We arrived early the next morning outside the Dairen breakwater. As there were nine other ships I wondered who would be cleared first when the customs launch came out. A large Japanese ship last to arrive was the first allowed in; we were the third. The Japanese officials were immaculately dressed and contrasted greatly with the sloppy Chinese officers of our ship, not one of whom had a proper uniform. I was disregarded entirely until just before the Japanese officers left. Then one of them told me, in English, that I must go to the police station. He said that two second-class passengers also had to go and that a boy from the ship would accompany us.

We anchored a few hundred yards offshore, and I managed to find the two other passengers who spoke English. I carried my cory (wicker suitcase) down the steep swaying ladder to a sampan packed with coolies from our ship. We landed on a muddy rock-strewn shore that proved to be over two miles from town. After a hectic twenty minutes, we reached a road of sorts, found a rattly old carriage and proceeded to the police station. Upon entering the examination room, I was given the usual questionnaire—how old, where from, how long a stay, what profession, etc. The Japanese officer spoke perfect English and even had a sense of humor, which is rare among officers.

I thought I would have to go to the Yamato Hotel, famous and expensive, but the Russian porter who was guarding my luggage suggested a Russian hotel, the Central, which was much cheaper. It was clean, at least, so I decided to stay there. The Central is one of those places to be found in any large city in the Orient, providing a home of a sort for people without a country.

I spent half an hour trying to locate the Texas marketing manager on the phone. Failing that, I got in touch with the terminal manager, Mr. Kull, whom I had met on the ship from Shanghai to Tsingtao. We arranged to meet after tiffin. I had a bath and shave, a change of clothing and shook off the effects of the night on the ship. I ordered curry rice, toast and beer for tiffin, which is always good and reliable even in the most doubtful place. I was just finishing my meal when Mr. Kull and Mr. Dougherty, a relief terminal assistant, came in. As my hotel wasn't very prepossessing, we went over to the Yamato Hotel to talk business. We walked a short distance down a wide avenue and across a park circle reminiscent of Washington, D.C. The people seemed equally divid-

Postcard of view from roof of Yamato Hotel in Dairen, showing Bank of Chosen.

ed between Japanese and Chinese. We spent an hour or so talking in the Yamato bar, chatting and watching a billiard game where the attendants were attractive Japanese girls in kimonos. Then we went for a tour. Dairen[2] is a progressive city with fine avenues, large public buildings and hundreds of good cheap taxis.

As Sunday was one of their few afternoons off from the terminal, my colleagues suggested going to a cabaret dance hall. The place was packed for the tea-dancing period, when dance tickets are half price and free refreshments are served. All the girls were Japanese or Korean, and all the guests were Japanese with the exception of a few foreigners. The band was good, and the eighty or so dance girls far prettier than the average.

There was a girl there that I'd back in any beauty contest, but one had to be a champion sprinter to get to her first when the music started, so I never found out whether she could speak any English. It was a pleasure just to watch her: grace, charm and beauty all in one and striking enough to make an impression a hundred feet across the room. They say perfection is like infinity, never attained, but I saw a close approximation in that Dairen dance hall.

Time went by very quickly. Suddenly it was late and I had to grab a taxi, pick up my bag from the hotel and dash down to the ship. It was a relief to be on the *Kyoto Maru* instead of the wretched ship I came on. No one spoke English, but the stateroom was spotless and there were clean white sheets on the bed. By eight o'clock in the morning I was back in my hotel ready for breakfast and the day's work.

It was a pleasant weekend in Manchukuo.

---

2. Dairen, originally called Dalny ("faraway" in Russian), was founded in 1899 by Nicholas II, Russia's last czar. It was lost to the Japanese, along with Port Arthur and the whole Kwantung (or Kanto) Peninsula after the Russo-Japanese War of 1905. In 1945 it was reclaimed by the Russians and then given back to China in 1952. It is now called Dalian.

10

The Railway Points
in the Heart
of Shantung

Tsingtao, February 15, 1937

OVER HERE MONEY GOES FARTHER but it also goes faster. Everything is paid by signing a chit, so it's a headache when the various chit coolies come into the office at the end of the month. The only money you have to carry is enough to pay rickshaws, tips and stamps.

Chinese New Year has been banned by the Nationalist Government in an attempt to switch over to the Western calendar, but it is still the real holiday for the people. Most business comes to a standstill for a week to ten days, and in some cases much longer. It is the time when all accounts for the year are settled and every Chinese who can possibly make it goes back to his hometown. Even the restaurants are closed. The first day of the New Year was February 1, but the fireworks were popping about the eighth. The heaviest snowfall seen in years in Tsingtao came on the tenth, which made it a little hard on the firecracker industry, but seemed to be considered good *joss* (luck) nevertheless.

Most of the Chinese spend the holidays staying up all night playing mah-jongg and other games, holding family feasts, calling on friends and visiting the cabarets. Servants are the unlucky ones as they only get New Year's Eve off and have to work the next day. They wear their own gowns for that day and collect their annual *cumshaw* (tips) from the members.

Wednesday night we watched a Chinese play in which Y.F. Li had a part.

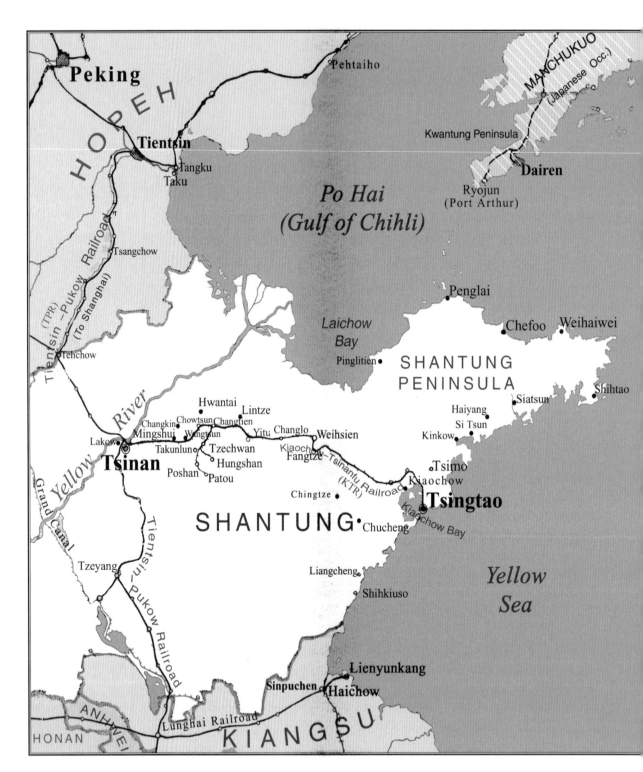

Shantung Province in 1936 showing towns visited or mentioned by the author.

Many of the costumes are beautiful and the fight scenes lively, but the music and singing are incomprehensible to Westerners. The whole show wasn't over till 2:30 in the morning, and it began at 8 in the evening!

The office staff had tiffin at D.F. Lee's house on Thursday. They have four small boys who are bright and attractive. Mrs. Lee looks like a girl of sixteen and speaks a few words of English.

We have a new arrival with the company, an Edward Martin who comes from six years service in Haiti. His wife and mother-in-law are with him, and they are feeling the cold. He is relieving Walt Powell, who is to go to India. This makes a temporary total of eight Texas Company foreigners. I'll be sorry to see Walt go as he and Bob Tam, a Chinese, and Rudy Müller, a China-born German, and I have made a foursome and have had a lot of fun together. Poor Rudy! How serious and offended he becomes when we argue with him about Hitler. He has never been out of China but is probably one of Hitler's strongest backers.

Then there is Davis, the English chap living at the Pension Victoria who works for the British American Tobacco Company; he has been out here eight years in all the ports on the China coast. I have a varied lot of acquaintances and friends, which adds to the interest of everyday life.

February 17

I had news late this afternoon that I am to start out again the day after tomorrow for a trip likely to last six or seven weeks. I will be visiting (again with Y.F. Li) the group of agencies called the railway points. They are so-called because they follow along the K.T.R.[1] to Tsinan, but there will be little train riding and a great deal of bus, rickshaw and sedan chair travel. The towns are incredibly poor and small. Y.F. has already warned me that accommodations will be awful. Fortunately, winter is on its way out and by the time I come back, it will be spring.

---

1. Kiaochaow-Tsinanfu Railroad, or Tsingtao-Tsinan Railroad, was built by the Germans. Begun in 1899, it has connected Tsingtao to the provincial capital since 1904. It was strongly opposed at first by the people of Shantung, where growing resentment against foreign control and the missionaries helped fuel the rise of the Boxers at the turn of the 20th century. All work on the railroad was interrupted for a while in 1900 during the Boxer Rebellion.

February 19

I met Y.F. at the railway station and left at 7:20 A.M. We traveled second class because Y.F. cannot put a first-class ticket on his expense account. It is perfectly comfortable, however. We arrived at Mingshui at 5:30 and took a rickshaw to town—about three li from the station.

Tsingtao Railway Station, from 1920's guidebook.

Mingshui,
February 21

I am writing this in a funny little room facing on the court of our agent's shop. Across the court is the main shop where the clerks and apprentices are noisily busy at a mah-jongg game, banging each piece on the table. I can hear a couple of coolies working in the courtyard preparing for tomorrow, which is George Washington's Birthday for us but market day for them. The huge heavy gates, which give the only access to the streets, are bolted and barred for the night, a necessary precaution as bandits have attacked the town recently.

This accommodation is better than usual as there is a little coal stove and the floors are brick instead of mud. Yesterday we took a trip to a coal mine, thirty li south of the town. They have an eighteen-gauge rail track and we rode standing in the back of an empty coal car. It had a little toy engine rather like one in an amusement park. The whole trip took seven hours.

The next day we visited the springs for which Mingshui is named (clear water), with a bamboo grove and temple nearby. We have been fighting with the agent steadily from 2 P.M. to 10:30 at night, without any success. We want to close the Safe agency and transfer stock to the Yinfoo godown.

We traveled first class on the train to Tsinan as the second and third class were filled with people returning after the New Year celebrations. The crowd in the station was out of luck. I was surprised to run into an old friend, Gordon Ingham (I haven't seen him for four years), who was traveling with a party of twenty. I had dinner with Y.F. at the T.P.R. (Tientsin-Pukow Railroad) hotel; the next morning we were up at 4:30 and took the bus to the station. I spent half an hour in the observation car talking with Gordon. He likes the group and said they had a great time in Japan and Peking. He asked me if I didn't get dysentery living as I do and eating everything, but so far I have been lucky. We arrived at Tsao Yuan Su at 8:45 A.M. and took the bus to Changkin, a small crowded town where it was market day. We took a rickshaw back to Mingshui. The trip took an hour and a half over a wretched road in bitter cold.

February 26

We left Mingshui and arrived in Chowtsun an hour later. It was a big fete day in Chowtsun, which is a much bigger place than Mingshui.

Our agent here told me through Y.F. about the lantern festival. It is an old

Keeping a watchful eye in Mingshui, a village near Tsinan.

festival that was abandoned about twenty years ago. The military authorities encouraged its revival to celebrate United China. The agent, like most businessmen, considers it a nuisance, an expense and a fire hazard. Many firms are closed from a few days before New Year's until the twenty-fifth day, while some factories don't open till the second moon. During the four days of the festival, our agent is entertaining about one hundred relatives at different times. It seems that it is the only time when young girls and women are allowed out on the streets. The rest of the time they may only go out of the house to visit the home of a near relative and then only with their parents. Even now, in the rural sections, bride and bridegroom never meet till their marriage day. Among the more modern people in a town like Chowtsun, they are allowed one meeting.

After tiffin, we fought our way through the crowds to the bathhouse, where we had an excellent bath in real comfort and cleanliness and I had a shave. Each customer has a comfortable private room with bed and a private bathroom across the corridor. I felt much better afterward and we looked for a place to put me up as there was no room at the agent's. I finally found a place in the Catholic mission, but no one seemed to be around, perhaps because of the festival. The streets are especially lively. Each village in the surrounding countryside sends a group to parade in fancy dress. Lanterns take all sorts of forms, from simple lights to huge structures.

All the grown women and most of the girls, who looked about fifteen or sixteen, have bound feet. How they can keep their footing in the pressing mobs is a mystery, for the crowds are just like those in the tunnels at the Bowl in New Haven at half-time. They hobble along on their heels: it looks as difficult as walking on stilts. Unlike the women in the large cities, none of them wear gowns but all are dressed in trousers bound at the ankles and short jackets. The old women wear black or blue but the young ones wear bright blues and reds.

Back at the agent's shop, they are sleeping three and four in a bed, so I guess that I am better off at the mission, although I have seen no one but the boy. Y.F. met me there and we set out for Hwantai. The first section by rickshaw is thirteen and a half miles and it took three hours. The road was jammed with people coming to Chowtsun to celebrate. Hwantai's main street is picturesque with massive pailous that are carved with dogs of Fo and are profusely decorated. I was told that they are about three hundred years old and are in honor of the many high officials claiming Hwantai as a birthplace.

We went to the main shop of our agent and had an excellent meal. Then we set out with him for Chaho on bicycles as the rickshaws take so long. We made the nine miles to Chaho in a little over an hour. We rested a little while, counted stock and returned. Our rickshaws met us on the way back but we preferred to cycle. We had dinner with Mr. Chang in Hwantai and then the rickshaws took us back to Chowtsun at 8:30. Usually, it is dangerous to be on the roads so late, but because of the festival there were many extra police.

As the crowds in the streets were worse than ever, we had to abandon our rickshaws as soon as we came to a main street. We gave the coolies four dollars each for the twelve-hour day; they surely deserved it. Each had pulled a full rickshaw well over thirty miles including their trip out to meet us on the road to Chaho. That would be a killing day's work for a normal person on a smooth road; these roads had to be navigated as they are full of ruts.

Y.F. and I talked a good deal during the ride back, swapping stories and talking about China in general. One story he told me was hardly in the mood of the beautiful star-filled night but concerned Hwantai, the place we had left. It seems that several hundred years ago at a crossroads just outside the town, there lived a very wicked woman who owned an inn where many travelers stopped for food and rest. She had the pleasant habit of killing her lodgers and after cutting them into small pieces, cooking them and serving them as *jowsahs,* little balls of chopped meat wrapped in a cover of dough. Her nefarious practice was finally disclosed when one of her guests found a fingernail in his *jowsah.* She was executed by a special messenger of the emperor himself, and a large stone tablet still stands that tells the story.

I came back tired and stiff from cycling. The agent's house was still full of people. I didn't want to go back to the empty Catholic mission, and the Protestant mission was too far away. Finally, Y.F. piled in bed with two other people and I took the cot.

February 28

We were up at nine but I was still stiff and sore. I didn't get much sleep as I had spent the night fighting off a flock of fleas. I wanted to go to the bathhouse and clean up but it was full. They said they would let me know when there was a place. We were able to do little or no business as every shop was full of visitors.

March 1

We were up early and managed to call on about twelve customers before catching the train to Changtien. Most of our customers are in the dyeing business for which Chowtsun is noted—silks dyed for funerals are sent to all parts of China. The Chinese wear bright colors when they are babies, then black or dark colors, and when they are buried they wear bright blues and pinks.

The station was jammed with people going home and carrying bedding. In the mob with us was a Catholic priest, a young handsome fellow with whom I exchanged greetings. He was also heading for Changtien, which is his mission,[2] and invited us to dinner. He was swept away in the crowd but we met again in the first-class coach when the train finally pulled out. It had been impossible to get second-class tickets.

After spending a couple of hours with our Changtien agent and checking stock and calling on a customer, I went to Father Roland's mission and had a friendly reception from him and Father Rudolph, who was visiting for a few days. Before sitting down to dinner, Father Roland showed us the mission. The church is of gray stone and in appearance looks like a fairly well-to-do Catholic church in a medium-size town in the States. On one side of the church is Father Roland's house and on the other side a long low building where he takes care of thirty orphaned girls. Three sisters, one foreign and two Chinese, have charge of the orphanage and help teach in the school that lies to the rear of the grounds. In the school, there are eighty boy boarders and thirty girl boarders as well as quite a few Changtien children. Since the orphans are taken care of free of charge, while the school boarders pay only $8 Mex. per semester, food is one of the big problems. They help to solve the problem by a fine large garden where the children do most of the work. There is also an extensive flower garden and an orchard of foreign fruit. Father Roland is happy in his work and took a pardonable pride in showing me over the place.

He spends at least half of each month traveling around his territory and living as I do in little villages. Father Roland has two advantages over me—he has a motorbike and knows the language. I don't envy him the motorbike as

---

2. Probably of Sacred Heart Province, a Franciscan order of friars from Illinois that established a mission in Changtien in 1924. Most Catholic missionaries in China at this time, however, were European; more than half of the Protestant ones were American.

CLOCKWISE FROM TOP LEFT: *Donkey caravan in village near Haiyang; fishing boat in Weihaiwei; singsong girl in Shitao; preparing the caravan in Sitsun, with Y.F. Lee at right with Stetson; pailou in Haiyang, with Texaco sign at right; the author's caravan setting out from Kin Kow.*

The Railway Points, Central Shantung

ABOVE: *Village worthy, and top left, inner gate at Mingshui, near Tsinan.*

ABOVE: *Railroad car from Poshan to Patou, in the coal region of central Shantung.*

RIGHT: *Temple complex near Chaho, with Y.F. Li, next to bike, and Texaco agent.*

In Mingshui, near Tsinan: TOP, *outer gate;* ABOVE, *shrine to treasury god during the Lantern Festival.*

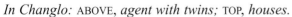

In Changlo: ABOVE, *agent with twins;* TOP, *houses.*

Lily Lee, the beautiful Chinese friend from Tsingtao with the "green Chrysler Imperial roadster (the best car in town)," was a popular stage and film actress of the 1930's.

the roads are so bad. We had a simple but welcome foreign meal served by a boy in an ordinary gown but wearing a felt hat. After dinner was cleared, seven or eight bottles of Japanese beer were brought on, and Father Roland, Father Rudolph (who was visiting) and I talked all the evening in front of the fire, even touching on U.S. politics. It was a treat for me.

The two priests are young men in their thirties, vigorous, robust fellows with no holiness about them except their devotion to the job of doing good. They had lots of interesting stories to tell and were good company. The atmosphere of the Protestant mission I visited in Tsimo in January was more austere; I didn't dare light a cigarette. I can see why so many people claim that the only successful missionaries in China are the Catholics. The Chinese like jollity.

Some of Father Roland's chief troubles are right in Changtien. He told me that in walking to his church from the station, I had passed through the section of the town devoted to opium dens and red-light houses. There are some two hundred Japanese families in Changtien, and with the exception of a few employed by the cotton mills, they are all directly or indirectly in the dope business. It is common knowledge that up and down the whole China coast, the bulk of the narcotic trade is in the hands of the Japanese. Most people believe it is a semi-official movement to undermine Chinese morale and counteract the possible effect of the recent strict laws made by the Nanking government. In this part of China, at least, it is certainly true that the worst offending towns are those with an appreciable Japanese population. The authorities have been executing Chinese dope peddlers since January 1, but the major offenders in the selling line go scot-free. The Japanese rarely use it themselves.

Three weeks ago a Chinese known to Father Roland was seized peddling dope in Tzechwan, a town a little to the south of Changtien. Father Roland visited him the next morning, finding him in good spirits and expecting to be released provisionally that afternoon. When Father Roland arrived back at his mission, word had already been received that a telegram had just been sent from Tsinanfu ordering the man's execution. The family, ashamed of the disgrace, would have nothing to do with the body, so Father Roland sent some men down to bring it back for burial. The authorities pay no attention to bodies at all, merely pick out a convenient spot for execution, shoot the prisoners, and leave them. This particular man was shot with two others under a bridge at the city wall. When Father Roland's messengers arrived, no one had taken care of any of the three bodies, that is, no one but the town dogs. Of the three men who had been alive that morning, only part of one skull remained. Not a pleasant story but very Chinese. On the lighter side, we talked about "face pidgin" and "friend pidgin" and how they sometimes work. In the afternoon, I had difficulty with our agent in town; he didn't want to report a stock shortage as sales and I demanded that he do so. After much talking, he agreed. The reason was to give me "face" because it was my first visit to him.

Father Rudolph contributed an interesting story in connection with his task of distributing alms to needy families. One of his flock came to him one morning and begged him to help out a friend of hers, saying that this friend (also one of Father Rudolph's congregation) would starve unless help was forthcoming. She pleaded and pleaded, but the priest was a little uncertain and decided to investigate a little more. The woman made every effort to get the money for her friend but finally gave up. That same afternoon, she returned and told him that he had done quite right—that the person hadn't needed money at all. She said she had to make the attempt out of "friend pidgin" but that she was glad he had held firm. The same type of thing occurred a while ago when Father Roland fired a servant who was worthless and disliked by everyone, including the rest of the staff. For two days after his dismissal, all the others came to

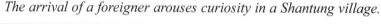
The arrival of a foreigner arouses curiosity in a Shantung village.

Father Roland begging him to take the fellow back and telling him what a fine chap he was. After the two days, they felt their duty was done and told him what a good job he had done in firing the worthless one!

March 3

I left the mission after an early breakfast and with a bearer went down to the station where I met Y.F., who had spent the night at the agent's shop. The early morning train for Tzechwan has only third-class accommodations, but they were quite all right for the hour trip. Tzechwan turned out to be one of the most picturesque towns I've visited. Commanding a fine position on high ground and protected by a massive well-preserved wall that seemed a couple of miles square, it looked more like an imaginary setting for a medieval romance than a real town. As usual, the railway station is out of sight across the plain from the city, so the picture is not spoiled. Also, as usual in the larger towns, business areas lie outside the walls—in this case, below the town and across the stone bridge that spans a moatlike stream flowing along one side. This was the bridge of Father Roland's story the previous night, and it was a little hard not to think of the gruesome details as our rickshaws carried us across.

With our work done at the agent's, we set out for Hungshan, where there is a large Japanese coal mine, a possible red-oil customer.[3] Their plant was the scene of one of the worst mine disasters in history when ten years ago, an underground flood drowned eight hundred men and five hundred donkeys. After the disaster, a Japanese firm took over and has since been trying to get the mine back in condition. They are still pumping water out and probably will be for a long time to come. Underground, the situation must be horrible, but on the surface the Japanese have done a characteristically good job of improving conditions and appearances.

A fine new wall, many miles long, encloses all the mine property, and in the enclosure thus formed is an almost parklike atmosphere, contrasting

---

3. From 1899 until 1914, the German-founded Shantung Mining Company attempted to develop the coal fields and mines of central Shantung, joining forces with the K.T.R. railway in the process. Tsingtao, the railway and mining and commercial interests would all fall into the hands of the Japanese at the outbreak of World War I, only to revert to the Chinese in 1922.

sharply with the drab squalor of the town of Hungshan. There is even a Japanese temple in a grove of small trees. It is sad to think that along with their industry and the comparative beauty they have brought to squalid surroundings, the Japanese have also applied their knack of marketing narcotics to the Chinese. Hungshan, where one would think that self-interest in the matter of labor supply for the mine would prove a check, is one of the worst of Japanese dope-infested towns in this section.

So, back in our rickshaws to Tzechwan and the train to Takunlun, a dirtier, far less interesting town. We were now getting into the heart of the coal district, each mile finding the scene grimier and more ugly. At Takunlun, after a long hour and a half waiting in the office of a Chinese coal company, we were able to climb on an empty coal car and ride out to the mine on the company's own narrow gauge railway. This was a large mine and one of Y.F.'s big calls, where he becomes more polite and obsequious than a peasant before a king. The managers and the head engineer were a strange lot, wearing their hair long in Western fashion to show their modernism. But they rose grandly to Y.F.'s absurd length of politeness, and the rushing around with tea and cigarettes was something to behold. While this was going on, I was trying to let my tea cool down. Another mine official came in and was introduced. Without warning, he picked up a full cup, tossed the contents on the floor and then refilled it from the pot. This happened three times before I was allowed to drink it.

We were saved from riding back to Takunlun on a loaded car by the generous gesture of our hosts, who some time before we were ready to go telephoned the other end of the line and ordered the water car to be brought for us, which was considerably cleaner than riding on top of a coal heap.

Back at the station there was a gang of at least three hundred begrimed coolies loading main-line cars by basket. They looked like an army of chimney sweeps. I was told that each coolie makes the sum of fifty cents Mex. per day, but if he has work one day out of two he is lucky.

Another short ride and we arrived at Poshan just at dusk. The Yinfoo agent was there at the station, smiling and bowing to lead us to his shop. As we walked through the streets, I thought I had never seen a filthier city. The following morning, the sun failed to improve the scene; I knew we were in the very center of the coal pile that is central Shantung. Only one mine among dozens surrounding the city has a rail spur. From all others the coal is brought by wheelbarrows, passing through the business section of the town on their way to the coal yards and station. The noise from squeaking wheelbarrows seems to dominate the city. One of the main streams of this incredibly dirty, noisy traffic flows through the street where our agent's shop is. From four o'clock in the morning to seven at night, there is scarcely a break in the steady plodding file. The product of these mines, for the most part, isn't what we, at home, call coal. It is like damp fine black sand that clothes in grime all the streets, houses and most of the people. When it rains, there are pools of black water. Standing in the doorway of the agent's shop, I saw scores of children making coal cakes out of layers of damp soot in the street, stacking them in baskets to take home for fuel.

It is difficult to know what is going on politically. I discovered much later that on the day after Chiang was kidnapped in Sian, New Yorkers were able to read more complete and accurate news in the *Times* than we in Tsingtao had available two days after the event. I, like almost every foreigner in China, have a great deal of respect and admiration for General Chiang (pronounced Jong), but since the Sian affair, I am a little less positive in my feelings toward him. He is wasting time and extending the period of uncertainty by his repeated declarations of resignation. These undoubtedly are for the sake of face, that bugbear of Chinese life, but they are out of place in the present mess things are in. I feel that while he was in Sian he made some sort of deal with the Communists. I am almost certain that he believes that China cannot face Japan without Communist support. Whether he will be able to control that support is a question.

The Generalissimo and the Nanking government are the recipients of a patriotism and loyalty no other government has received. The celebrations for Chiang's birthday were fervid and apparently quite spontaneous, but to think that China would rise in strength and toss out the Japanese is wishful thinking. Life is so difficult for all but a fortunate few that the bare problem of getting enough to eat develops a self-interest overshadowing the common cause.

While the Chinese are talking in Nanking, the Japanese are organizing and aiding the Mongols and the Manchucowans in their attacks on the northern borders and have landed a thousand marines at Tsingtao. I think that foreigners will be no more than tourists in ten or twenty years' time. Either China will be strong enough to get rid of us or the Japanese will be in charge.

My impressions of China in general are really not impressions "in general." There are many Chinas, and each one is different, like the story of the blind man describing the elephant. Peking is a glorious China and then Shanghai is a modern Baghdad, a cross section of the world, a combination of New York and Main Street. Since November I have been living in two very different Chinas: Tsingtao, which is an important outpost, and the interior villages and towns, probably the truest China of all. I enjoy them both and like the way my time is divided between them. Life in Tsingtao is easy and comfortable. I enjoy the club, the companionship of several nationalities, the work at the office and outdoor hikes and horseback rides in beautiful surroundings. But it is the life up-country that I'm here for; its appeal is entirely different. It is as uncomfortable and as lacking in luxuries and even necessities as could possibly be imagined. It's also strange and different beyond anything I had ever hoped to encounter. It is the enjoyment of meeting people in their own backyard, so to speak, that makes me like it so much. I work with them, live with them and eat with them twenty-four hours a day. The only mar is that I have a small, slowly growing vocabulary and have to use an interpreter for conversation.

These Shantung merchants among whom I live and at whose shops I spend the night are a fine lot. For the most part they are much larger in stature than the average, many of them being strapping six-footers. They are shrewd but open-faced, jovial and friendly too.

Kiaochow, March 21

Palm Sunday and I am hard at work as usual. This day started at 5:45 A.M. at a place called Chucheng, where we had to catch a bus for Chingtze, stay there a while inspecting and calling on customers, then get another bus to Weihsien,[4] where we caught a train for Kiaochow. Now I am in our agent's shop and there is no decent table or light. It is an uncomfortable place, but we have just been to the bathhouse so I feel a little cleaner than usual. It looks as if we will get back to Tsingtao on Good Friday.

I would like to have ten days or two weeks to rest up for the next trip. But I know now that it is to be the Yellow River points and the sooner we get at it the better off I'll be. It is the worst section imaginable; if we are still out there

---

4. Weihsien: After the outbreak of war with the Allies in 1941, the Japanese interned American and British civilians in a former mission compound in this town on the Tsingtao-Tsinan Railway.

when the heat and bugs come it will be unbearable. Y.F., hardened campaigner that he is, dreads the trip. It will take at the least five weeks—five weeks without a bath, with nothing but small towns where decent food is impossible to get, let alone a bathhouse. The agents and the people in general are especially backward and primitive, and sanitary conditions are worse than in the rest of the province, which seems hard to believe.

Kiaochow, March 22

It is night again, and I'm back under the same candle. Things are not looking so good here. Our agent, who initially seemed as honest as could be, has been

After two months on the road, the junior marketing assistant soldiers on in Yitu, despite the cold, less than ideal travel conditions and ignorance of the language. Notice the author's shoes.

a perfect host. Yesterday after our arrival he ordered a good meal for us and afterward took us to the bathhouse, even paying the bills. He made himself pleasant, talking about the old days in Kiaochow when it and not Tsingtao was the big port. Before dark yesterday, we checked stock, finding a large amount on hand and apparently in order. This morning, however, as there were some damaged tins that had been made at the Shanghai terminal, not at ours in Tsingtao, we decided to go over the stock, tin by tin, identifying marks on the bottoms. We had the coolies shift each tin, Y.F. looking at the marks and I listing them. We found a total of one hundred and sixty empties, which meant that the agent had sold that many without reporting them sold and remitting to us. It is the first time in six years of inspecting agents that Y.F. has ever had an agent falsify his stock position during an inspection.

This agent is unsound financially because of an enormous debt incurred by his no-good son. He has a large past-due account in addition to this shortage that he must pay for. We have no place to transfer the stock, so we must remain to guard our stock until we can move it or until the agent pays what he owes.

It is interesting to see how the Chinese react to being caught out in outright dishonesty. The agent said it was all due to the carelessness of his godown clerks. He knows that we don't believe that, and yet Y.F. pretends to believe that it is so. No mention is made of dishonesty. Y.F. proceeds to the matter of paying up in a calm, slow manner that drives me crazy. He would not make Mr. Kwang lose face for anything. He will do a good job and protect the company's interest fully, but he won't interpret for me if I get brusque with the agent.

This place is the limit for comfort. There is only one bed; I sleep on it and Y.F. sleeps on the cot we carry along with us. There is no space in the room for my bag, which must stand under a shed in the compound. The bed is at least two feet too short for me and as hard as a board, which, of course, it is. All my clothing must be piled on the bedclothes when I sleep. There is a tiny stool that only accommodates our overcoats if they are carefully folded. There is no fire at all, not even a charcoal brazier. If I have to stay here during a three-day holiday, just an hour and a half by train from Tsingtao, I'm going to be sore.

11

The Coronation Ball, Tsingtao

Tsingtao, March 26, 1937

BACK IN CIVILIZATION and it is grand. It is a perfect day, with the birds singing, and from my window the bay is blue as blue. I have a different room at the Victoria—a room that was too cold in winter but is really much nicer, with a direct view of the waterfront and the town.

Mr. Keefe at the office sent for me to return. I tried to get the holiday for Y.F. as long as the Kiaochow (pronounced Jow-jo) business was settled, but Keefe decided he should cover the four towns on the itinerary before coming in. I felt sorry leaving Y.F. in that awful place. The next four towns were to be just as bad, with miserable bus trips in between.

All is changed at the office. Ed Martin, who came in a while ago with his wife and mother-in-law, was just getting settled when he received instructions to go up to Chungking, 1,500 miles up the Yangtze River. His wife and mother-in-law must have had fits! As Powell is due to leave for India, I am learning

Japanese destroyers in Tsingtao Bay. The dark flat craft right of center is an aircraft carrier.

and working for him so I'll be able to fill in if necessary. Our district accountant was transferred to Shanghai while I was away. The office has a new chap by the name of Taylor, a Ph.D. from Heidelberg!

March 30

We have as our guests in the harbor sixty-five Japanese war vessels, the Grand Fleet, as they call it. They are putting on a searchlight show right now, a really magnificent spectacle far beyond any night display I've seen. Looking out of my window I can see the ships spread out in all directions—some behind the town in the harbor and some in front along the waterfront, with a long line of the larger ones stretched out along the coast for miles. The brilliant beams of white light seem to come from every point of the compass, while many are aimed lower and sweep the thousands of red roofs of the town. I can imagine how thrilling it is to the Japanese residents and how proud they must be.

The fleet arrived this morning, and by afternoon the town was packed with Japanese sailors and marines—about forty thousand of them, an orderly, clean-looking bunch, neat and militarylike. The visit is one they pay each year and has no special significance beyond Japan's continuous parade of strength before the supposedly awed eyes of the Chinese. Naturally, the whole setting we are in is a perfect setup for an "incident." None will occur, of course, if the Chinese have their way—or the Japanese, too, for that matter, for I believe they will not want trouble now. But I hate to think what could happen to this town if some crazy band of irresponsible Chinese started something.

April 5

Saturday I bought a bike! Rickshaw is rather slow and I needed more exercise. It's a pretty one, Chinese made but equipped with a coaster brake, which is unusual. It was $32 Mex., but I talked the fellow at the shop into throwing in a bell and lock and letting me have it for $30. That is U.S. $9.

I have finally decided that I must learn Chinese. I can get a teacher to come to the office for an hour each day. D.F. is interviewing prospective teachers for me now. Y.F.'s name, Chinese style, is Li Yung-fu and D. F. is Lee Ding-fong.

April 9

My lessons, which I take in the morning at the office before working hours, are going along fine. I think that my up-country trips helped me even though I didn't seem to be learning much at the time. My teacher, a fine old gentleman, correct in black gown and jacket and little round black skullcap with top-knot, is from Peking, and Mandarin is his native language. Educated people all over China know Mandarin, so I will be understood anywhere in Shantung, except perhaps by coolies. It will be difficult learning Mandarin while hearing Shantungese all around me.

April 28

All Tsingtao is looking forward to the Coronation Ball on May 12, when the British community will host a large dinner and dance at the Edgewater Mansions, a fine summer hotel. Each principal nationality in town gives one party a year for all the others, usually at the club. This will be the British contribution for the year, with each British subject being assessed fifty dollars for the occasion. The Americans gave theirs on Washington's Birthday while I was out in the country. The Chinese members of the club also gave a party that I missed because I was in Chefoo.

Census figures are practically impossible in any Chinese city but most estimates place the population of Tsingtao from a quarter to half a million. This is about the size of St. Paul or Minneapolis. It seems much smaller to me. The Chinese, of course, form the great bulk of the population. After them come the Japanese, with between twenty and thirty thousand.

Then come the Russians—I have no idea how many there are, probably a thousand or so. Then come the Germans, who used to control this whole region. There are probably about two hundred of them, most of them not well off but still far above the Russians.

After them come the British and the Americans, maybe two hundred of these last two combined. Apart from the banks (National City Bank of New York, Hong Kong and Shanghai Bank, Chartered Bank of India), the Big Four in the East are the Standard Oil Company, the Texas Company, the Asiatic Petroleum Company (Shell) and the British American Tobacco Company. These four account for a good proportion of the British and American foreigners in China. Then, of course, there are several large British shipping firms: Butterfield & Swire; Jardine, Matheson, etc. Also important is the Chinese Customs, which is still run by foreigners.

All these outfits do a lot of shifting in personnel, and after a person has been out here a few years, he is bound to know half the foreigners in China. Harbin, Mukden, Dairen, Tientsin, Tsingtao, Nanking, Shanghai and Hong Kong are, in a manner of speaking, adjacent towns, in that most people have served time in most of them.

My mother is planning a trip to China and will be landing in Kobe soon. It would have been more pleasant to go to the Imperial Hotel in Tokyo for the first night in the Far East instead of the gloomy Oriental Hotel in Kobe. Kobe is probably the least attractive city in the country and the most foreign. I don't like it except for the scenic mountain trip up to Rokko-san behind the city. The Motomachi-dori is an interesting shopping street, but I hope she does not do too much shopping there. She ought to spend a lot more time in Kyoto than I did. That was one of my big mistakes.

View of Chungshan Road, Tsingtao's main street, in 1937.

Tsingtao, May 6

A gold filling came out of my tooth in a sticky piece of candy, so I have been going to a dentist pretty regularly for the past few days. Dental work is expensive. The fellow I am going to is supposed to be the best in town, but I have little faith in him. He is a Russian who learned his dentistry, according to Powell (who knew him in Harbin), in a six months' course in Harbin.

Last week I also developed a bad rash on my right hand and some on my face. It was a little like poison ivy rash, but the blisters were smaller. After I went to see Dr. Lew I learned that along with five or six other people who had dropped in at Pop Kane's bar for a glass of beer last week, I had Ningpo varnish poison. Pop had just varnished his bar with the stuff, which was a little sticky. Some people got it much worse than I did; fortunately I was there for only a few minutes. It is a queer thing about the varnish, which is supposed to be the best and hardest there is, but once in a while it plays mean tricks on people who touch it before it dries thoroughly.

Yesterday morning we had a little excitement. Looking out from the office windows we saw two bandits being driven on a police-filled truck through

Chungshan Road to the execution place. I haven't seen an execution yet and don't care to, but there are plenty for anyone who has an interest. They are done in a crudely informal manner, the victims being tossed on the ground with hands tied behind their backs and ankles tied together. While they are lying face down on the ground, a policeman goes from one to another firing a pistol into the back of their heads at about two inches distance.

National Archives

The USS Canopus *with submarines.*

Imagine the execution of a hundred and twenty prisoners in that way during a single morning, as happened in Peking the week before I arrived last fall.

This is Friday the seventh and part of the U.S. Asiatic Fleet arrived this morning. The flagship, the *Augusta,* will not be in for another four weeks, but we have the *Canopus* and several submarines. The destroyers, which have all just come from the Philippines by way of Shanghai, are just arriving in Chefoo.

The trees are now getting green, flowers are out, and the temperature the last couple of days has hit 85 degrees. Spring has arrived for sure. It is hard to believe that just a short time ago I was freezing to death in places like Lo-an and Lingtze. With the leaves out and perfect weather, Tsingtao is marvelous. I do hope I can get some time off and meet my mother in Peking when she arrives in China.

The Coronation[1] is almost here, and the British Committee has all sorts of plans. This is a small place though, and I would enjoy seeing the celebrations in Shanghai or Hong Kong, where they have British troops and hold a tattoo, as they call it. All Shanghai is decorated for the big event. Well, we will have our big ball anyway, and it should be fun. The town is getting livelier all the time, with new places opening and visitors arriving. The officers' families are here and there are quite a bunch of them.

A branch of the famous Jimmy's Kitchen in Shanghai opened the other

---

1. Of George VI.

day; one can get a real ice-cream sundae, also hot cakes and proper sausage, and ham and eggs American style.

May 12

Coronation Day! We are one of the few foreign firms who are not having a holiday! Socony is taking the afternoon off, but I guess we are going to work on through. Coming to the office this morning along Pacific Road, we had a splendid sight offered by some British and Japanese warships with their "dress uniform" on—flags and pennants all over from stem to stern. The Union Jack is flying from the main-mast of the Japanese destroyer, and I imagine that it is also in the place of honor on the U.S. ships in the back of town.

Deke Erh

The surprisingly modern Edgewater Mansions Hotel was built in 1937; above, a present-day photograph.

With several receptions at the consulate, a church service, a sailing regatta and quite a few "high teas," the British community is well occupied, while we poor Yankees attend to business.

Tonight is the huge ball (dinner too) at the Edgewater Mansions. With the officers from our fleet and the British ships in port, and the newly arrived sprinkling of summer visitors and navy wives, there will be almost six hundred people attending, which includes Chinese and Japanese officials and influential townspeople.

We are to have a buffet dinner at 8:30, after which we will go out on the balconies overlooking the bay and watch a fireworks and illumination display

The Charleston bar and cabaret in Tsingtao.

put on by HMS *Medway* and some submarines. At eleven o'clock, when the military band stops for the evening, there will be dancing.

May 21

The Coronation Ball was a splendid affair with a dozen nationalities represented and many, many uniforms. Chinese and Japanese officials are impressive at a formal occasion like that. Many of the Japanese women wore kimonos—there were some beauties. All the Englishmen were decked out in their war medals, and it was a sorry man who didn't have at least three. After a buffet dinner, preceded by twenty-five hundred martinis, we were to have gone to the veranda of the hotel for a fireworks display put on by the British ships in the front harbor. But a fog came in, and it was no use. The dancing lasted till about three, when the gayer spirits went down to the various cabarets to finish off the evening. I went down with a crowd to the Charleston, a Chinese cabaret, but came home fairly shortly. I was the only foreigner in the office who showed up for work before 10:30.

That was bad news about the *Hindenburg* and surely a serious blow to this type of transatlantic service. I hadn't realized they were still using hydrogen. I would not care to cross an ocean in a hydrogen bag.

Aside from missing the newspapers and the new shows, etc., I haven't experienced a moment of boredom since I set foot on China over half a year ago. From this side, the U.S. is not looking so good: high taxes, labor troubles, dust storms and endless political bickering that will probably amount to nothing. Here, on the other hand, there is no fear of labor unions, no annoying political dissension and the weather is fine. Above all, foreigners have more individual freedom than any group of people on earth. They pay no taxes and are practically lords in their own right. They enjoy extraterritoriality, which means that the folks at the U.S. Consulate are the only officials in Shantung who can bring me to justice.

June 2

After waiting for two months, wondering when I was to go out, I have just received the news that I am to leave at one day's notice. I am taking tomorrow's plane to Haichow, down south of here along the coast. I will work there for a while and then make my way back home by bus and rickshaw. It is odd to think that a person who has lived so near the flying fields in Long Island should take his first flight in China!

Ever since the Chiang Kai-shek kidnapping last December, shipments on the Lunghai Railroad up to Sianfu have been disorganized, piling up at Lienyunkang (near Haichow) waiting for cars. The Texas Company has had a Chinese inspector down there for five weeks trying to persuade the railway to give us cars, but without any results. When, or if, I can get our stock loaded, I have to go to Sinpuchen, also near there, and try to get the agents of all the oil companies to get together on a price. They have all been selling below the price, which they must give the companies, and have been cutting one another's throats. I hope I can persuade them to cooperate, but it won't be easy. The managers of Socony and Asiatic Petroleum in Tsingtao have complained to Keefe that our agents are the worst offenders. I have to travel lightly as it will be warm. I'm keyed up to go and should have an eventful but difficult time.

Lienyunkang, June 7

Thursday morning I was so busy rushing around to get to the airport on time (where I learned that the plane was delayed in Tientsin because of bad weather), that I didn't have time to think that this was my first flight until I was in the air and Tsingtao harbor was right underneath. It was a small Stinson cabin plane with a foreign pilot and a Chinese co-pilot, the regular system followed all over China. Twice a week, large Douglas planes make the route but they do not stop at Haichow, my destination. My fellow passengers were a young Frenchman and a Chinese, both from Peking and bound for Shanghai. The land beneath us was cut out into small rectangular patches of shades of brown and green while on my left was the rocky shore and the blue Yellow Sea. I was surprised by the roughness of the plane, which jolted, slipped and bumped in a crazy fashion because of a strong head wind from the south.

A year or two ago the airport was moved from Haichow to a flat field two or three *li* outside Sinpuchen. When I stepped out of the plane, the ground underneath was like a living, jumping brown carpet: I had run into my first grasshopper swarm. It was a strange sight and made for unpleasant walking.

I was met at the airport by Mr. Kiao, our inspector, and two Socony inspectors, Mr. Chang and Mr. Hsen, who had rickshaws waiting to take me to Sinpuchen. They had been out to meet me twice because of the delay, but from their polite greeting and smiles, one would never have known. The maneuvering and dickering connected with getting five different agents to come to a price accord were complicated, but by eleven o'clock that night the agreement had been written and the last of the agents had put his chop on it.

I was able to sleep on my rock-hard bed in the funny little Chinese hotel with a feeling of satisfaction. The next morning, before the bus left for Lienyunkang, I had a chance to look around Sinpuchen, a rather unattractive place with dirty streets, brackish water and pigs living with the families.

I had quite a surprise the night before, just as I was going to bed, when eight soldiers marched into my room and demanded my *huijo* or passport. Mr. Kiao was found, however, and he got rid of them, still grumbling as they went out. It seems that I do not have a Chinese interior visa for Kiangsu Province, nor does my passport indicate that I am a resident of Tsingtao—a matter I must attend to when I return. The soldiers were unpleasantly officious.

Lienyunkang, June 12

It is one of those evenings when I feel far from home and all that I love and know. The air is warm and springlike, and I can hear the somewhat strained music of a Chinese fiddle coming in the open window. Down the hall of my *fan-tien* or hotel comes the noise of a late dinner party being held in one of the rooms. I have just returned from a lonely stroll down to the cliff overlooking the harbor and the tea-*fan* has brought me my tea. Next door Mr. Kiao is playing mah-jongg and asks me to join in his party, but why should I spoil their

A Texaco gas station in Tsingtao.

game by having them try to put up with a novice who can't speak the language? In short I feel hemmed in by the strangeness. There is nothing in which I can enter fully, neither conversation, nor games, nor eating. So here I am at ten in the evening, while in Hempstead on the other side of the world, it is morning, but it is also spring.

While I was writing, another group of soldiers came charging into my room and demanded my passport. I told them that they had seen it last week, but the spokesman said it was a different man and he had gone away, and that furthermore my inland visa was dated for the year 25 (of the Chinese Republic) and this was the year 26. So I had to get Mr. Kiao again from next door, who said that as I didn't have the visa for Kiangsu Province, I would have to return directly by ship to Tsingtao and get the necessary chops on my passport.

Tsingtao, June 28

On top of all the trouble about the passport, I came down with food poisoning and spent a day and a night in the American Missionary Hospital in Haichow. I decided to go back to Tsingtao by land with the Chinese inspectors of the other companies and have a joint inspection on the way home. It was an awful trip and took seven days instead of four.

12

Tsinan, Floods and the Outbreak of War

Tsingtao, July 5, 1937

I AM GOING to the Tsinan office for a month. In the Yellow River hot belt, Tsinan is a large city of half a million people or more, with a handful of foreigners—just men now as the women are always sent to Tsingtao for the hot months. There is a small club, with perhaps a dozen members, and a tennis court, so I have bought a racket in preparation. I will live in the Stein Hotel, run by an old German who has clean rooms and good German food; the living will be fairly comfortable.

The work, however, will be different from what I am used to and difficult. Since there is a lot of price trouble in Tsinan among agents of the three oil companies, I will have to hold up our end against the "old hands" of the other companies (Socony and A.P.C.), both of them foreigners long in service. Then, too, the Tsinan office controls all our agencies along the Tientsin-Pukow Railroad in this province and all those along the Yellow River, besides some along the western end of the railroad from Tsingtao.

Today at noon all the American men in Tsingtao, including the senior officers of the Navy, were up at the consulate for a champagne toast to our country and the President. To celebrate the Fourth of July, sailors have been shooting off firecrackers for two days.

Tsinan, July 14

I am hoping that the affair at Marco Polo Bridge[1] will be relegated to the long list of "incidents." I hope so with all my heart, but I am afraid this time the lid is off. In Tsinan, over three hundred miles inland, and on the line of the railroad to Tientsin and Peking, our small community is watching the affair with great attention. Strangely enough, the people in the States seem to know more than we do. There was a "Stop Press" item in the *Tsingtao Times,* which arrived here this evening, saying that a couple of bombs had gone over the wall in Peking at 12:16 yesterday noon, but that is the latest we have. Most of the information is practically two days old.

Needless to say, with the current situation I am worried about my mother's trip, scheduled to start two weeks from now. Perhaps it would still be possible for her to visit Japan and probably visit me in Tsingtao as long as the Texas Company is still doing business here, but as for Peking, that's another question.

It is hard to realize that possible war is at hand. When Bell of Socony and Richard of Asiatic Petroleum Company and I made a joint inspection today of Chowtsun and Mingshui, I thought it would be hard to imagine a more peaceful-looking country. Crops were growing in well-taken-care-of fields; children were playing; shopkeepers were doing "business as usual"; coolies were working, sleeping in the shade, sitting on their haunches by the roadside, smoking their long-stemmed bamboo pipes. In short, a poignant picture of China everlasting.

Japan will never get China—*never*—but China must fight. It may be defeated this time and even for the next ten years, but eventually Japan will be driven out of China, out of Manchukuo and back to its own islands, where it

---

1. Marco Polo Bridge Incident , July 7, 1937: A clash between Chinese and Japanese soldiers near Marco Polo Bridge outside of Peking escalated the conflict between China and Japan.

belongs. A while ago, Chiang Kai-shek made a ringing speech saying that China would not cede an inch more territory to Japan. If it comes to real war now, I feel sorry for China. In the north the Twenty-Ninth Route Army is ill equipped, poorly officered and perhaps with pro-Japanese men in command. To the west and southwest of Hopeh are the armies composed of bandits, Communists and bandit-suppression troops, all three of which are interchangeable.

In Shantung the army is directly under General (and Governor) Han Fu-chu, who is jealous of the Central Government and who would not send his troops north even if China declared war. Then farther south comes the fairly small army spread along the Lunghai Railway, the boys that gave us trouble in Lienyunkang. Beyond them is the Nanking army of the Central Government, General Chiang's own crack troops, but so far away. And even if they were to move north, who would defend the Yangtze?

Yesterday the Chinese started erecting the old sandbag fortification in Chapei, that section of Shanghai memorable for the "war" in 1932.[2] Cargo from Japan to China is now being insured at wartime rates. Furthermore, the Japanese Embassy in Peking is preparing to give shelter to all their nationals in the city. The Japanese emperor, returning to Tokyo from a vacation, says that the affair must be settled once and for all. Japanese troops and planes are pouring into the Tientsin area from Manchukuo and Japan. With the Chinese press clamoring for war, the situation is tense tonight.

In spite of everything, life goes on at our little club, and the very English Mrs. Nash is giving a cocktail party tomorrow. I have just had a fine dinner at the Stein Hotel, but how pointless everything seems now. I am especially worried about my mother's trip to the East. I hate to think of the uncertainty and disappointment that must be on her mind when it is so near the sailing date. Although it will be a terrible disappointment, I do not think she should come to China now.

When Y.F. Li looked at a photograph of my mother, he said how young she looked and that he wanted to give a dinner party for her. He surprised me by saying, "She doesn't look down on the Chinese does she?" I quickly reassured

---

2. The "Shanghai Incident," Jan.-May 1932: Japanese naval forces bombed the Chapei section of Shanghai after a Chinese boycott organized to protest the Japanese occupation of Manchuria at the end of 1931, and an attack on Japanese monks on a street in Chapei. Thousands of civilians were killed.

him. I did not tell him, however, that she has read so many novels about China that she tends to put the Chinese on a pedestal and have unrealistic views.

July 22

The uncertainty about this present crisis is nerve-racking for everybody. Each day finds new rumors circulating, and so far yesterday's rumors have proved to be the following day's news.

There are many Japanese in Tsinan, perhaps two thousand, and many, including most of the women, have already left for Tsingtao. The southbound trains passing through here are jam-packed with Chinese, and many Chinese are leaving Tsingtao for Tsinan.

If the fighting should come, our consul, John Allison, says he would first call in the missionaries into Tsinan and then if the situation warranted, we would have to go down to Shanghai on the Tientsin-Pukow Railroad. Reports are rampant now that the Japanese are about to land two divisions (forty thousand men) at Tsingtao to move westward through Shantung and meet their men from the north here. There will be much bloodshed before they get to Tsinan, if they ever do.

There is no thought at all of any actual danger to us here, but when you feel certain that the country in which you live and work is about to go to war and the decision is slow in coming, it is hard on the nerves. Then, too, being in charge of an interior station in north China at this time presents many problems. I must see that we have enough stocks in our godown here to last out awhile in case rail communications from the Tsingtao terminal should be interrupted, and that we have the right stocks for an emergency.

Stars and Stripes over Texaco godown in Tsinan.

If it comes to war, we will be able to sell every unit of gasoline we can get up here. Yet if I order large stocks now and nothing happens, we will suffer great leakage loss before we can dispose of the gas through normal channels.

I must also consider the possibility of looting, always the bugbear of oil men in China in perilous times. As the Socony man said yesterday at the club, in the matter of ordering stocks "you're damned if you do, and damned if you don't." I've had no news today from the north, but yesterday things looked worse than they have any time before.

This time, if there is to be peace, Japan must back down, and I am afraid this will not happen. It would mean further loss of face, which is more precious in the Orient than respect for human life.

July 28

On Saturday I cabled my mother not to come. The following day, however, everything was so peaceful that I nearly changed my mind and seriously thought of sending another cable telling her to take a chance.

Monday I was making a call on a large cotton mill outside the city when a wire came for the manager telling him that fighting had broken out again at a town between Peking and Tientsin. The next day, yesterday, the news by radio was even worse. At the club yesterday afternoon, John Allison, the American consul, showed us copies of the official dispatches he was sending to our embassy. I hadn't realized till then that we are practically in the middle of a war. John had called Governor Han Fu-chu in the morning and had also talked with the Japanese consul. The opinion of the Chinese authorities is that Tsinan will be one of the first objectives of Japanese bombers when the fracas gets under way. Chiang Kai-shek himself wired Han Fu-chu yesterday morning to push preparations to the utmost limit because the Japanese would invade Shantung within ten days. This was stated not as an assumption but as a fact. It seems to be certain that Tsingtao will be attacked within a week. Central Government troops are coming into Shantung all the time and are joining Han's army near Weihsien, half-way between here and Tsingtao.

Governor Han also told John that he wanted all the foreigners to be ready to get out at a moment's notice, and John is asking the embassy for instructions. Up to yesterday, the Japanese consul here has been optimistic about Shantung not being involved, but yesterday morning he practically admitted there was little hope of avoiding conflict.

The consuls in Tsingtao must be nearly crazy with worry for they have thousands of summer visitors on their hands from Shanghai, a semi-transient group hard to keep track of. We have thought all along that there could never be much trouble in Tsingtao because the Japanese could take it so easily. Things look different now. There are tens of thousands of Chinese troops in the country right outside the city; the story is that they will defend Tsingtao. If the Japanese have to bring their navy into play to capture the city (which means shelling), goodness knows what will happen.

Nothing could have been more dramatic than what happened this morning in the Tientsin-Peking district. The night before last, the Japanese delivered an ultimatum to the Chinese demanding that all Chinese troops evacuate the whole area up there by noon today. This morning before time was up, the Chinese, with excellent strategy and daring, launched an attack on the Japanese that, according to our reports, cleaned out the thousands of Japanese troops between Tientsin and Peking. All are reported to be killed, wounded or captured! That is hard to believe; we are impatient to see the Tsingtao paper tomorrow morning. If this war comes, I am on the side of the Chinese.

Right now, the chances seem a little more than fifty-fifty that we foreigners will have to leave Tsinan in a few days. We would probably have to go south to Shanghai or Nanking, perhaps to Tsingtao if we go soon enough. Most of my clothes are hanging in the closet in the Victoria there, and I have a trunk that is locked. I wouldn't like to be in Shanghai with all my belongings under fire in Tsingtao. I will write to Bernard and ask him to take care of my things.

The Japanese have promised the foreign powers not to bombard Peking, which is good news. The currency fell six cents to the dollar between yesterday and today—$3.41 now, had been $3.35. I'm glad my money is in gold.

We are getting little news in Tsinan, especially as the trains are not coming here from Tientsin any more. The situation in Tientsin, according to the *Tsingtao Times*, must be awful: bombs, street fighting, artillery and all sorts of confusion. The Japanese are holding some sections of the city and the Chinese others. A shell crashed into the Tientsin Country Club, of all places!

The only local news is that most of the Japanese consular staff in Tsinan has left the city for Tsingtao. That is a bad sign because the consular staff usually remains till the last moment.

I've played tennis daily for a week now. I take clean clothes up to the club with me and have a shower and change after playing. We usually play in the evening from about 5:30 to 7:30. Most of the bunch have their boys bring their

dinner over to them, and everyone sits around a big table and eats his own dinner. Quite often I eat with them, sharing several people's food, instead of going
back to the hotel. We never eat till almost nine, so we have a nice long afternoon after the sun goes down. I don't believe anyone but a China resident
would play in such heat. We get absolutely drenched in perspiration after the
first game, but one soon gets used to it and can forget the heat.

The service one gets in China is unbelievable. You never have to walk a
step to pick up a ball. Each side has two ball boys who keep the court clear and
toss you balls when you are serving. I played tennis one day last week out at a
missionary college outside of town. Even the missionaries have ball chasers!
If I were at home, I would probably not be playing tennis, or I would have to
go to the state park to play. A year in the Orient certainly changes one's expec-
tations. On the other hand, while the club is good and the service fine, that is
all we have. You can't go for a pleasant drive into New York for dancing, etc.
Clubs in China have to take the place of a lot of things; no wonder they are all-
important and fitted out as well as possible.

There was an earthquake here at 4:45 this morning. I woke up with a start
at what I imagine was the first shock. My bed was rocking just as if I were on
board a ship, while out in the street there was a great running and yelling. The
quake continued for a minute or two with a considerable rumble, and then after
a five-minute interval came another tremor. I got out of bed to see if I could
stand; it rocked me back and forth. The Chinese, and I too for a while, thought
we were being bombed. The city didn't settle down for hours. The old German
hotel manager, who has lived here since 1914, said this was the first earthquake they have ever had. Several houses had cracks on the inside walls.

Because the station is not far from my hotel, I could hear trains leaving and
going through all night. Sixty trainloads of Central Government troops are supposed to have gone through within the past forty-eight hours. According to
reports from the front, however, Central troops have taken little action up
there, which might mean that Chiang is going to let the Japanese get away with
it again. Some rumors even say that he is waiting until the Japanese destroy the
Twenty-Ninth Army, since he has never trusted it anyway. This sounds crazy
but anything is possible in China.

Four or five miles outside of town at a place called Lakow (where we have
a company godown), there is the bridge across the Yellow River for the
Shanghai-Tientsin line. That might be the object of an air attack, but I can't see

why they would want to bomb Tsinan. Out at Lakow, the Chinese have Central Government antiaircraft guns and have declared martial law, one of the rulings being that no lights must be shown after 8 P.M.

Neither side has declared war yet, and through Chiang's inaction the whole thing might still blow over, with the Japanese satisfied with Hopeh. Only in a full-blown war would Shantung be invaded, I believe.

We had the usual evening at the club last night. The whole eighteen of us were there from about 5 till 1 A.M. We played tennis, had cocktails and ate there. Dick Nash brought his radio over, so we listened to the English broadcast from Tokyo and then later on the news from London. We all gathered around in great excitement, but they just talked about preparations for Bank Holiday and then about scientific excavations in Ireland! It was exasperating. When the announcer finally talked about our side of the world, he knew little more than we did. The broadcast from Tokyo was just as unhelpful.

We had another earthquake while everyone was at the club this afternoon. We kept on playing billiards until the balls went haywire. All the British and American women and children are being evacuated to Tsingtao tomorrow. The streets are full of turmoil and the temperature must be at least 104 degrees.

August 8

I have been busier than ever before in my life and I am enjoying it—working ten hours a day while most of the foreigners take a siesta. Y.F. Li and I have been getting practically all the war orders. We have sold forty thousand gallons of auto oil to the army. According to George Bell of Socony Vacuum, competitors didn't even know about our sales until they received letters from their Tsingtao office asking about it. In the middle of the week, on top of all the work we have to do (we do the same work as Socony with a staff of less than a third of theirs), we were notified that the China National Aviation Corp. planes (partly owned by Pan Am) were about to start daily flights to Tsinan, and we must give them fuel. The little military airport that they use here is seven miles outside of town, via a road in awful condition. I went out there to meet the pilot and make arrangements when the first plane arrived on Friday. I have to arrange for storage of a few drums at a time, and we will have to ship stock out to the airport by man-drawn carts. Besides this, we are in a terrible situation about our godown here in Tsinan. We store our stocks right in the middle of town, and the city fathers are worried about having such a dangerous cargo in their midst in case of a bombing raid. They have taken up the matter with the American consulate, so it looks as if I'll have to be looking for a new godown outside the city. What a terrific bother that will be.

Early last week we had scenes of panic; about half the population left town within three days. It was terrible. I'll never forget those never-ending streams of heavily laden rickshaws carrying frightened Chinese with all their movable property to the station, fleeing to their ancestral homes in the country. They quickly lose their supposed calm and fatalism. There is a temporary lull now but no one considers it anything but temporary.

I went to the cinema last night with Mr. Chen, the local manager of the Bank of China. He had just been talking with Governor Han, who said that right now the Yellow River is worrying him a great deal more than the Japanese. Things certainly happen in bunches in this country. Here we are in the midst of a war scare, with hundreds of people fleeing in all directions, others digging what they consider bomb-proof shelters, and gas-attack warnings on the cinema screens, etc. And then we had the earthquakes, and right now perhaps comes the climax of trouble: the Hwang Ho (Yellow River) is higher than it has been in seventy years. The river is practically in Tsinan's backyard.

We are afraid that our company godown on the dike at Lakow may be swept away. Having been out there several times in the past few days I have seen what is probably one of the secondary wonders of the world, the Hwang Ho in real action. The men worked all last night piling sandbags on our property. (The water is now even with the top of the dike.) What a scene: mud huts being washed away, temporary shelters for the homeless, and right beside you, level with your feet, the raging water rushing along like the rapids above Niagara. Only this water is yellow and muddy. A few people are starting to leave Tsinan, but I doubt if the water gets to the city.

August 12

The road to Lakow is under water, three feet of it! Since the godown is in danger I ought to move stocks, but there is no way to get them out. There are fourteen thousand gallons of kerosene sitting on top of a dike about to overflow!

In the morning yesterday, my time was filled with hectic attempts to arrange for gasoline deliveries to the military here and down the line at Weihsien. I was on the phone with the Tsingtao office and competitors half the time. The military is frantic about getting gasoline here before the Tsinan-Tsingtao railway line is cut.

Yesterday, when I conveyed the news to Governor Han's office that the order must stand pending a day, he raised a terrible fuss. At the same time, he warned his own men and purchasing agents that anyone causing a delay in getting that gasoline here would be beheaded. Knowing how things are done here, that is no idle threat. Lucky I have an American passport.

The floodwaters are now filling streets and mills in the northern part of the city half a mile or less from our office. The telephone line to Lakow collapsed the night before last, so yesterday afternoon I went by bike with Y.F. to see what was happening to the godown. We went along the railroad track, which is the only way. What a sight! Flood refugees living under tables and cloth huts

"Mud huts being washed away": Devastation from flooding in Lakow.

Tragedy in Shanghai, August 14, 1937: A press photograph shows the devastation outside the Cathay Hotel on Nanking Road after Nationalist airplanes accidentally dropped bombs intended for the Japanese flagship anchored off the Bund. All told, more than a thousand people were killed and hundreds were wounded.

besides the tracks; water on either side of the track embankment all the way there; houses, factories all under water. Women struggling along on the way to Tsinan, carrying week-old babies; old men with white beards, unbelievably thin and scrawny of limb, hobbling to safety. Poor China!

Fortunately Lakow godown was still there. We came back to Tsinan after a three-and-a-half-hour struggle with the crowds—and the bicycles we should never have taken.

We all knew the International Settlement in Shanghai *could* be bombed by accident or otherwise, but when it actually happened, it came as a dreaded surprise. I knew, of course, that the fighting was going on in Shanghai, but I thought it was taking place in the Chapei section as in 1932. When I got to the club, the fellows had already had bad news from both Tokyo and London. The Chinese had attempted to bomb the *Idzumo,* the Japanese flagship lying off the Bund, but instead had hit the Cathay Hotel, the Palace Hotel and the Jardine wharf. Two hundred or more persons were reported killed around the corner of the Bund and Nanking Road where the two hotels stand facing each other.

The A.P.C. oil tanks were hit and were burning last night. Tokyo reported that ours and S.V.C.'s were hit too, but London said only A.P.C.'s. An unknown number of foreigners were killed; at least three American bodies have been found. We hung around the club, playing billiards and poker until midnight, when we went over to the American consul's to hear London again. The news was about the same except we heard that two Japanese marines were killed yesterday afternoon at Tsingtao. That was an unpleasant shock, for it means that the Japanese will probably insist on landing now. If they do, there is a serious chance that the Tsinan-Tsingtao railroad will be closed, bottling us up here.

Already, of course, it is impossible to reach either Tientsin or Shanghai from here; if the railroad is closed, we will be entirely cut off. John Allison, the consul, advised me to go to Tsingtao. He is sending out letters to all missionaries, etc., in his area conveying the same advice, but he himself is staying on awhile, as are the A.P.C. fellows, Dick Nash and Jim Pullen. George Bell of S.V.C. went down the night before last for his vacation. Whether another man comes up here to relieve him is problematical. The British American Tobacco people have moved their entire accounting department down, and instead of four foreigners, there is only one left. Today, except for the consul and a teacher at the missionary college outside the city who is staying with him, I'm the only American in town, although one B.A.T. American may return this evening.

Peter Kengelbacher

The Japanese flagship Idzumo *off the Shanghai Bund in August 1937.*

John says that he does not believe there is any actual danger to Tsinan, and his advice about leaving is only to avoid being stuck here if the Tsinan-Tsingtao line should be closed. He says he will order me to go as soon as he hears the Japanese consul is leaving, and at that time he will leave too. We all plan to catch the same train. I'm in the office waiting for a promised call from our manager, Frank Keefe, who will inform me if the Japanese have landed.

August 17

The time has come for me to be evacuated. The Japanese consul and all remaining Japanese in town are leaving on a special train at 6:30 this morning.

My train will leave at 10:10 tonight and get in Tsingtao about 8 tomorrow morning.

We have had the greatest assortment of people popping into Tsinan from all over the country during the past week. The other day, there were two Germans at the hotel trying to get to Shanghai from Nanking. Nanking to Shanghai is about two hundred miles; they were taking a twelve-hundred-or-more-mile route via Tsinan and Tsingtao. By the time they arrived in Tsingtao there were no ships going to Shanghai, so I wonder what happened to them. There are no ships to Tientsin either; communications have broken down everywhere. Yesterday a foreigner from our Tientsin office arrived in town from the country south of here. He was up in Kalgan, way up northwest of Peking, when he was cut off from Tientsin by the fighting. He finally worked his way south and after traveling a few thousand miles on all sorts of trains and other conveyance, reached Tsinan and left for Tsingtao last night.

Capt. Frank Dorn,[3] a U.S. Army observer in town to watch activities, thinks we might be in for a two-year war of major proportions. Now that the Japanese have left Tsinan, all government and military offices are open only at night for fear of bombing.

The floodwaters have risen again around Tsinan. One foot more and we lose the electric lights. The scene from our office window is typical. All traffic moving to the left is laden with people and their belongings headed to the Shanghai-Tientsin line station to leave town. All traffic going in the other direction is crowded with people trying to get out of the flooded sections of the northern part of the city just half a mile away.

Although I hate war and killing, I must admit I find there is quite a zest to living over here just now. I'm getting my bit of adventure at any rate and wouldn't trade my position for a humdrum job in an office at home for any amount of money.

3. Frank Dorn, 1901-1981, was a soldier, linguist, author and painter. He served in the United States Army in China under Joseph W. Stilwell when Stilwell was senior attaché in Peking and later chief of allied staff attached to Chiang Kai-shek. The two officers were involved in the defense of Burma against the Japanese. Dorn became a brigadier general in 1944.

13

Waiting While the Japanese Advance

August 20, 1937

H ERE I AM back in Tsingtao, and what a situation. Over three-quarters of the Chinese population have left, practically all the stores are closed, everything is on a cash basis, and no one has any money. The food problem is getting tough as the farmers won't bring in anything. The Japanese had six big ships in today moving out the last of their women and children. No business is being done except making collections if possible, and the boys in our office have disappeared. The big British American Tobacco factory has closed down, as has every other factory in town. You can't buy anything except essentials and then only for cash. The huge number of vacationers up from Shanghai cannot return: with their cash running low, and not being able to cash checks, they are in an awful spot.

The American consul and American Navy have prepared a plan of evacuation for us. When we hear the ships blowing continuous S.O.S.'s or see red rockets at night, we are to rush immediately to the Edgewater Mansions Hotel, which is out at the beach. We are to be checked by the already appointed squad leaders and taken to the ships by small boats. And then where? Perhaps to Manila, but no one knows.

On Aug. 20, 1937, the USS Augusta, *on the Whangpu River off the Shanghai Bund, was mistakenly hit by a Nationalist antiaircraft shell. One seaman was killed and seventeen were injured. Eight years later, on August 7, 1945, President Truman announced the bombing of Hiroshima aboard the* Augusta, *which was taking him back to the United States from the Potsdam Conference.*

People are begging for space on ships to leave but practically no ships are available. The Japanese ships are taking only Japanese passengers. Yesterday a British ship sailed for Shanghai loaded with 650 members of the Shanghai Volunteer Corps who were here on vacation. That is the only passenger ship that has left for Shanghai since the big trouble began there. It will later be escorted up the Yangtze by British destroyers.

This might mean the end of the white man in the Orient, and it might mean a world war. The Chinese and Japanese are no longer negotiating; it's all fighting from now on, and it could last a long time.

There is no particular news in Tsingtao, which is continuing to live in dread of something, although there are no signs of anything about to happen. I think that the Japanese will have their hands full. In fact, it seems as if the Chinese are winning for the moment in Shanghai, although it is amazing that they can't hit that Japanese flagship, the *Idzumo*. It was pretty grim for a while at the Pension Victoria just after news came through that the USS *Augusta* had been hit. Most of the people there are families of the men on board the *Augusta*, but the report came in shortly after that no one with relatives had been wounded.

Meanwhile, any ships leaving Tsingtao for any ports are crowded with people. Some go to Manila, some to Hong Kong. Men who are due for home leave within a year are trying to send their families back to the States or England. Business will soon be at a standstill. There is no telling what action the company might take if there is nothing for its employees to do. It had already issued instructions that wives may be sent to any place requested, at company expense, if a ship is available. So far none have left. Since Mrs. Keefe has terminal cancer it would be undesirable to move her and make her more uncomfortable than she is.

Everyone hopes that something will happen soon. There is nothing worse than waiting in this state of tension. The foreign banks in Shanghai are supposed to open up today. We are all anxious what the rate of exchange will be after this ten-day lapse.

September 3

The last of the Japanese residents, including the consul, have left, which means there won't be a single one in Shantung, where ordinarily there are about 20,000 of them. Leaving has meant considerable hardship for the Japanese, some of whom have been here fifteen and twenty years and haven't returned home until now. This was their home, and they have had to leave on the spot, giving up everything they couldn't carry. Everyone is wondering what the evacuation of the Japanese means. The Japanese authorities claim that by leaving they are cutting down the chance of having the fighting spread, but most of us don't believe this. They have turned over their mills and property to the Chinese, and Mayor Shen has accepted the responsibility. The night before last he threw a big dinner party for the Japanese consul, Otaka.

The news is now that Tsinan is having air-raid scares, with Japanese planes getting very close. Canton, Foochow, Soochow, Nanking, Hankow and Shanghai have already had air raids, and now Tsinan. So far, Tsingtao has been fortunate. Everything is so confused and mixed up in China now; if Roosevelt decided to declare war, I wouldn't even be surprised.

For the moment, however, life continues as usual. In the evening I usually eat at the Tsingtao Café Pavilion, which has a balcony porch right beside the water, overlooking Tsingtao Bay—the prettiest spot in all China. I feel as if I am living like a millionaire, but I can't get worried about it.

Hundreds and hundreds of Shanghai people are up here whose vacations were over weeks ago and who can't return. Some of them get money from friends, but many are penniless. We are holding a ball at the Edgewater Mansions Hotel tonight to raise money for relief, mostly for the Russians. There is practically nothing to do at the office except trying to cover our finan-

The Sincere Department Store on Nanking Road in Shanghai was hit by a bomb on Aug. 23, 1937. There were hundreds of casualties.

cial position with our agents and making deliveries to the military. We hear that the U.S. is sending out four more light cruisers, which is good news for us. Tsingtao has certainly turned out to be the best spot in China right now—we are lucky to be here. But it is possible that every white person in China will be moved out within a month.

President Roosevelt has declared that all Americans still in China are there at their own risk. We were notified that the U.S. Navy is prepared to take all Americans away within a couple of weeks. Many women and children have already left.

A dirty little freighter left for Shanghai today loaded down with 1,200 passengers, almost all Russian women who had been stranded in Tsingtao. It was a crime to let a ship sail like that. She has just three cabins and six lifeboats and so much superstructure that there is hardly any deck space. The trip down will be a nightmare even if everything goes well. If they should hit a typhoon or bombs, it would be disastrous. Hong Kong seems to be just as bad as Shanghai, with overcrowded conditions, typhoons, cholera and dysentery.

Foochow and Amoy have been bombed again, and even the American consuls there have closed up shop and cleared out. We are all amused at the statements put out by the Japanese, trying to defend their actions against the Chinese. They are complaining about the "lack of sincerity on the part of the Chinese"! They are giving the English trouble too. They stopped a British merchant vessel and searched her. Yesterday, they fired on and sank a Maritime Customs cruiser with an Englishman in command.

Because the servants have left ("gone Ningpo more far"), some women here, believe it or not, are cooking their first meal in years. People everywhere meet to compare hardships: at the club, on the beach and at cocktails.

Taylor, our accountant here, has a big house and up to now four servants: a cook boy, a No. 2, an amah and a coolie. Actually, the last named is not a coolie but is called "a small piece," a young boy who does the same work as a coolie but who can be hired for $6 or $7 Mex. per month. That is economy since a full-grown coolie can command twelve or fourteen. What a country.

This war has developed into one of the most inhuman struggles ever waged. Tsingtao is the only major city in China, except for Chungking and Chengtu (1,500 and 1,600 miles up the Yangtze), that has not been bombed. From reports we have had through Reuters News Service, the New York and London papers are thoroughly aroused about the intensive bombing of noncombatants. The Japanese have already bombed Lienyunkang and Tsinan and several other points I have visited in the past, and now it looks as if all Shantung is to be subjected to what Canton, Nanking and Hankow have experienced. Tsingtao has regained a little composure in the past few weeks; although it is still very empty, there is a little more life and action about the place. We know that the Japanese planes could be here in a few hours, and we expect them at any time.

The main news for me personally is that Harry Bernard has been transferred to Shanghai, and that so far no one has been assigned to take his place. If no one is sent, it will be a great stroke of luck for me as I shall be No. 2 in Tsingtao (Shantung District) in less than a year. I was trying to make myself not think about it, but it is pretty hard not to hope.

October 7

With its northwestern border already overrun by the Japanese army, Shantung is definitely involved in the struggle for the first time. The Japanese vanguard is now only forty miles from Tsinan, with nothing but an evidently disrupted Twenty-Ninth Route Army and the swirling Yellow River in between. For a long time, the old Twenty-Ninth held the Japanese way up north, just a short distance outside Tientsin, but in the past two weeks the Japanese advance southward has been very rapid since the Chinese have not done much fighting. They put up a pretty good resistance in Tsangchow and Tehchow for a time, but without any artillery, not even antiaircraft guns, their position was hopeless from the first.

The Japanese are using as many planes and artillery as can be brought from Tientsin along the railway. The Chinese with their big swords, rifles and hand grenades have been murderously outclassed. The Japanese can bomb the Chinese from the air with no fear of reprisal, and can blast them from ground positions at a safe distance. An Associated Press representative, however, who had visited the lines while they were still up in Hopeh said the Chinese fighting spirit was phenomenal, that officers and men alike had no interest in food or sleep or rest—they just wanted to fight.

The Twenty-Ninth Route Army has often been accused of being pro-Japan. There is still an almost complete lack of cooperation between it and Nanking.

It looks as if Nanking has decided to let it be wiped out while the Central troops form a strong line farther south. At any rate, Tsinan is ready to fall, and there is no evidence that Nationalist troops in any great number are going to defend the city.

Of course, we have some government troops in the province who came up a couple of months ago, and they, along with Han Fu-chu's 60,000, are moving toward Tsinan, presumably to join the Twenty-Ninth. But I don't know if this will do any good. We all feel sure that Tsinan will fall within a few days. When it does, we will probably find out at least what Japan is planning to do about Tsingtao. I personally believe that the Japanese must take complete control of the Tsingtao-Tsinan railway to keep their troops supplied as they move farther south. They are already very far from Tientsin, their base of supplies, and by shipping supplies to Tsingtao and then up the railroad line to Tsinan, they would not only have an additional supply line but a faster one. The next week should clarify matters and end this long suspense that has kept us in the dark for so long.

It was a little disquieting to learn the other day that the general in charge of the large body of Chinese troops outside Tsingtao is that shifty old fox General Yu , who was one of Chiang Kai-shek's kidnappers last December. He has a bunch of his Shensi troops with him who are distinctly of the bandit type. It is said they are waiting outside the city limits in constant readiness to swoop down on the town and that they could be here in practically twenty minutes. We know that in spite of our sympathies for China in the general outcome, we have more to fear from Chinese soldiers who will want to destroy the town long before the Japanese take it. They are right, of course, for it is perfectly ridiculous for the Chinese to be protecting and patrolling the Japanese mills in Tsingtao, while Japan is doing all the damage she can all over China and is now actually invading the province.

A few days ago, the police at the Public Works Division distributed bags of sand and large barrels of water at even intervals all along the streets. These are to be used in dousing fires caused by incendiary bombs and have a rather sinister look.

Last night we saw our first evidence of the Japanese in a long time when about ten of their ships put on a searchlight display about five or ten miles out. We have known for a long time that they have a fairly sizable fleet lying outside our harbor, because the naval ships and others coming into port have seen

The cruiser USS Marblehead.

them. But this is the first time they have come close enough to be noticed from the land.

There is a small French destroyer in now, also a few British destroyers, and the U.S. cruiser *Marblehead*, which could take us all out to safety in a few hours. The British aircraft carrier HMS *Eagle* is in Weihaiwei and could steam down in no time.

The *Marblehead* is not quite as large as the *Augusta* now in Shanghai, but it is a pretty good-sized ship with a complement of perhaps five hundred men. It's nice to have it here and to see American sailors on the streets and officers in the club.

The workmen on the *Tsingtao Times*, our only newspaper in English, went on strike last week because of what they termed the anti-Chinese policy of the editorials. I believe they are mistaken, since Little, the editor, while something of a pompous Polonius, has said nothing they should have taken exception to.

How I would like to read the *New York Times* each morning. America seems getting nearer the point where, along with other nations, she might use economic force on Japan. Even so, I can't imagine Japan quitting. She has gone too far and would lose too much face and prestige.

October 18

I have just received a batch of letters from home. Letters sometimes take three months to get here. My parents are worried, of course, and it is a shame that the newspapers sometimes make matters sound worse than they are. We have been expecting things to happen in Tsingtao for months now, and until four days ago practically nothing happened except panic among the people and a general exodus. Thursday night we had an air-raid drill that had been announced the night before. Sirens blew and every light in the city went out for fifteen minutes, while all traffic was stopped and any people on the streets were herded into prearranged quarters.

Everyone laughed and joked about it, but the next day we had a real warning. I had just returned to the office when the sirens blew. From our fourth-floor balcony at the office, we had a bird's-eye view of Chungshan Road. Police with drawn pistols and rifles with bayonets attached drove people off the streets in no time at all and then ran hither and thither themselves, acting very important and looking up at the sky all the time. By then the streets were cleared, we had our terminal on the phone and learned that our watchman out there had spotted two planes heading toward the city. It was all very exciting but I didn't see the planes. Finally the "all clear" whistle sounded, and the streets filled up again. On Saturday there was another warning, but again, downtown, we saw no planes.

Huge piles of sand and barrels of water are everywhere on the streets now, and a few more of the remaining American women have decided to leave for Manila or home. The USS *Chaumont* is coming through here on its way to Japan late this week, and the USS *Canopus* will pick up some more people for Manila next week. According to the executive commander of the *Marblehead*, our protection ship, there are still over four hundred Americans in the city, which surprises me, but he must be right.

I expected to hear that Tsinan had fallen, but the Chinese are holding their own for the moment and have pushed the Japanese back some fifteen miles, which means they are still about forty miles from the city.

The three oil companies are now the source of gasoline for practically all of the Chinese armies. During the past two weeks we have shipped hundreds of thousands of gallons to Tsinan and thence down to the Nanking area. One night last week when it looked for sure that the route would be cut off by the fall of Tsinan, we kept our terminal open all night: making tins, filling them with gasoline, roping them and getting them ready to load onto the railroad cars in the daylight. Keefe, Bernard and I took four-hour shifts to help the terminal manager in case of fire or other emergency. It is against company regulations to handle gasoline at night, and Sansome, the terminal manager, would not take the responsibility unless one of us was out there all night. My shift was from two to six in the morning, and it was exciting in spite of the lack of sleep and the chill.

The workers and coolies have already worked about twenty hours and were to go on for sixteen more, but their spirit was wonderful; they did a great job getting that shipment ready. We made, filled and stacked 20,000 five-gallon tins—100,000 gallons! Sansome told them that every tin they filled was going to help fight the Japanese (and make more money for the Texas Company!) and they surely went to work with fervor.

I made continuous rounds during my shift into the noisy can factory where the sheets of tin are cut, stamped, punched, soldered and put onto the belt. Then it was out into the darkness to the filling room where the gasoline is fed into the tins, still on the belt, and they are capped. From there the tins are conveyed to the testing room where they are tipped sideways and upside down automatically while workers watch for leaks. Then the belt carries them into the huge godown where a crew of ten coolies tie straw rope around each tin diamond fashion and stack them in piles that rise almost to the ceiling. I would check all the fire equipment with my flashlight, take a look at the filling tanks and go upstairs in Sansome's flat for a cup of hot coffee. Ten minutes, and I'd be out on the rounds again.

The three companies loaded and dispatched 700,000 gallons of gasoline

A press photograph showing the Chapei section of Shanghai burning in the background. After intense, systematic bombing by the Japanese, retreating Chinese troops set fire to the area, north of the International Settlement, in late October 1937.

during three days last week, and now we are getting out more. The price is $1.05 per gallon, fifty cents of which is, of course, duty.

Nothing has been heard from Shanghai regarding the No. 2 job here, and Bernard will be leaving at the end of this week. It looks as if I might be elected and, if so, Shanghai will have to send word soon authorizing my signature for depositing funds, etc.

I rented a car early in August at $50 per month. It belongs to Kishimoto, a Japanese customs official who had to leave with the rest of his countrymen. It is handy to have and much quicker and better than rickshaws. Without a car of one's own, a lot is spent on rickshaws and paying the monthly chits for the hired cars. Gasoline is quite expensive, but I figure the money I spend on the car is worth it. I was asked to try out for a part in the Tsingtao Amateur Dramatic Association play this year, *The Patsy* by Barry Connors, and got it. Tomorrow, I have been invited out on the USS *Marblehead* for dinner and a movie.

October 30

I have just come from the regular free bar tiffin at the club—about forty or fifty men were there, which is usual for Saturday. It's getting so that we hardly discuss the war any more except when something happens, such as the three British soldiers being killed in Shanghai last night.

The people there are having a terrible time, and Harry Bernard is caught up in it now. He sailed on the SS *Shentien* on Wednesday and arrived in Shanghai on Thursday afternoon. There was a big party down on the ship when he left, according to the good old custom. Ship sailings, always lively affairs, are part of the fun of life in a China port.

Thursday night I had dinner out on the *Marblehead*. How strange it seemed to be waited on by black stewards in actual American surroundings. After dinner we had movies on the afterdeck right between the airplanes the ship carries. It was a beautiful night and in spite of the war, I enjoyed watching *Mickey Mouse* on the deck of a United States cruiser here to protect us, with the lights of Tsingtao off in the distance, under a starry sky.

Last night, Jim Avent, the Standard Oil manager, gave a huge cocktail party out at his house for all the officers and invited about ten or so Americans.

There must have been forty of us altogether; we had a grand time. Jim, a typical Southern host, entertains well in his beautiful home. His wife is one of the many who have been evacuated. We had a buffet dinner; countless dishes and every one of them perfect. It is so easy over here; all Jim had to do was to tell his No. 1 boy to have chow for forty people. Parties like this cost enormous sums because of the liquor, but he is getting at least three thousand a month, so it doesn't matter.

A letter came for me from our Shanghai office a few days ago notifying me that I have been put on "home leave basis." That means I no longer have the stigma of being "Shanghai hired" and am on the same basis as fellows hired in New York and sent out. It means that when my year is up, I will be promoted to a fully fledged marketing assistant, which is one step under district manager—usually a long jump but not necessarily so. Someone in Shanghai was nice enough to give me that basis long before it is usually granted.

Harry Bernard was not given that rating for over two years after he joined, and then he had to wait till he had five years' service before he got leave. I am put on the regular three-years, eight-months basis just like Keefe and the rest. July 1940 sounds like the next century and I am not sure that I want to wait for it, but I'm glad that I'm being considered in a favorable light. I have been lucky for someone just eleven months with the company.

This afternoon I am going to see *After the Thin Man*, and tonight there is a dinner party at the American School. Then we will head over to the Tsingtao Café, where everyone will be—as usual on Saturday night. I am to escort one of the teachers, and my German friend, Rudy Müller, is going with another teacher. The British vice-consul, Ken Bumstead, will be there with a girl from Tientsin.

Tomorrow morning, if the weather is good, I am going to drive out to Laoshan, a beautiful mountain district about forty miles away, with a Chinese friend[1] in her green Chrysler Imperial roadster (the best car in town!).

Life is still very pleasant here, in spite of the war. Sometime I have to face the question whether I want to live a life outside America, separated from my parents. If I could go home two months a year, I would be very happy with this life.

---

1. This is the author's first mention of Lily Lee, a stage and film actress with whom he would have a serious affair and whom he later hoped to marry.

Hill of Longevity at the Summer Palace, showing the Pavilion of Buddha's Fragrant Incense and the Marble Boat, foreground, a favorite of the Dowager Empress.

Begun in the third century B.C. and reconstructed during the Ming Dynasty in the fifteenth and sixteenth centuries, the Great Wall was built to keep out northern invaders.

ABOVE: Tsingtao, "a pretty red-roofed town passed down from the German occupation of the port."
BELOW: Edgewater Mansions Hotel in Tsingtao, site of the Coronation Ball in May 1937, "a splendid affair with a dozen nationalities present and many, many uniforms." Both postcards issued in Japan.

It is a lovely fall day, almost reminiscent of spring. I am doing all the regular work now as No. 2 and have been for some time, with an office of my own, two Chinese clerks as assistants and a stenographer to answer my bell. It is an important job and I like the work.

We have had no air-raid alarms lately. Except for the fact that the number of soldiers one sees on the street is increasing slightly day by day, the town is very peaceful.

The situation in the western part of Shantung is still confusing. I think the Japanese, who seem to have come to a standstill in their drive toward Tsinan and the south, are probably trying to make a deal with Governor Han, who may be forced out of power by Nanking. The central government troops and those who are patriotic among Han's troops are going to fight the Japanese in a big battle north of Tsinan within ten days. There are so many rumors and guesses circulating around town.

The rehearsals for the play are proving to be fun, especially since I have a very unimportant part with nothing to worry about or to learn. There is a club dance tonight and I don't have a date—Tsingtao is getting back to its winter form with very few girls around.

Another week has gone by and Tsingtao seems less and less likely to be included in this war. There is certainly no reason, however, why we alone of the entire coast should feel safe. After all, a Japanese bomb did land just ten feet from the door of our godown outside Tsinan.

I am working hard trying to get used to my new job. Next month, because of the job, I should be getting the car allowance. That is forty gallons of gas free each month and thirty-five dollars for upkeep.

Rehearsals for the play are taking a lot of my time. Last night, we were at it from six to ten. Usually the rehearsals are from six to eight, but they will probably be longer now as the production date gets nearer.

Yale seems to have a fine football team this fall; I wish I could see some of the games. I am getting the scores from the fellows on the *Marblehead* every

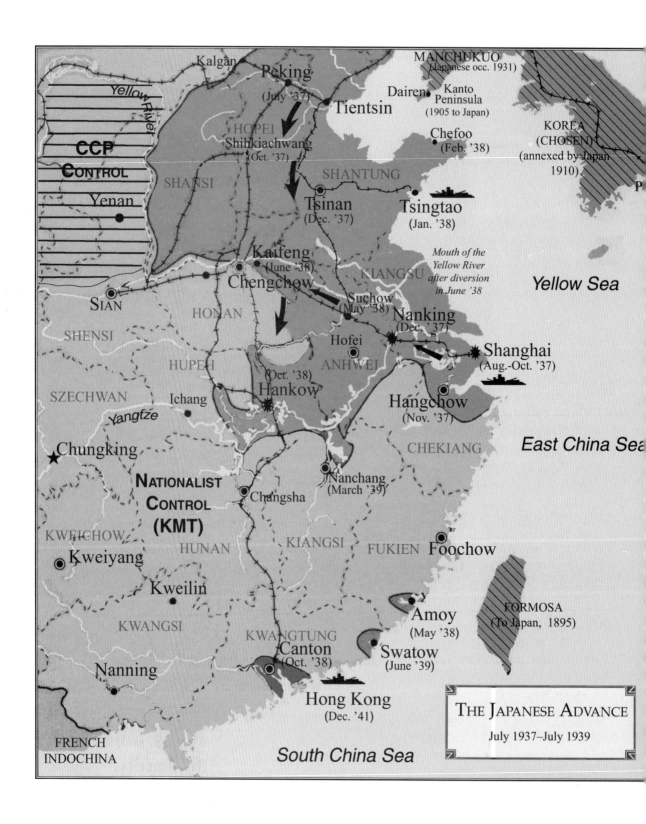

Kalgan

Peking
(July '37)

Tientsin

MANCHUKUO
(Japanese occ. 1931)

Dairen
Kanto
Peninsula
(1905 to Japan)

Yellow River

CCP
CONTROL

HOPEI

Shihkiachwang
(Oct. '37)

Chefoo
(Feb. '38)

KOREA
(CHOSEN)
(annexed by Japan
1910)

SHANSI

Yenan

SHANTUNG

Tsinan
(Dec. '37)

Tsingtao
(Jan. '38)

P

Kaifeng
(June '38)

Chengchow

Mouth of the
Yellow River
after diversion
in June '38

Yellow Sea

SIAN

HONAN

KIANGSU

Suchow
(May '38)

Nanking
(Dec. '37)

SHENSI

HUPEH

Hofei
ANHWEI

Shanghai
(Aug.-Oct. '37)

(Oct. '38)
Hankow

SZECHWAN

Ichang

Yangtze

Hangchow
(Nov. '37)

CHEKIANG

East China Sea

Chungking

NATIONALIST
CONTROL
(KMT)

Changsha

Nanchang
(March '39)

KWEICHOW

HUNAN

KIANGSI

FUKIEN

Foochow

Kweiyang

Kweilin

KWANGSI

Amoy
(May '38)

FORMOSA
(To Japan, 1895)

KWANGTUNG

Canton
(Oct. '38)

Swatow
(June '39)

Nanning

Hong Kong
(Dec. '41)

THE JAPANESE ADVANCE

July 1937–July 1939

FRENCH
INDOCHINA

South China Sea

Monday. Last night I went to see *Les Misérables* again. They also had a revival of Disney's *Water Babies,* which is beautifully done. The American consul is having a cocktail party Saturday night, and the officers of the *Marblehead* are entertaining the club members Tuesday night. On Wednesday, the German Club is giving a concert for the benefit of the Chinese Red Cross. Saturday night, the Russian community is holding a bazaar for the same cause. Soon Thanksgiving will be here and the famous German Bazaar at the end of the month.

I am studying Chinese quite a bit these days, and with so much practice with a Chinese friend[2] I am really making headway. I can't follow a regular conversation, but if I can keep the conversation within certain limits, I can talk a little.

November 17

Tsingtao is near the panic stage again. Tsinan is as good as lost. The Chinese have been destroying all Japanese property since before noon today. The famous Yellow River Bridge at Lakow, built by the Germans years ago, has been blown up in an attempt to prevent the Japanese from crossing.

The day before yesterday, Mayor Shen of Tsingtao said he would be responsible for the peace and safety of the town for three more days and that he would level Tsingtao to the condition of mud before handing it over to the Japanese. Calling on the American consulate this morning, he said he hoped every precaution would be taken for the safety of our nationals. The consul, Sammy Sokobin, admits for the first time that things look very bad.

Governor Han[3] has instructed Mayor Shen to destroy all Japanese property, and if he refuses, Han will send his own people to carry out his order. The Nanking government is making a last desperate effort to get gasoline through. I have been working in the rain at our terminal since four o'clock this morning. The coolies have been working since seven yesterday morning—twenty-

---

2. Lily Lee, who would later say that her English greatly improved after meeting the author. At about this time Jim informed his parents of the affair and a possible engagement. Because of the slowness of the mail, he would not receive their answer until the following March.

3. Governor Han Fu-chu, warlord of Shantung, would be shot in 1938 for deserting his army.

one hours. In the can factory five or six little urchins no more than seven or eight years old are shifting tins on the racks. They look as if they have never smiled in their lives, and their eyes are almost closed. To say the least, it's a crime. They get six and a half U.S. cents per day but actually receive less when the squeeze to the No.1 is subtracted.

Yesterday, we loaded twenty-five fifteen-ton freight cars with gasoline, and the competitors another thirty-eight between them. That is 65,000 tins or 315,000 gallons in one day, each gallon $1.08 paid before delivery. It is hard to believe that any more shipments can get through, but as long as China is willing to try it and pay in advance, we will load stocks. With our Tsinan office now closed, the staff is in Tsingtao. No more trains are entering or leaving Tsinan; all shipments throughout the province are at a standstill, except for these gasoline cars for Nanking. We are thankful for tonight's rain since it is saving us temporarily from trouble in Tsingtao. I just had a phone call at 3 A.M. from a Chinese friend, telling me that Mayor Shen had at midnight been persuaded to promise that he would do nothing tonight. He refused to promise the same for tomorrow, but perhaps he will change his mind. I am awfully glad I have no family to worry about. Keefe and Taylor are both very worried right now—and so, with more reason, is D.F. Lee, with his wife and four sons.

November 23

We have another period of tense waiting, with nothing happening. Our staff is ready to flee to the interior, and we were forced to pay them their November wages before time. I can't blame them a bit for worrying. They know that Chinese men, women and children are being slaughtered by the hundreds in Nantao in Shanghai today, after a whole week and a half have slipped by since the fall of the city. If the Chinese in Tsingtao damage the Japanese property (worth at least U.S. $100 million), the Japanese will come in for vengeance and we will have the same scene here.

Christmas does not seem very real with the prospect of martial law in a day or so. No one knows what the provisions will be. We don't know if we shall be here for Christmas or if we shall be under a Chinese or Japanese administration. The Japanese are reported to be landing at Chefoo today and also at Shihkiuso down the coast. This morning, there was a fire in one of the

*A press photograph of a Chinese civilian
executed by Japanese soldiers.*

Japanese cotton mills, which the municipal government claims was accidental. It caused quite a stir; we expected martial law to be slapped on us.

How I hope that the trouble that is spreading all over the world today never comes close to home and my parents. It's frightening to think that it ever could, and I have become convinced that the only way to stop it is to build up the most powerful defense ever seen, whatever it costs. How clear it is today that man is not even close to the point where cooperation and mutual trust can keep the peace.

November 29

Friday evening a huge explosion occurred downtown, just before curtain time of our play. Some of the coolie soldiers were moving dynamite, presumably to one of the Japanese cotton mills, when an accident occurred, and the whole lot went off. Several people were killed and wounded, and there was a panic, as no one knew what it was. We gave the play, however, in front of a packed house, and everyone said it was the best play given here. It was fun in a way, but it took way too much time.

Local conditions are worse than ever. This morning, the municipal government ordered all people living in the Saufong area (where the mills are) to leave within twenty-four hours. The Chinese seemed determined to blow the place up. They are also getting ready to do something to the harbor, for all the junks were made to leave last night. A British steamer that docked last night at five was told to go out at midnight. It is back again this morning at the dock, but through passengers for Shanghai were warned that they came ashore at their own risk and that the ship might leave at one hour's notice.

The USS *Marblehead*, our noble protector, is nowhere to be seen. It was scheduled to go out for regular maneuvers today but left unexpectedly last night leaving some of her men on shore. We keep looking out of our office windows, scanning the harbor to see what is going to come in—the *Marblehead* or the Japanese. The rumor is that ten or fifteen Japanese destroyers are on their way here from Shanghai and another bunch coming from Dairen.

The Japanese took over the telegraph facilities in Shanghai late last night and imposed a censorship on all messages. The Chinese staff walked out, and now there is no service at all. The last wire to come through was from Lefevre, our general manager in Shanghai, telling Keefe and Taylor that he urgently advised them to send their families away. Whether they can do it or not is another question.

There are no accommodations to be had, and even if there were, we expect the harbor to be closed in a couple of days. It looks as if the Chinese are planning to sink some old ships there or else blow up the wharves. Everyone feels so uncertain about what the next hour will bring, and with no business to do, it's nerve-racking. We can make no shipments at all now to any point, and since this morning we can't even communicate with our head office. Food is shooting up in price, while coal has gone from $18 per ton to $30 per ton in eight days. The Chinese have destroyed the Japanese-owned mines in the interior, and between that and the disruption of rail service, we are expecting an absolute lack of coal in a short time.

Just now, we have learned that the local government received a wireless

*Chinese fleeing Tsingtao for Shanghai in early December 1937. Because
of overcrowding, they had to stay on deck for the duration.*

message from Japan at noon today giving it twenty-four hours to clear out. I'm
going down to the club right away to see what is going on. All Americans are
ordered to have forty-eight hours to get ready—food on hand, eating utensils
and two blankets—to go to the meeting area at Edgewater Mansions Hotel.

December 3

The tension has calmed down for the moment. Apparently Chiang Kai-shek
sent a wire telling the people in Tsingtao not to start any trouble until the
Japanese actually land. The big thing is Japan's encroachment now on foreign
rights in the International Settlement in Shanghai. The Japanese realize that the
powers are afraid to take any decisive action, and so are doing as they please.
France alone is putting up a stand as regards her concession, which is actually
a French colony.

December 7

I'm getting used to the job, but I'm not very busy. Business has almost stopped; except for small local sales and regular reports to Shanghai, there is nothing much to do. I can't keep my stenographer busy even half the time. As I haven't been officially notified of my promotion from Shanghai, I imagine in the present situation they are just letting things ride for the moment. I was told that I would be sent to Shanghai for several months to get some intensive lube oil training and then be sent back to a district. That, also, has been postponed.

We had great sport last Sunday afternoon when the British from HMS *Suffolk* put on a schedule of races with the lads from the *Marblehead*. There were races for all sailors and races for stokers, petty officers and officers. There was even a race for bearded sailors, but the only entrants were British, because our men aren't allowed beards. A lot of men fell from their "horses" and the whole afternoon was one laugh after the other. The famous German Bazaar, held last Saturday, was as much fun as last year, which meant a lot to those attending.

USS Panay, *gunboat of the Yangtze Patrol.*

Y.F. Li is going back to Tsinan this evening to reopen our office and godown there. He feels rather nervous about it. Keefe and D.F. Lee are going to Chefoo for a four- or five-day trip, so I'll be in charge for a while.

December 16

There has been considerable excitement since the sinking of the USS *Panay*[4] on Monday. The British, after all the insults they have swallowed in the past months, get quite excited over the fact

---

4. The *Panay* Incident: On December 12, 1937, Japanese aviators sank the U.S. gunboat *Panay* on the Yangtze outside Nanking without warning, killing two people and wounding others. It was packed with diplomats, journalists, Western and Chinese refugees escaping from Nanking. The incident caused an uproar in America. The Japanese government apologized and said it was a mistake.

that we don't seem to be prepared to fight a war even though our ship was sunk. The Japanese certainly went crazy up the river.

I would not like to be here if and when America and Japan start a war. We would be seized by the Japanese and put into a concentration camp for the duration, and that would not be pleasant at all.

We have a serious relief problem in Tsingtao as a result of the confusion. The International Relief Committee is raising money all the time and operating soup kitchens for the destitute. In Shanghai they are trying to keep a few hundred thousand Chinese from starving in the streets. Things are awful in China and will be getting worse. It is insane for the Japanese to try to conquer the whole country, and their disregard for foreigners is equally senseless. The work of years has been destroyed—buildings, wharves, ships, railways—all the material things that have been built up with such effort under Chiang Kai-shek's government. For the past five months, the Chinese "Republic" has been a nation for the first time. The semi-rebellious south, the Reds out west, and other groups who have never cooperated are willing to cooperate behind Chiang. But I fear that with Nanking[5] lost as well as Tientsin, Peking and Shanghai, morale is going to snap.

December 18

Yesterday, Dick Nash of A.P.C. gave me the first hint of more trouble: he had heard that Han Fu-chu was leaving Tsinan with all his troups.

Today, out of the clear blue sky, all ships were ordered out of the harbor at 4 P.M., and notice was given that a strict curfew would be enforced at 6 P.M. I went to the club around 4:30 and sat in the bar with Rudy Müller. The place filled up gradually, but by 5:30 men began to scurry off to get home before the curfew. After 6 o'clock I was absolutely alone except for the white-gowned boys, who were frankly scared. The town had heard of course that tonight was the night for the destruction of the big Japanese mills. There had also been much talk of the Japanese having already landed at Laoshan Bay, east of here.

---

5. Rape of Nanking: More than 40,000 Chinese (the Chinese figure is 300,000) were slaughtered after Nanking fell to Japanese forces on December 12, 1937. The Chinese government moved further up the Yangtze, first to Hankow (now Wuhan) and then Chungking.

At seven o'clock I heard someone enter the club, and into the bar stamped old George Griffiths, the "Welsh Consul," as we call him. He was cheery and talked about his three-block walk from his hotel to the club, during which he had been stopped four times and had a bayonette gently nudged against his stomach. But old George is the type of harmless, blustering old chap whom authority can never check. Knowing not a single word of Chinese despite his eighteen or twenty years in the country, he had waved the marines aside in outraged dignity and doddered on his way.

You can't talk to Griff for five minutes without learning that he is Welsh and proud of it. Having discovered that I have a strain of the blood through my grandfather, he has called me Lloyd George for the last year. This night, in his eyes, it was a case of two Welshmen sticking it out in the face of fierce odds. We shook dice for a drink as he rambled on and on about the Welshmen holding down the fort.

At 7:30, Tite, the young English chap with B.A.T., came in wearing a dinner jacket and unable to make a supper engagement in another part of town because of the curfew. So there we were, the three of us, when just as eight struck we heard a deep-sounding boom. We ran out into the gateway of the club and could hear repeated detonations from the north, evidently in the Tsankow and Saufong districts, where the mills are located. By 8:10 we could see a huge red glow covering half the sky from our vantage point at the rear second-story windows. We felt a bit anxious as we ran from that view to look out over the water from the dining veranda. But it was the same old Yellow Sea, with a beautiful path of yellowish silver moonlight streaking across from the distance. Not an invader to be seen. So we went down to the billiard room for a game.

December 23

The explosions continued throughout the night on Saturday and flared up stronger than ever just at dawn, when the Chinese navy was sunk down at the wharves to close the harbor. At that time, we heard planes, and a minute or two later a Japanese bomber and pursuit planes appeared and circled around. Alarm sirens added to the confusion.

Sunday was grim throughout, with three more air alarms and planes appearing each time. We were certain that the Japanese would come during the day and were disappointed when they failed us. The fires in the mills continued through most of the second night.

Curfew has been enforced every evening since Saturday, and marines and special guards, all heavily armed, are much in evidence.

The looting started on Monday in the downtown section quite near the office. At first the marines and police took their share and were using the butts of their rifles to smash in boards and windows.

By Tuesday, however, the uniformed men were more or less in control and had orders to

Chinese residents fleeing Tsingtao.

shoot looters on sight. The bodies are left exactly where they are as a warning to would-be looters, not a very pleasant sight on the streets. Between our office and the Chartered Bank along Chungshan Road, there were six poor chaps stretched out in the gutter, one of whom was shot just as I left the office on Tuesday.

Every once in a while the police or marines capture a whole group and throw them into the back of an open truck with their arms bound. The officials then stage a parade, with bugles playing to attract attention. When the truck comes to a likely corner, one of the poor devils is dumped out, made to stand up—usually grinning from the dope he has mercifully been given—and then shot in the head. He sprawls bleeding on the pavement, and the horrible procession drives to another location where the job is repeated. It's sickening.

Monday, our consul had a wire from the State Department again urging all Americans to get out. I rushed around until curfew time finding out who among my list would go on the transportation provided by the Navy. Half of the three hundred Americans are prepared to go. The *Marblehead* and a destroyer came up from Shanghai to take care of the situation, but they have no instructions concerning taking people away before the trouble starts.

The Chinese are planning to blow up the rest of the Japanese property in town, but just when we do not know. I wish they would do it and get it over with, and then the Japanese would come in. We are all tired of the air-raid alarms and curfews and shootings on the streets. What a Christmas season! Food is getting scarce, and we expect the water and lights to be shut off when the Chinese do their work on the Japanese-owned power plant. The harbor, of course, is entirely blocked; the people fighting to get on the few ships going to Shanghai or Tientsin must reach them by sampan.

December 27

The curfew was on as usual on Christmas Eve, but I took a chance and stayed up at the Keefes' house until a little after midnight. I sneaked over the hill with-

"Fires blazed all over town and the explosions were frequent and very loud": The Chinese destroyed property in Tsingtao before the arrival of Japanese navy forces on Jan. 10, 1938.

out being stopped. They don't have enough men left on duty to patrol the residential district thoroughly, but it is impossible to get around downtown.

Christmas morning, we had the regular big party at Keefe's for the members of our staff and other employees. It was quite a success but not the same as last year. Evening parties are out because of the curfew, and few would have the heart for them anyway. After Keefe's party, I went to the Taylors' for dinner and had a nice "homey" meal. They had told their boy the day before to get a goose for dinner, but when they went out to the kitchen Saturday morning to look at it, they discovered that the boy had a swan! We ended up with chicken.

There is no communication with Tsinan; one can only guess whether it has fallen. There is talk now of a volunteer armed corps of foreigners. The regular government has practically ceased functioning, except to enforce curfew and keep the streets clear during the innumerable air-raid alarms. Sandbag defenses have been erected along the shore, including the Bund in front of the club.

Sunday, January 2, 1938

Tuesday night, fires blazed all over town and the explosions were frequent and very loud. Wednesday was tense, but except for sporadic shooting, all was quiet. When we awoke in the morning every single official and employee of the government had cleared out! From the mayor down to the lowest street-sweeping coolie, the whole outfit was gone. Not a soldier, not a policeman, not a fireman! By seven A.M. the looting had started, and practically every Japanese shop in town was ransacked by noon.

Fires and clouds of smoke were to be seen in all directions. The remaining Chinese, maybe twenty or thirty thousand, were in a panic—if they were not looting, and probably even the looters were in a panic too. Japanese planes flew over regularly throughout the day, unheralded by the usual air-raid sirens because no one was left on duty to blow them.

Before noon, the foreign volunteer corps had been called out and was patrolling the streets in cars and carrying arms. The Americans had been refused official permission by the consulate to join the volunteers, and only a few whose homes are here participated at first. Antossovitch, the German police captain who has been the only foreign member of the city police for the past eight or ten years, was still in town. He somehow secured the services of the 120 railway police, a crack outfit in a way; some of them were converted into firemen. On the whole, the volunteers did some very good work at stopping what might have been an attack on all property, not just the Japanese property.

Wheeler of the Customs Service was in the hospital, and Mrs. Wheeler was catching the *Fausan* for Shanghai. They had to leave their home, which is in the Japanese end of town, and have been living in a pension near me. She had to go back to the house and pack Friday afternoon. I drove her there in Wheeler's car and stood guard for a couple of hours while she supervised the packing. I had Keefe's automatic revolver and a couple rounds of ammunition and got quite a kick out of the whole business. There were several fires blazing in the neighborhood and scattered shots were heard, but no one bothered us.

Ten of us broke the volunteers' curfew and celebrated New Year's Eve at the club with the help of a portable gramophone. I was missing home too much to feel in a good mood, but under the unusual circumstances it wasn't such a bad evening, or night rather, for we didn't break up until 4 A.M. Because the club is one of the volunteer patrol headquarters, we were able to keep in touch with the shootings and the fires. I wonder when I'll have another New Year's Eve like this one. I'm sure that even in 1980 on December 31, I'll think of that party in the club, with the town being looted and burned outside.

I feel that this foreign volunteer business is wrong. By force of arms, Germans, British, Russians and now Americans are protecting Japanese property from the Chinese. The trouble is that some of the more unruly Chinese would not have stopped at destroying Japanese property. The poor Chinese have seen their own government officials dynamite the Japanese mills, blow up cable stations, wireless offices and water works, but when they try to grab pieces of silk and other things from shops belonging to the enemy, they are set upon by armed foreigners who actually have no business interfering. I also felt that a good many of the volunteers were in for the "sport" of the thing and enjoyed riding around town with a gun and making arrests. It seems a little senseless too, that if our lives and property were in such great danger, then why hadn't the sailors and marines from the *Marblehead* and *Dorcestershire* landed?

On New Year's Day in the morning, Sam Sokobin, our consul, received a cable lifting the ban on American participation. The reaction at the club bar, always the "Parliament House" for foreign Tsingtao, pushed a great many Americans into the "Vigilantes," as the Shanghai radio calls us. I realized that the company would lose face if we did not have representation, so I phoned Keefe and told him he had better come down. He wanted to avoid the whole thing and yet show we are taking some action by forming our own guard for our terminal and tin factory. It was better for Keefe to have the desk duty where

he could keep in touch with his wife, who is very ill. So we went to headquarters and signed on. We were given armbands and assigned duty.

My first shift was at midnight for four hours, which I spent at the telephone exchange with a Chinese police rifle on my shoulder. My companion was an old Russian who knew about fifty words of English and very little Chinese. It was freezing cold and there wasn't even a brazier in the whole building. We have a dial telephone system here, so there wasn't a soul stirring, and the Chinese staff were stretched out on beds in their offices. Nothing at all happened, and at 5 A.M. I was back in bed at the pension.

The German Club in Tsingtao.

My next duty was at noon the following day. This time, I was in charge of a motorcar on patrol duty with a Russian driver, two Chinese railway police and myself. As the Chinese were both armed with rifles and the Russian had a revolver, I contented myself with a good heavy nightstick. From our substation quartered at the club, we have a large selection of town to cover, including the wharves, the junk harbor, the cabaret district and the entire Japanese section. Our orders were to cruise around in a fairly systematic fashion, break up any mobs, arrest looters and firebugs, and impress upon the populace that we are law and order and mean business.

Captured loot is to be taken to the German Club, where we already have tons of Japanese goods of every description from sewing machines to silk kimonos. We have to get out of the car on each round of our territory and make a tour of inspection on foot through the dockyards and godowns adjacent to the small harbor where the junks and sampans are. Looted property is obviously leaking out of the city by water or small craft, but catching anyone at it is another matter. In a four-hour shift, we make four patrols, going back to the club for hot coffee in between. The Chinese police are quartered downstairs in the Ping-Pong room. Two of these are always asleep on the table, and when we are ready to go out on patrol, we go down and shake a couple of them awake, leaving the rest to slumber on. The two chosen jump up, grab their rifles and climb into the car. I must admit I am rather enjoying it.

What wasn't so great, however, was getting out of bed at ten past three this morning and rushing down to the club to go on patrol till 8 A.M. The "dawn patrol" is the coldest and most dismal of all, and the town was dead as a grave-yard all the time I was on duty. I spotted an open gate at the side of the Japanese consulate grounds but drew a blank when we went in to investigate.

I have the duty from eight P.M. to midnight tonight, which is one of the best for not missing sleep. I won't have to go on again till noon tomorrow, so I am counting on a good rest. As the situation stands, the petty looters are pretty scared, and for the most part the town is dead quiet. You can drive for an hour through ordinarily crowded streets and not see a soul. The talk is now that the Chinese marines who were stationed here until last week have turned bandits and are organizing outside the city for a looting party. That would be disas-trous: our little Cox's army[6] would be worse than useless. The men from the ships would have to come in, and I am sure there would not be any nonsense about protecting anything *but* foreign lives and property.

We are all hoping that the Japanese will come in and take over from us— why should we get up at three in the morning to protect their property? They are probably having a good laugh at us, well content not to have to land now and provide a government and garrison with resulting expenditures. The for-eign community is playing right into their hands, defeating one of the purpos-es of the Chinese for destroying the mills, namely to divert Japanese troops from South China.

---

6. In January 1932 Father James R. Cox of Pittsburgh led an "army" of about 15,000 jobless men in one thousand trucks and automobiles to Washington, D.C., in a plea for federal relief.

14

The Japanese Take Tsingtao

January 11, 1938

THE JAPANESE FORCES are here at last. The news of the invasion, Monday, January 10, was in all the newspapers. It is a great relief to have the waiting over and not to have to be out all night patrolling the town with a squad of Russians, all of us armed to the teeth. Or to be stationed in lonely Litsun guarding the waterworks with a Mauser automatic on my hip and a Chinese Army rifle slung over my shoulder. It was quite fun for a while, but we were going around in a daze at the end of the week.

January 19

We have much to be thankful for in this town. Our harbor is still blocked, and now the British shipping companies have curtailed or temporarily canceled their calls on our outer harbor. To complete our sense of being cut off, the USS *Marblehead* sailed for Chefoo on Sunday morning, followed later in the day by HMS *Suffolk* bound for Weihaiwei. Japanese ships are as thick on the waters of our bay as their marines (and now soldiers) are on our streets. Curfew has not been lifted, and it is hard to recall the normal days when we could be out after dark. It's over a month now since we had that freedom, apart from the ten days when we were doing the patrolling ourselves. That was an awful time, and I'll never forget it.

In the main the Japanese have used great moderation in Tsingtao city itself, that is, compared with the terrible sacking of Nanking, but we are constantly disgusted by the scattered acts that are taking place. Less serious by far than the attacks on women, but annoying, is the petty thievery on the part of the Japanese soldiers.

They walk into the few Chinese shops that have dared to reopen (encouraged by the provisional government), order twenty dollars' worth of merchandise, toss twenty cents on the counter and walk out. The sentries steal all cigarettes and small bundles from passing Chinese. Our office staff is searched in a humiliating manner on their way to and from the office, and every possible insult directed at them.

A headline on the front page of the New York Times, *Jan. 11, 1938.*

TSINGTAO OCCUPIED BY JAPANESE NAVY WITHOUT FIGHTING

Sailors Landed From Twelve Warships Suddenly Seize City Blotted by Ruins

TOKYO TO STATE POLICY

'Strong Measures' Likely to Be Announced Today as Future Course on China

Japanese forces landed at Tsingtao yesterday, capturing the city without meeting resistance. They found property of their nationals widely devastated. Other foreigners were permitted to return to their homes. Forces pressed on to capture the Tsingtao-Tsinan Railroad, and others continued the drive on Suchow.

Two marines entered D.F. Lee's home the other day, sat down in his living room and demanded cigarettes and drinks. Fortunately, his wife had time to hide in a closet. They acted pleasantly enough, he says, and greatly admired some potted flowers in the corner of the room, but when told there was no wine in the house, they said they would be back at the same time the next day and that wine must be forthcoming. And of course it *had* to be. If he failed, they would have ransacked the house in their anger and found his wife. They know absolutely no law except their own wishes, and the Chinese have no power or redress whatsoever.

It is pitiful for a fine decent man like D.F. to have to put up with such treatment from ordinary coolie soldiers. Through a friend who had some influence with the Japanese, he was able to stop the calls on his home, but few people have been that lucky. In the villages and towns of the interior, the conditions are beyond description.

Among the foreigners here in town, the Japanese are obviously partial to

Press photo of Japanese marines landing on Tsingtao Beach, on Jan. 10, 1938.

the Germans[1] and just as plainly have little regard for the British. The British Chamber of Commerce made fools of themselves when they called en masse to pay their respects to the Japanese admiral. They were kept waiting half an hour outside in the cold on the administration building steps, only to be told in the end that the admiral was too busy.

I have been losing my respect a little for the Britons in general although Jim Pullen, the A.P.C. No. 2 here, who has been living in the room next to mine at the Pension Victoria, is one of the best chaps I've known. His wife sailed for England in November. We get along fine and talk and talk. In fact, I get along with most people all right; there are very few people I can't talk to. Mr. Keefe is one of them, and I don't know whether it's my fault or his.

I have just been advised that the New York office has approved a raise of U.S. $75 to my salary, bringing my new rate to U.S. $200 per month. With my living allowance figured in, I am now making $800 Mex. or about U.S. $230. I am tickled about it, especially as I have been a little worried during these troubled times that raises might be overlooked. It is nice to know that it has

1. According to a report in the *New York Times*, a group of German residents carrying the Nazi flag met the first Japanese contingent and escorted them to City Hall. When the Japanese took Tsingtao from Germany twenty-three years earlier, in 1914, they suffered severe losses, unlike the 1938 takeover.

Japanese marines enter City Hall; photo taken by the author.

been made retroactive to November 1.

Now with my home leave set at the proper home-side schedule and my salary advance in one year to 200 gold, I am easily on the same basis as anyone being sent from home. I have been so fortunate. Home leave is four months, China-to-China, first-class transportation costs paid. This includes family, but the company disapproves of men marrying during the first term. Mrs. Keefe is still living but is worse than ever. Her children are in Shanghai and also Mrs. Taylor. After I received the letter from the company, I went right to Peterhänsel's, a German tailor, and selected material for two suits at $136 each. It's fine English stuff and should wear for years. The Chinese tailors are much cheaper but they have gone "Ningpo more far" (i.e., into the country).

This afternoon, Doc Taylor and I went out to the *Marblehead* on the invitation of Commander Goodhue to look over the articles in the ship's store. We had bought the necessary U.S. currency at a bar patronized by sailors before we went out. I bought home-side underwear, five pairs of Navy black socks at fifteen cents a pair, Beachnut peanut butter, Whitman's peanut brittle and two cartons of Chesterfields at sixty cents per carton. I also bought a lot of other things such as toothpaste and Lux toilet soap. It was a fine opportunity and I'm glad I went. I even had a strawberry ice-cream soda for ten cents.

My parents, who are worried about the war situation here, would like me to go home. I haven't really decided to stay a full term but do not want to go home yet. I have a pleasant job and am having experiences that will be in my memory for a lifetime. Nor has a year and a half of time, and ten thousand miles of distance, made a commuter's job around New York seem any more appealing. But it seems heartless, as my parents are alone.

January 25

It looks as if I am to be transferred! Mr. Keefe told me today that someone by the name of Butt is due here to take over my job about February 1. Of course, it just might mean that they don't think I am ready for a No. 2 job in a big district and that I shall continue here as No. 3, but I doubt that. My guess is that I will either get a station office—which is an independent post (but still under a district office), like Chungking, Peking or Changsha—or that I will be sent to be No. 2 at a place like Saigon.

I am glad to be on the move and would be pleased with Peking or Saigon. Chungking, too, would be interesting. Changsha, I wouldn't care much about, or Nanking. I would hate to go back to Tsinan. Perhaps I will have to go to Shanghai for training, but the "bamboo wireless" (China Coast gossip) has it that I am scheduled either for the interior or outport. This fellow Butt who is relieving me has had one full term and is just returning from home leave. In the ordinary way, that is the only sort of person who gets a job like the one I have now, so I shouldn't complain if the change appears to be a demotion. I think I hope it will be Saigon.

It's been cold for a long time, and everyone is sick of it. Peking would be colder still, but how nice it would be in spring or fall. On the whole I would like to be in the tropics. They say it is beautiful country around Saigon and that you can make wonderful trips back in the jungle, even up to Angkor Wat. I would have to brush up my French, and best of all, my home leave might come sooner since the regular term in the tropics is shorter.

Conditions get better slowly. The railroad to Tsinan probably won't be open to business or passengers all the way for another three months because of the tremendous damage.

February 1

This is the last day of our New Year's holiday that started at noon on Saturday. It was quite different this year, with no parades or celebrations and not a single firecracker. How noisy it was last year!

This is the third three-and-a-half or four-day weekend we have had in just a little over a month—we surely have a lot of holidays in China, and the banks and some British firms take many more than we do.

My relief, Butt, arrived on the *Shenking* on Saturday together with Keefe's three children and several other returning refugees from Shanghai. It is a cold job meeting ships these days. Passengers and baggage have to go by sampans from the ship to the pier in front of the club, and each trip takes about fifteen or twenty minutes. I arrived on the pier just as the first passengers were leaving the *Shenking*, but it was only after more than an hour of bitter cold that Butt and the three kids were all ashore with the luggage. Passengers never seem to get in the same sampan as their bags, and it's such a nuisance.

I hope I don't have to go to some place inside the Chinese lines and have this to do all over again: the waiting and wondering when the Japanese are coming and having daily air raids, etc.

Now there is considerable talk of the possibility of an air attack from the Chinese. The Japanese are keeping on guard. They have relieved us of the curfew at last (after six weeks of it), but they have heavy sentry duty and patrols all over town. There are forty or fifty armed men to be seen from any given spot at any time of day. After dark they stop every car and inspect the occupants. Antiaircraft guns are mounted along the Bund and in other places.

The Chinese are strong at Hsuchowfu, where they not only have a real army but also many Russian-type (and Russian-manned, so they say) bombing planes. They could reach us in about three hours, and it is conceivable that they might try to launch their long-talked-of offensive.

The Shanghai office has just told me that I am to go to Chungking. I knew from my first reaction that I probably wanted to go there all along. Saigon and India can wait until I've had more time in China, and Chungking is a great place to put in more time. I remember reading just two years ago an article in the *Sunday New York Herald Tribune* by the drama critic Richard Watts, who had just visited Chungking. I can remember vividly the disappointment I felt in the realization that I probably would never get there on my trip. Then later, almost a year and a half ago, in Peking, I thought I had a chance to get way up the Yangtze but had to decide against it for reasons of expense.

When I get there, I'll be in charge of an office of my own, complete with clerks, accounting departments, statisticians, credit men, traveling inspectors and all the rest of it. I will be seven or eight hundred miles farther into the interior than any other Texaco foreigner. The nearest one is at Hankow. It will be rather nerve racking at first, especially with the shrewd up-country agents, who will try all their tricks and wiles on the new manager. At least I am told that my mustache adds several years to my age, in Chinese eyes.

I will also have to face the experience of managing a house. The company has a fine residence there for their manager, a real home from the pictures Walt Powell had of it. Walt kept eight servants, counting his chair coolies. Chungking is all hills, and the streets are all flights of steps. One gets around in sedan chairs supported by four coolies, on one's own regular payroll. I'll have to order food, watch expenses and keep the "squeeze" down.

I am taking over from Ed Martin, who came out from eight years with the company in New York and Haiti. He went up to Chungking last March taking with him his wife and mother-in-law. I believe the company wants to get a family out of there now and put in a single man who can be evacuated more easily and under almost any conditions.

My travels from Tsingtao to Chungking should be interesting and exciting. I'll start off late next week on a Butterfield & Swire ship to Shanghai, where I'll probably spend a few days getting instructions in the General Office and making arrangements about money. I hope I have time to see a few friends there. There is practically no chance at all to go up the river from Shanghai farther than Nanking, as the Japanese hold that city. I don't believe there is enough water at this time of year for the boats to get through, so a plane is more likely. My luggage could be quite a problem.

I regret in a way leaving Tsingtao, although it has been difficult here for the past several months. It has been hard getting around, and there's no place to go except the club. We had a seven-o'clock curfew for a month and a half, which became tiring before the end. Prices have gone up, and right now there is no running water except for about an hour in the evening. Coal has been so expensive that hardly a house in town has been warm enough. There has been no taxi service for a long time, and most of the rickshaw coolies fled to the interior long before the Japanese came. The mail situation is awful, the telegraph service useless. Nothing comes in or out by railway, and even now, five weeks after the Japanese arrived, the harbor is not open except for small ships, all of them Japanese. The arrogance of the soldiers is a thorn in everyone's side.

Many people think that the white man's day in the East is as good as ended. I firmly believe so, but think the demise will be a gradual one and extending

Postcard of Tsingtao waterfront in 1930's.

over several years. After all, the situation is an artificial one with scarcely more justification than the reverse situation would be in our part of the world. I doubt if China would have put up with us very long if she had been allowed to grow, so Japan's action is merely hastening the end. Foreigners are being crowded out of the Chinese Customs, long controlled by the British (the other nations have an interest too). There were six British customs men here in Tsingtao including the commissioner, and a week ago the last one of them left Shanghai for good.

I wonder if Tsingtao will ever be in its glory again, with thousands of visitors from the whole China coast. I hardly think the U.S. Asiatic Fleet will continue using this port as summer headquarters even if they stay in the Orient.

15

Destination Chungking, Via Hong Kong

On board SS Tjisilak,
February 23, 1938

I LEFT SHANGHAI this morning at eleven o'clock and am now heading south for Hong Kong with a stop in between at Amoy. This Dutch ship is cozy, with good food and comfortable accommodations. We have six foreigners among the ten first-class passengers, and there are about a hundred Chinese second- and third-class passengers.

I said my farewells after a George Washington Ball at the Tsingtao Cafe on Saturday night. The party didn't break up till five in the morning, so I was tired when we boarded the ship the next day.

I was disappointed at having only one full day in Shanghai. But it was fun being there again, and I saw a lot of people I knew, including my friends the Henkels. The only time I had at the office was about half an hour on Monday afternoon just after I got off the ship from Tsingtao. I had a good hour's chat, though, in the evening with Phil Le Fevre[1] (our general manager in China) and his wife at their home on Route Kaupmann in the French Concession. They are fine people and nice to know.

---

1. Philip F. Le Fevre of New Paltz, N.Y., became managing director of the Texas Company's China subsidiary in 1937. He had been in China since 1921 and with the Texas Company since 1920.

"We absolutely danced our legs off at the Park." Postcard of the Park Hotel in Shanghai, built in 1934 in the latest Art Deco style. It was later a favorite of Mao Tse-tung. The building to the right is the Foreign YMCA, where the author stayed in 1936 while looking for work in Shanghai. The Park's roof-top nightclub was a popular dancing spot in the 1930's.

I stayed at the Park Hotel on Bubbling Well Road, where I had a good room and bath. The appointments, the atmosphere and the service are just like any first-class hotel in New York. A single room such as mine costs eight dollars a day without food. Because I had such a short time there, I decided not to think of the expense of anything. I don't think I ate a meal except breakfast that cost less than four dollars. If a serving of asparagus, which I used not to like, cost $1.20, that was all right by me. I didn't even try to keep track of the money I spent, since I felt that on this trip I was entitled to spread myself before my term in a place like Chungking.

The destruction in and around Shanghai is a sight to behold. From the ship, one can see what weeks of intensive shelling and bombing can do. It was awful.

There was some trouble at Amoy, our stop on the way to Hong Kong; our ship received a message from the Japanese by wireless not to put into Amoy harbor until Saturday morning. As a result, we had to go very slowly not to reach there ahead of time. We won't get to Hong Kong until some time on Sunday, four days after leaving Shanghai. I hear that planes to Chungking are booked pretty solid by Chinese officials, so it is possible that I will have a delay in Hong Kong waiting for a reservation. I won't mind that at all.

March 4, Hong Kong

I have never had a boil in my life, but I came down with one on the first day out on the ship from Shanghai. It was low on my stomach and extremely painful. I had to stay in my berth the last three days of the voyage under the doctor's care.

When we arrived in Hong Kong, I was met at the ship by a chap from the company who took me to the War Memorial Hospital up on the Peak. I stayed there four days, leaving yesterday afternoon feeling pretty good but with a half-inch-in-diameter hole in my stomach that has to be dressed regularly for another week. I can walk fairly well now.

The planes to Chungking are full up; unless I get hold of a cancellation, I won't get out of here until the eighteenth, two more weeks. But I'm not complaining. Hong Kong is the most amazing place I have seen yet: immense mountains, tropical climate, blue water, palm trees—just beautiful.

That was a great blow to me when I was enjoying my trip so much to come down with that awful boil. The weather was perfect and the sea was a bright blue. On our right we could see the coastal mountains on the mainland, and as we lazed toward Amoy in an increasing warmth and balminess, life seemed perfect. Picturesque junks were all about, and every now and then we sighted a coast ship and twice, large Japanese destroyers.

Thursday night, however, I went to bed, not to get up again until Sunday afternoon, when we entered the wonderful harbor of Hong Kong. Mr. Decker, the company man who came to meet me, said the earliest they could get me a seat on a plane was March 11.

The young English nurses and Chinese boys made me comfortable in the hospital, a fine new stone building at the top of the Peak. Each room is large and has a private glassed-in porch to which the bed is wheeled in the daytime. From the windows, the view is sensational—the mountains, the clouds and two thousand feet below, the blue bay is studded with tiny spots of junk sails. Attractive homes, mansions really, with walls and gardens with flowers in bloom cover the many-ridged mountainside. The mountain area above Hong Kong is unmatched for its natural and man-made beauty. I stayed there from Sunday through Thursday, enjoying fine food, excellent service and little pain.

All the hotel rooms in the city have been taken for at least two weeks to come, so when I left the hospital I came to a large pension over on the Kowloon side (ten minutes ferry ride from Hong Kong), which is fairly comfortable. I would rather be in a hotel but this is not too bad.

I'll never forget my first night ride across the harbor to the Hong Kong side. As the ferry left our ship in Kowloon, we passed several hundred yards away from a large P.&O. liner destined to sail for England. Every light on the ship was on and then a seagoing junk with a huge rectangular sail went by. Although you can't see any buildings or land at night, the lights are wonderful: it must be one of the most famous sights in the world.

At night it was warm enough not to wear a coat, but downtown in the daytime it was too warm for comfort. It was a welcome change from the freezing weather in Tsingtao. I feel at home here already and keep running into people I know. Once a person is established in China, he meets friends and acquaintances in any ports he visits. It means that I would be more at home in

"Picturesque junks were all about": A 1952 photograph of Hong Kong Harbor.

Nanking, where I have never been, than I would be in a strange city in the States. It is one of the things that make life so pleasant here.

There is little for me to do in the office though I check in daily. The movies are good here and I enjoy sauntering around town. I drop in at the Hong Kong Hotel at cocktail time, when I can always find people I know. One would hardly realize there is a war going on. Sometimes when the wind is right, the bombing of the Kowloon-Canton Railroad can be heard.

We had a practice "blackout" the other night when I was in the hospital, and the nurses had to work by flashlight. I have been so lucky to be here; I'll probably pay for all my luck when I get to Chungking!

Hong Kong, March 9

I am having a hard time wondering what to take to Chungking and what to leave behind. I can only take in thirty-two pounds free and not much more by paying excess. The aviation company told me that if I come out to the airport next Tuesday with any more than forty pounds, I would have to leave it there.

I had tiffin with our manager here, Mr. Lawrence, and a tobacco chap who had just come down from Chungking. He said that I will want my tuxedo up there, and that was one thing I counted on leaving behind. He said there is no butter in Chungking, few cigarettes and little medicine. The river is too low for ships to reach Chungking from Hankow (there is no railway), and even if water transportation were possible, there is practically nothing left in Hankow in the way of supplies. So the only way to get things to Chungking is by airplane from Hong Kong and what little they can get from Hankow by air.

I think that the social life will be pleasant for there is a small crowd, rather like Tsingtao. Barthay of the Tobacco Company tells me that there are about thirty-five foreigners, mostly men. Two American girls work in our consulate and are now living in the Texaco house with Mr. and Mrs. Martin. I suppose they will have to find other quarters when a bachelor arrives to take over.

I have enjoyed the life in Hong Kong, the efficiency and civilized aspect of all things here as compared with the somewhat haphazard life in Tsingtao. Most of the buildings here have an open porch on each floor, which is the most striking architectural difference from other cities. In South China, there seem to be as many women coolies as men. One sees many Indians with their head-dress of white cheesecloth with flowing streamers. The poorer people wear Japanese-style slippers, which make a clip-clop noise on the sidewalk. The Star Ferry runs a fine service from Kowloon across the harbor to Hong Kong. The clean, comfortable ferries run every ten minutes all day long and every five minutes during the rush hours.

Before I left Hong Kong, there was the usual scurrying around, changing money, getting my trunk into storage and saying good-bye to friends. The next day, I was up before daylight and was off in a taxi to Kai Tak Airport, which is on the outskirts of Kowloon, a good twenty minutes' ride from Star Ferry. At the field, a big tri-motored Junker belonging to Eurasia Airlines was warming up under the care of German pilots for its run to Hankow. My even larger Douglas DC-2 was standing on the runway.

In the office where I had to be weighed and have all my bags weighed again, I met Chuck Sharp,[1] the pilot whom I knew quite well from Tsingtao when he used to do the Shanghai-Peking run before the war. After all the threats, the airline (the China National Aviation Corp.) was generous about my

----

1. Charles (Chuck) L. Sharp was a pioneer airline pilot in China. He flew the first flight over the Hump (from India to Free China over the Himalayas) in November 1941 and the last C.N.A.C. passenger flight out of Hong Kong in 1941.

Tsim-sha-tsui area of Kowloon; Peninsula Hotel is at center. Taken by the author on a China National Aviation Corp. DC-2 from Hong Kong to Chungking, March 1938.

excess baggage although I had to pay three Hong Kong dollars per kilo on each of twenty-five kilos excess.

Then a taxi pulled up and Lily stepped out. It was still twenty minutes before seven, when the plane was to leave, and there was the usual desultory, meaningless conversation that is the curse of delayed farewells. In one corner of the small waiting room, a French couple were having a bad time of it. The girl's tears were making a sorry mess of her rouge. Later, spotting her in the seat across from me on the plane, I could see that at least half of her makeup had been transferred to him. When the plane finally took off, I had one last look at Hong Kong from the air. It was a marvelous sight. As we headed north, I took a last glimpse at the Peak and the harbor studded with junks and steamers. Then we crossed into Chinese territory.

In Tsingtao, since the tenth of January, I had been as much in Japanese territory as if I had been in Japan. It was difficult even for neutrals to pass from one side to the other during the war. During my stop in Shanghai, in the Settlement, I was on international ground surrounded on all sides by Japanese-occupied territory. In Hong Kong, up to the present, one is surrounded by land still held by the Chinese, so it is often bombed by the Japanese. Because we were in a Chinese commercial plane, which is legal prey to the enemy, it was a bit worrying. An hour and a quarter after leaving Hong Kong, we circled over Wuchow and settled down on the small field on the bank of the Si River. The planes refuel at Wuchow even though they use little gasoline in the short run from Hong Kong, to give them an extra margin of safety. There were light brown patches in the field where sand and gravel had been used to fill up bomb holes made the week before, when Japanese planes had paid a visit. No plane had been on the field at the time, but the C.N.A.C. field attendant had been caught without shelter. Though he made a running dive for the tall reeds growing along the river, he had his clothes burned off by a bomb that landed within thirty feet of him.

The more up-to-the-minute news that Chuck had for me was that he had just heard by wireless that a squad of Japanese planes had crossed our path about five minutes behind us, forty miles back. I noticed that Chuck was keeping a pretty close watch on the sky to the southeast. I asked him what our plan of action would be if we saw them coming in our direction.

He replied quickly: "Run like hell for the riverbank!" Chuck's advice turned out to be unnecessary. When our fuel tanks were filled to the brim, we headed for the next stop, Kweilin, which is the last stop before Chungking.

The country below became increasingly wild and rugged. We flew through clouds for safety most of the time but on one long stretch without clouds, we had a view of the strangest country I've ever seen. The steep conical mountains so characteristic of Chinese landscape paintings were right below us, hundreds and hundreds of these weird mountains. They are like stalagmites rising from the floor of the largest cavern in the world. That section of northern Kwangsi up near the Kweichou border is in many ways as inaccessible and remote as Tibet.

At Kweilin[2], the only thing of interest was the group of fake airplanes made of scraps of wood to act as decoys to the Japanese bombers and make the enemy overoptimistic in his count of the number of Chinese planes destroyed. It looks like a child's game but may have value. From Kweilin to Chungking was an uninterrupted flight of about two and a half hours. Because we were flying in bright sunshine over an unbroken bank of clouds, we could not see anything, and it was rather boring. I had thought we would hit the Yangtze

---

2. Now Guilin.

some distance below Chungking and follow it up to our destination. But the city and the river came into sight at the same moment, and almost before I knew it, we were finishing our big circle of the city in the glide down to the field on the island in the river.

The office expected me two days later, so there was no one there to meet me. After filling out a long form for the police at the airfield and having my baggage examined, I finally managed to get up to the city and located the club. I introduced myself to the chaps, had some food, inquired about directions and walked over to our office.

Coming to Chungking in little less than six hours is like cheating nature. One simply doesn't appreciate the distance and inaccessibility one has over-come. A few years ago, the quickest trip from Hong Kong to Chungking would be just under three weeks. I imagine the only proper way would be to take the long steamer ride winding across the country and after going through the gorges and past Wanhsien, arrive at one's destination in Chungking.

C.N.A.C. poster of the mid-1930's.

V

CHUNGKING

重慶

16

Chungking, War-Torn Capital of China

March 31, 1938

I T IS QUITE A PROPOSITION running a twelve-room house and eight servants (counting my four chair coolies) as well as an office of my own. I'm having an interesting time although business is slow by ordinary standards.[1] Conditions at the office are unusual enough to be fairly exciting even to an old-timer. The currency is apparently going to pot. When I received a wire from Hankow to increase prices $3 per unit of ten gallons, it caused havoc among the agents, who had to cope with furious customers.

To add to my troubles, my No. 1 godown keeper is in the missionary hospital with typhus. When I found him at home, looking on the point of death, surrounded by friends burning joss sticks, I bullied him into seeing a foreign

---

1. Jim arrived in Chungking on March 15, two days after Anschluss, the annexation of Austria by Hitler on March 13, 1938.

doctor. Dr. Gentry of the mission made the trip across the river and persuaded him that his only hope was to have treatment at the hospital. He went in three days ago and appears to be all right, which is fortunate for me because I would be responsible for moving him to the hospital against his wishes. His concubine was looking after him (his wife is in his native home of Dairen) and would surely hound me for coffin money and expenses for shipping the body back to Manchuria if he died.

April 13

I feel I should have more time to write letters and handle current matters, but my days are full. My "boy" awakens me with a glass of orange juice at 7:30 A.M., and at 8:45 I'm on my way across the river to my office. I go to the International Club for tiffin then back to the office. About 5 P.M. I cross the river with Stephen Cumming on the Butterfield & Swire launch. My Chinese teacher comes at six, and dinner is at eight. Because I need a full hour to go over my Chinese lesson, there seems to be no time for exercise. Something has to be changed soon. Life in an outpost should be free, easy and social—not this New York rush-hour business.

We have all been rubbing elbows with the famous for the past few days. The new British ambassador and his family arrived by plane on Saturday to present credentials to the president of China and are not leaving until tomorrow, Thursday. The club dance Saturday night was literally overrun with colonels, wing commanders and first, second and third secretaries of His Majesty's Embassy, not to mention Sir Archibald[2] and Lady Clark-Kerr. (The *e* in Kerr rhymes with the *a* in Clark, Hempstead's Dr. Kerr notwithstanding.) To add to it all, along with the Embassy party came Peter Fleming,[3] the writer whose *Brazilian Adventure* I got such a kick out of several years ago along with so many other American readers. It was a best-seller for several months. To add another touch to the glitter of our guests, young Mrs. Fleming[4] is a well-known actress on the London stage. Fleming himself looks hardly older

2. Sir Archibald Clark-Kerr (1882-1951), later Britain's wartime ambassador to Moscow.
3. Peter Fleming, brother of Ian Fleming, author of the James Bond series.
4. Celia Johnson, later star of the 1946 film *Brief Encounter.*

than I and though very English is a good sort. The real sensation, however, for Chungking is Lady Clark-Kerr, who is very young, very beautiful and very wealthy in her own right. She is also very blond, very well dressed and very well educated. Add to these attributes that she is an ambassador's lady and the result would be a sensation anywhere, let alone Chungking. Sir Archibald is a real gentleman, the perfect type, in my mind for an ambassador. He is easy to talk with, friendly and commands respect in a natural and unassuming way.

April 16

The British ambassador's party left Thursday morning early by ship for Hankow. In the afternoon, Commander Harvey Overesch, the U.S. naval attaché, arrived to join up with Colonel William Lovat-Fraser, the British army attaché, and Colonel Sabatier, the French army attaché, for a cross-country trip to Yunnanfu.[5] I had Overesch stay with me Thursday and Friday and enjoyed his company. An all-American football player for the Navy in 1913, several years ago he was graduate manager of athletics at the Naval Academy in Annapolis and was responsible for the series of games with Yale that started with the one in 1935, which I saw with my father. Overesch was there too.

Last night he and I were invited to dinner at the "Bastille," which is the name given to the French naval post. It is an hour's ride from by chair at night, a rather hair-raising trip. Miraculously, those chair coolies keep their footing in the dark, going up and down stone steps and over rocks where there isn't even a path. After dinner, Colonel Sabatier came back home with us, and I put him up too. They were up at 4:30 this morning to meet Lovat-Fraser and get an early start on their five-day auto ride to Yunnanfu. Lady Clark-Kerr and Mrs. Fleming are going by plane from Hankow in a day or two to meet them in Yunnan and go down to Indochina with them and then up to Hong Kong from Haiphong. I envy them their trip and would have given a lot to start out with them this morning.

Yesterday we had a jolly time when I had Mr. Mills, the British consul general, at my home for tiffin with Overesch. Life is certainly interesting. Commander Overesch has been living for some time with our ambassador,

5. Kunming.

Nelson T. Johnson, in Hankow and says that the ambassador is all set to move the embassy up here on a moment's notice. We will be fortunate if the move is made for they are a swell crowd, from Johnson on down. Tentative arrangements have already been made for some of the party to live with me if they move to Chungking.

The past two days have been wonderful for weather. Yesterday morning I took a three-and-a-half-hour hike up into the mountains, which made my legs stiff. It's a delightful country—mountains, paddy fields, pagodas and the most beautiful flowers growing everywhere. I have lovely roses in my garden and poppies, daisies and marigolds. Fruit trees are in flower and nature is at its best. It is time to join the others at the launch to cross over. This being Saturday, the whole community will gather on the British gunboat for a curry tiffin, a regular weekly event. It is hard to realize that tomorrow is Easter Sunday.

April 17

I am lounging around at home and trying to get my large, open second-floor porch ready to live in. The coolie is scrubbing the floor and Tien is busy giving him instructions, which is as close contact with actual work that his dignity as "boy" will allow. The screened-in section of the porch is about 40 feet by 15 overlooking the garden in the front of the house; I'm planning to fix it up as a combination dining room and bedroom. The great heat that will start in a few weeks and last through September will be as bad as if not worse than any I encountered in either Nebraska or in Tsinanfu, so I'm going to make myself as comfortable as possible.

There are three electric ceiling fans in the house, and I will have one installed on the porch. These and a General Electric table fan should be able to stir up quite a breeze. The Electrolux refrigerator will keep me supplied with cold drinks and I have enough servants so that I never have to lift a finger! I am certainly better prepared to combat the heat here than I was in Stein's hotel in Tsinan.

Most of the foreigners will soon be moving up into the bungalows in the second range of the mountains, but I have decided that I would rather put up with the heat on the foreshore than spend approximately four hours traveling to the office and back, which is what the others will have to do. They read and

The Texaco house, or "Red House," on the South Bank, just right of center, with pillars. The Wanhsien, *a Butterfield & Swire steamer that brought hundreds of refugees from Hankow, is visible to the right of warehouse, with white forecastle.*

sleep in their chairs, of course, but even so I think it is too much of a waste of time. They must be carried over hundreds of stone steps and narrow mountain paths to make such a trip, but perhaps they get used to it. It makes life tough for the chair coolies, although that seems of no consideration.

My house, known as the "Red House" because of the red stucco or cement, is well known by everyone in Chungking and is easily one of the most distinctive landmarks of the South Bank. Right on the shore, about 120 feet almost straight up from the water, and rather imposing against the green background of the trees, it is more prominent and distinctive from the city side of the river than any other house. In the high-water season later on in the summer, those 120 feet will be reduced to 30 feet—a change of 90 feet in the water level.

The house has an interesting history, having been built by Archibald Little, the pioneer merchant of the Upper Yangtze whose story is supposed to be the foundation of Alice Tisdale Hobart's book *River Supreme*. It is either the oldest or next to the oldest foreign residence in all Chungking. At one time it was the American consulate, at another, it was the office of a private Chinese bank.

In more recent years it has been used as an officers' club for the United States Navy Yangtze Patrol when they have a gunboat in port. Last summer, it was the residence of Captain Hughes, commander of the ill-fated *Panay,* and his family.

There are twelve to fifteen rooms and servants' quarters, which are semi-detached. I am living on the second floor and haven't been in all the rooms yet as I have no call to visit any of the downstairs ones. There is electricity but no running water, which seemed bad when I first learned of it, but actually I don't mind it now. The bathrooms are supplied with decent commodes, and as for a water supply, my coolies take care of that. All the water used in the house for drinking, cooking and washing is carried up in buckets from the Yangtze. It does not look appetizing when it arrives, but by the time it has been run through the sand cleaner and boiled, it is just the same as any water that comes through a pipe. My bath is generously filled each morning, and the water is perfectly clean. The No. 1 servant and benevolent tyrant of my household is the cook, Yuan, a wonderful old chap with a tremendous amount of natural dignity and a pleasing way about him. He does the cooking and meal planning and supervises the other servants. His wife lives with him in the servants' quarters and helps with work on occasion although she is not on the payroll. They are a nice couple and I'm glad to have them.

The "boy," Tien, waits on table, serves tea, calls me in the morning, supervises the care of my clothing and passes on orders to the coolie. The coolie is the one who really earns his pay. He hauls water, does the heavy cleaning, all the odd jobs and carries messages. The amah does all the washing and ironing, keeps my suits pressed and my clothes mended. She also does any sewing that is required. I give Yuan $25 Mex. per month, Tien $20, the coolie $12, and the amah $10. They supply their own food. I could cut the salary of all of them except Yuan, considering there isn't much work with just one person in the house. But it would save very little money and would make a difference for them, so I'm going to let it run along as it is for the time being.

My servant bill runs to $67 Mex. per month or approximately U.S. $19. On top of this, there are four chair coolies. The No. 1 gets $12 per month and the other three, ten each. That is $42 Mex. or U.S. $11. It would seem rather amazing back home to have eight servants for a total of $30 a month, especially as they supply their own food and never have a day off.

Of course, when they are buying food for me, it is not difficult to squeeze in a little rice and vegetables for themselves and almost certainly a little extra squeeze in addition, but that is considered legal enough and part of the game. My bills are reasonable, and I can rely on Yuan to be moderate in his squeeze. Prices of imported foods like tinned goods are high, but there is such an abundance of good local food that it is not necessary to buy the other. Large, delicious oranges are about seven U.S. cents a dozen, eggs about nine cents; all the spinach I could possibly eat at a meal costs a cent and a half. An excellent filet of beef costs less than a dime. Milk is about seven cents a bottle and Yuan makes our own butter. My food bill runs between twenty and twenty-five U.S. dollars per month. It takes about a ton of coal per month to run the kitchen stove, and that costs about $4.50.

I had to buy china, glassware and kitchen utensils from the Martins when they left and will pass them on, at a small depreciation, to my successor when he comes. I like the furniture supplied by the company, especially the fine beds with their Simmons mattresses. I have a decent establishment and find little to kick about. The location of the house is excellent as far as the view of the river and city goes; it is also handy to the boat landing where I cross every day. The Chungking Club, which is for foreigners only, is just a three minutes' walk up the hill. The garden, pleasant and tropical, is cared for by a gardener in the pay of the owner of the property, who rents the house for $150 Mex. per month. The library at the club is not as large as the one in Tsingtao but there are plenty of books. We get all the magazines, *Time, Saturday Evening Post, Fortune, Illustrated London News, Punch*, but they are about two months late.

Chungking never gets very cold, but in summer it is one of the worst ovens in the world. The city itself is about six or seven hundred feet above sea level. There are fewer hours of sunlight here per year than almost any place in the world. In general, it has the reputation of having the worst weather in China.

May 1

My godown keeper, who has fully recovered from typhus after his stay in hospital, is now back on the job. Smith,[6] an American pilot here, was not so lucky.

---

6. Harry G. Smith, at one time operations manager of China National Aviation Corp. and later personal pilot for Chiang Kai-shek.

Chair coolies for the Asiatic Petroleum Company (Shell).

He caught the disease at the same time and died within eight days in the same hospital. It was an awful shame. He was a peach of a fellow with a wife and three children in the States. I had asked him to share my house with me.

My chair coolies have been after me to buy them uniforms. I broke down last Thursday. Olive green with red borders and a big red "T" for Texas Company on the backs inside a red circle, they should be ready tomorrow. Most of the companies have uniforms, and my coolies were wearing their most ragged clothes to help me make up my mind about buying them. One argument they made that seemed plausible is that a uniform will help them escape the press gangs that periodically round up bunches of coolies for military service.

It is getting really warm again. The river has risen twenty feet since I arrived and is now on its way to high level, which is anything from sixty to a hundred feet. It was at two feet when I came, so the scenery has changed a great deal.

May 4

One feels remote from the rest of the world in Chungking. It is fifteen hundred miles up the Yangtze into the interior of China, and only a little over two hundred miles from Tibet. The city is located on the north bank of the Yangtze at a point where the Kialing River flows in and joins its bigger brother, bringing with it a steady stream of junks and sampans from the center of the province. Part of the city is below the juncture of the rivers, but the principal and larger section is on the high bluff above.

Chungking seems to be a typical oriental city, teeming with life. I don't know what the population figure is but it must be enormous. Formerly, a wall completely surrounded the city; on the riverside it ran along the edge of the bluff, rising almost sheer from the water. This wall is scarcely to be seen now, but the various points where the several stairways reach the top of the cliff are still called "gates" or in Chinese, *men*. At Tai-ping-men, where I land daily, three hundred stone steps have to be climbed to reach the city from the water's edge.

On either side of these stairways, and indeed all along the face of the almost vertical bluff, are ramshackle huts made mostly of thatch and bamboo and odd pieces of wood. They are of the flimsiest possible construction, held together by rope and supported in thin air by tall poles whose bases are wedged in crevices in the rock further down. They look like the cliff dwellings in the picture books. It seems impossible that they can raise small children in these places without losing them over the side. It can only be luck and the curious will of the gods that keep these poor people alive. As the river rises in June or July, the cliff dwellers fold up their houses and crowd together a little higher up. Finally, there is no more room at all as the river nears the top of the cliff. Where they go after that is a mystery.

Tai-ping-men and the sights there on the steps are probably the most vivid recollections that foreigners carry away with them from this strange river city. Seen twice a day, week in and week out, it is a hard place to forget and seems like a symbol of the city as a whole. The slimy, filthy, worn steps; the wretched hovels on either side; the gigantic and disgusting pigs that overrun the area; the mangy *wonks* (dogs); and the endless stream of coolies grunting their way to the top under crushing loads—all this is very little different from any of a thousand byways of the city up on the top. Water for most of the city is carried up by coolies, each with two wooden buckets on a shoulder stick. A step at a time, swaying their load to give them momentum and grunting at each step, they work slowly to the top. Their buckets emptied, they go to the bottom again, wade in the river up to their calves, fill up and start the painful climb again. They do this their whole lives until they can't work any more. Will the time ever come when millions of coolies don't have to work like slaves for a wretched living?

The city on the top has few level stretches and rises to a crest twice as high as the cliff on the riverbank. In the past several years a great amount of effort has been expended in leveling off space for one or two motor roads. But the great majority of streets or alleys are made up in large degree of series of steps and thus can be traversed only on foot or in one of the thousands of two-man

CHUNGKING

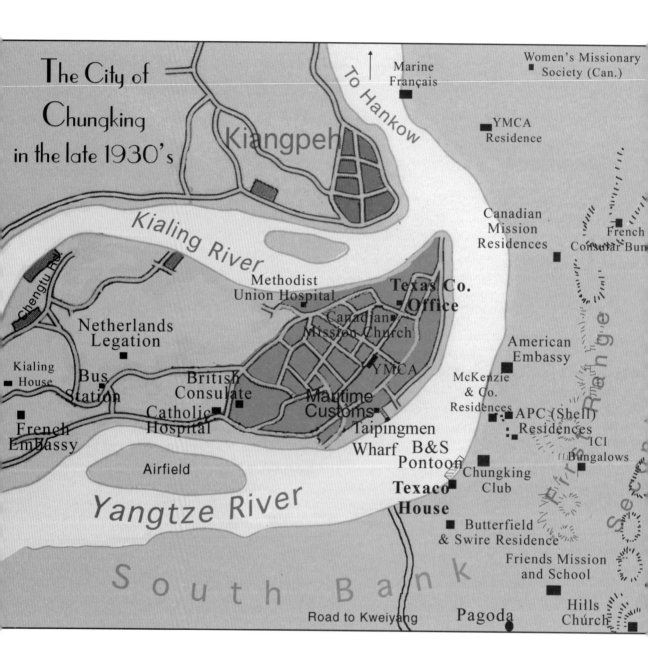

Map of Chungking, showing the city proper, on the peninsula jutting in between the Kialing and Yangtze Rivers, and the mountainous South Bank, where most of the foreigners had their residences.

sedan chairs. Many of the more permanent foreign residents here can remember when it seemed impossible that Chungking would ever have motorcars or even rickshaws. There are hardly any cars and probably fewer rickshaws than chairs. The rickshaws here are the worst I have seen; I think it is probably their last resting place. Discarded by city after city farther down the river, they have at last reached Chungking in such an awful condition that sensible people fear to ride in them except on uphill or level rides.

The street life and the life of the shops have a closer similarity to South China city life than to that of the north, although Chungking is so far west that one expects to find a culture and set of customs entirely different from either type. It is disappointing to find that Chungking street life is according to the regular Chinese pattern, aside from an extra-special daub of filth. Here are the same hordes of street vendors, from the chap whose whole stock in trade consists of handy little tools to clean out one's ears to the fellow who carries about a complete restaurant, stove and all, on his shoulder pole. Here, as elsewhere in the northern cities, the shops and one-room handicraft factories have no front walls at all; what goes on inside is as much a part of the street scene as the passing sedan chairs. Except along the few motorcar roads, sidewalks do not exist at all, and the average street width is probably no greater than ten or twelve feet. It is a mystery how such tiny shops and such narrow streets can accommodate so many people.

Conditions of life in this city, which is practically bulging with humanity, are wretched for the most part. From the pleasant distance of my porch across the river, the whole hill on which Chungking rests looks like one large festering sore. It doesn't always seem that bad, but on some days when I leave my office and ride through the city in my chair to Tai-ping-men and go down the steps, I feel I cannot take a deep breath until I am in the launch and out in the middle of the river.

I am fairly used to China smells by now, but these in Chungking get me down once in a while. And I don't think I'll ever get used to the horrible beggars. One feels pity for them but also disgust because they make themselves as hideous as possible to further their profession. The Chinese have so many good qualities, but compassion for the sufferings of people outside their family group does not seem to exist.

The airfield is on a flat island in the river. When the river rises much over thirty feet, this island is under water, so another airport has to be used about ten miles down the river from the city. In the old days it used to take as long to get to the city from this airport as the flight from Shanghai, because the only way to the city was by boat through the swift river current. A motor road has been built recently that obviates this situation, and sometimes a seaplane can be used as a taxi in from the field, but it depends on the river.

The south shore of the river and up in the hills behind my house is a charming section, except for the ugly blotches where the villages stand. Where nature has been left alone or only tampered with to the extent of making paddy fields in green valleys, or where foreigners have erected homes and gardens, Chungking is still beautiful, but the city is a picture of filth and ugliness.

At night, when viewed from this side of the river and all you can see are electric lights, it makes rather an attractive picture somewhat reminiscent of Hong Kong seen from the Kowloon side. But in the daytime, even from this distance, it is ugly. There is not a spot of color or brightness. The whole place is a mass of nondescript browns and dirty grays, here and there a smudge of sooty white. Always low-lying over all like a dirty blanket is a cloud of gray smoke from thousands of evil-smelling fires. Although Chungking is an ugly city, it does not mean that it is not interesting, and life is often pleasant and enjoyable. I am glad to be here for a term but hope my stay doesn't turn out to be too lengthy.

As I sit and write, a slight breeze is blowing in my porch doors from the river. I can hear the beating of drums and gongs from the city side, which never seems to stop. The din is not unpleasant when you get used to it and fits in well with the chirping of crickets on this side. I am now so used to the gongs that I scarcely hear them, but the sound comes across the river distinctly and is loud at times. Most of it is for funeral wakes. One night after a death in the Chinese house behind mine, I had to listen to the drums all night long. They sounded right in my ear.

June 4

It has been extremely cold the past several days, and now our rainy season has started. I have been using blankets—I almost felt like having a fire in the fireplace. The river has risen to a level of thirty-eight feet, which cuts off a few of the steps on each side, but that doesn't make much difference to me, as I have

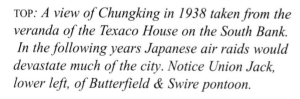

TOP: *A view of Chungking in 1938 taken from the veranda of the Texaco House on the South Bank. In the following years Japanese air raids would devastate much of the city. Notice Union Jack, lower left, of Butterfield & Swire pontoon.*

ABOVE: *Maifeng Bank, site of Texaco office.*

RIGHT: *The Butterfield & Swire steamer* Wanhsien.

CENTER: *Landing at Tai-ping-men steps.*

ABOVE: *Passing a water carrier while riding on a sedan chair on the streets of Chungking.*

CENTER RIGHT: *Haulers on the Yangtze.*

RIGHT: *Landing at Tai-ping-men steps.*

ABOVE: *A village in the hills behind the Texaco House on the South Bank of Chungking.*

BELOW LEFT: *From left, Ed Rowland; Geoffrey Aldington, the British vice consul; and the author enjoying tiffin on HMS* Gannet.

BELOW: *Chair coolies prepare for morning commute to the office.*

RIGHT: *The author at home, posing in colonial garb.*

been using my chair right from my door to the launch and from the launch to the office without walking at all as I used to do.

Chair riding is more nerve-racking in Chungking than anywhere else, particularly going up and down stairs in the rain. You are completely curtained in on all four sides when it is raining, and expect to be tossed over an edge or drop backward a hundred steps or so at any time. In some places, the angle is terrific and your feet are almost level with your head. You wonder what would happen if one of the coolies slipped, but somehow they never do. I have finished with any nervousness about it and spend my time in the chair reading, whether we are going up and down steps or on the level. When you cross the river in a sampan, your chair is placed lengthwise, resting on the thwarts, and you sit like a king on his state barge.

June 15

I have heard that I am going to be transferred, but there is no definite news. There seems to be confusion in Shanghai about my being available for transfer. I am working along on the assumption that I am to stay in Chungking until all my stock is sold. Things are in such a terrible condition that it is hard to keep abreast of happenings without Shanghai's evident misunderstanding about my availability. The market is upset with rumors that the government is about to forbid any sale of gasoline that is not for military use. It is more and more evident that what little gasoline is in Szechuan now is all that anyone will see until the war is over. As the exchange has been dropping we have had corresponding price increases every few days. This morning I had a wire from Hankow telling me to stop all sales until further notice. Then, later in the morning, I had news that I could sell small quantities at an increase of $5.75 per unit of ten gallons. That would be an increase of 57 cents a gallon in one day. When I arrived here, three months ago, the price was $15.30 per unit, which seems high after the Tsingtao price of $10 or so per unit. The price is now $28.75.

Every sale we make is a twisted confusion in itself. There are so many angles to Chinese dealings and corruptness that sometimes I get sick of the whole mess and wish I could expose it all. Money that is so badly needed to win the war oozes out every time a purchase is made for the government. Everyone along the line has to be paid their squeeze. The smallest parts come out of our agents' commissions from us, but the largest share comes out of China's public funds. People say that China has gone away from the old idea of squeeze and that it is only the old-type officials who continue to bleed the country according to time-honored custom, but I see that it is not true every office day in the year. It is such a relief to take a hike up in the mountains and into the country on a Sunday and see the farmers and their families working in the paddy fields totally unconscious of gasoline, bullets and squeeze, and even, for the most part, entirely unaware of the war. There, everything is green, healthy and growing. There is peace, pleasantness and probably honesty.

We haven't had uncomfortably hot weather since the end of May. There has been a lot of rain and the mosquitoes are out in droves. My screens seem to do no good because it has been impossible to sit in the living room in the evenings. I stand it for a little while but then go to bed under my netting. I have found some mosquito incense that comes in a coil like a snake and burns slowly. Happily, it seems to help. The first time I saw anything like it was in the Oriental Hotel in Kobe. That seems back in another century.

The bombing of Canton continues. It doesn't seem likely that there will be any city left by the time I get there. I learned today that there is no seat on the plane to Hong Kong until the seventh of next month so it looks as if I'll be here till then at least.

A letter from "Doc" Taylor in Tsingtao arrived this morning informing me that Mrs. Keefe died on May 9. It is certainly just as well as she was in great pain, but it is tragic that such a thing should have happened to a lovely woman with three young children. Poor Frank, I must write to him, but I dread the job.

On the lighter side I have just heard from Ed Martin in Tientsin that Harrison, our district manager there, has left his wife and run away to England with a Russian woman. What a thing for a successful middle-aged man to do!

This is a real tropical rainy season we are having, and it is just as depressing and unpleasant as it sounds in the books. We have had only one clear day since the end of May, and ordinarily it rains most of the twenty-four hours. The motor launch I usually cross the river in is under repair, so Cumming (B.&S.) and I share a sampan each morning. It makes a queer picture in the pouring rain: our two chairs side by side in the sampan with our curtains shutting us off entirely from all vision, our eight chair coolies huddled together under their huge rain hats and the rowers working for all their worth to reach the other side without being swept too far downstream by the terrific current.

The water is so yellow and muddy that even the drops splashed up by the paddles are a heavy dirty brown. When we reach the other side, one of our coolies takes away our front curtain, and we dash out onto the muddy shore standing there in the rain till our chairs are off the sampan. Then into them in the semi-darkness and off we go up the three hundred steep, slippery steps.

I just received a letter from D.F. Lee in Tsingtao. He has become a father again and now has five sons! Business conditions there remain hopeless because only Japanese are allowed to use the wharves and the railroad to Tsinan is used only by the Japanese for war supplies. Tommy Shields from our Shanghai office has gone to Nanking with one Chinese to see what the chances are of opening up there again. I haven't learned whether or not anyone has been sent to Canton and have no news at all about what I am going to do when my stocks are gone. The new British gunboat is in port; I had dinner on board last night. Today they are inviting the foreign community for curry tiffin.

It has been about two years since I left New York. Everything now is very confusing—I would not be surprised if the company decides to release me. I am still the youngest and newest in the organization, and staff reduction looks like an economic necessity. Chinese staff that are being released get three months' salary in advance. I hope I do too, if I am released. They might even pay for my passage home.

June 21, 1938

Since May 29, over three weeks ago, we have seen the sun just once. When I cross the river twice a day, there is a mist or teeming rain. Most days, from the river and foreshore, it is impossible to see the first range of mountains, where the people have their bungalows. A mixture of fog and dirty smoke and smells lies over the whole city like a blanket. I am now inoculated and vaccinated against typhoid A and B, paratyphoid, cholera and smallpox.

It is hard to realize that practically a million Chinese have been drowned in the floods of the Yellow River.[7] The Japanese too have suffered heavy loss-

7. In June 1938, the Yellow River was temporarily diverted south of Shantung by the Nationalist Government, which blew up the river's dikes in Honan in an attempt to stem the advance of the Japanese. This flooded an enormous area at the cost of about one million lives.

es. Both sides blame each other for purposely opening the dikes, but no one knows the truth of the matter.

Wonder of wonders, the sun is out, and I am able to write outside in my porch again. Tien is busy brushing all my clothes and hanging them out in the sun. It was just in time as they were beginning to show a trace of mold. When I look at all my clothes there, I wonder how I could have brought so many up to Chungking. There is my double-breasted suit from Macy's, my tuxedo, my old Harris Tweed jacket, etc., and I am wearing a pair of Florsheim shoes, which still look new, and my old brown Walkovers.

When I write to my parents in Long Island, I start off telling them about the things that I really like here, such as a trip down the mountain by chair after a tennis tea at someone's bungalow. The stone steps through the pines and the lonely stone tombs overrun with grass, and wild flowers are beautiful in the dusk. Every once in a while, there is a coolie sitting on his heels on the steps putting a pinch of tobacco in the tiny bowl of his long bamboo pipe. There are paddy fields on the open space on the side of the mountain with a hundred different levels and shapes. The water is very skillfully trapped in every little field on its zigzag course down the mountain. As you enter a little dirty village, there are palms and patches of bamboo and a small roadside shrine with sticks of burning incense. In the growing darkness, it is a more pleasing scene than in the light of day. You can overlook the mangy dogs and the runny noses of children, but the gutters that are used for toilets for everyone up to the age of about twelve are unpleasant. I always end up by writing about the disease, neglect and filth, which you can't get away from in China.

July 5

Yesterday, it was foggy as usual in the morning, and then when I was halfway up to Jones's house in the hills, the rain started teeming down; it has been raining ever since without a letup. Besides Jones and myself, there were three British American Tobacco men, two of them visitors from Hankow, so we sat around and heard the latest news about Hankow. After dinner we played Monopoly, which I haven't done since leaving home. When it was time to leave at 10:30 the weather was so awful Jones insisted that we stay up there and come down in the morning. He finally persuaded the other three, but I wanted to get back to my own bed. The trip down the mountain is seldom done after dark, and I was foolish to try it. The steps are steep in places, and sometimes there is a terrific drop beside the narrow path. In the rain and the dark, it was a horrible experience.

*Traveling by sedan chair on the
South Bank.*

17

Long, Hot Summer
on the South Bank
of Chungking

July 9, 1938

IT IS TWO HOURS after sundown, and I can see the lights across the river while I am writing on my porch. It is hot, so I have the ceiling fan on over my head. Just below my porch at the riverbank, a B.&S. steamer is unloading a cargo from Ichang. The yo-hoing of the coolies mixes with the chirping of thousands of crickets. Sometimes I can hear the beating of gongs across the river and occasionally, the terrified squeal of a pig as it is carried upside down with its feet tied together on a bamboo pole. Outside the porch screen a lizard is chasing a moth. The incense coil is burning away to discourage the mosquitoes, which can make life unpleasant. Tien is preparing my bed for the night with the netting. It is one of those nights when, in spite of a few discomforts, one feels that life is good.

I played six sets of tennis in the broiling heat this afternoon up at the B.&S. house with Cummings and the British gunboat officers, returning shortly after seven for a cold tub and a whiskey soda before dinner. For dinner I had cold chicken, potato salad, fresh tomatoes, sweet corn on the cob and approximately three buckets of iced tea. I feel better than I have in a long time and could almost, but not quite, decide that Chungking is a decent place to live. I don't know why but I have not been well lately. I hope the tide has turned and I can enjoy everything more.

Three days ago the B.&S. steamer *Wanhsien* arrived in port from Ichang with many hundreds of war refugees from Hankow and points east. That steamer is not supposed to carry passengers, but because of the war, it decided to take up to one hundred and fifty each trip. Every time a steamer sails from Ichang there is a great riot as men and women fight to get up the gangway. With the only alternative throwing them off the ship by force, B.&S. has been compelled to carry four or five times the number it decided on. The conditions on board are terrible. With no cabins for them, the refugees must stand on the deck, so crowded together that only a few can lie down to sleep at night. The British skipper told me that he was disgusted by a number of men who took the space to stretch out while the women in their families were forced to stand up all day and night, many of them nursing babies.

Just below the city, about two miles down the river, there is a large Buddha in a niche in the bank who is the god of this section of the upper Yangtze. Every junk coming up, without exception, stops there while the crew take time out to burn incense and pray for a safe journey. Even on the foreign steamers the native crew invariably light firecrackers when they are opposite the Buddha.

The animosity of the river population against the steamers has often lead to drastic action. Undoubtedly a number of junks have been sunk from the wash of the steamers operated by the two British shipping companies (B&S and Jardine Matheson), but it appears that if a junk is lost in the ordinary vicissitudes of the dangerous passage through the Gorges, and a foreign steamer merely happens to be in sight, a fantastic claim for damages and loss of life will be lodged against the steamship company. The theory seems to be that these foreign steam devils have no right to be on the river anyway, and that their presence is greatly offensive to the river gods who mete out fate to the junk men.

It is only rarely that a steamer can make the trip from Ichang to Chungking without being fired upon from the shore or from boatloads of freelance soldiers who think they are in danger of being swamped. Shortly after my arrival, there had been so much trouble of this kind with the officers and crew of the steamships having had such near escapes from bullets pinging against the bulk heads, that something had to be done.

Large white signs with two-foot high characters were hung across the bridge of the vessels. These characters could be read at a considerable distance and said in effect: "Don't shoot! We are going slowly and carefully. Watch us. See that this is true." In spite of this, the game of taking potshots at the ships continued. When the British Ambassador sailed down to Hankow after presenting his credentials in Chungking, the Chinese authorities spent the days prior to his sailing in frantic efforts to cajole the people along the river to allow this one ship to make the trip without being shot at. No shots were fired at the ambassador's ship, to my knowledge, but after this concession to diplomacy, the game was resumed with gusto.

Now that my stocks have all gone, I have been searching the market for a decent price for my empty wooden cases and iron fuel-oil drums. I sold out the entire batch of 17,000 cases today at a price slightly better than that authorized by Shanghai. As for the drums, I have been trying for weeks to get a decent bid on the 540 pieces I had and couldn't get a better price than $7 a piece. This morning, just after selling the 17,000 cases, a customer came in who wanted the drums. I quoted $8, and he countered with $7. Finally, I offered him the drums at $7.75 and he went into the other room to think it over. When he was there, a chap came in from Ming Seng, the big shipping people, and said his firm needed the drums badly. We had approached him last week but he wasn't interested. I quoted him $11 per drum, last price, take it or leave it, and much to my surprise he took it. I was sorry I didn't say $12. I have had my salesmen out scouting the market for weeks, and the best bid they could raise was seven dollars. Then suddenly this man dropped in and wants to take them all. The buyer was a graduate of the University of Chicago by name of Kelly Wen, printed on his card.

Yesterday, while riding in my chair from the office to the International Club, on the city side, I was watching a man walk along the sidewalk with a tame monkey on a string. A street hawker with a basket of Chinese plums came along in the opposite direction. As the two came abreast, the monkey, with a quick movement, snatched one of the plums and started eating it. There was a terrific rumpus while the hawker tried to get the owner of the monkey to pay for the plum; a crowd gathered around to see what would happen. My chair passed out of sight, however, so I didn't see the end of the business.

A number of shops in town specialize in supplying gold teeth. They are not dentists, more like beauticians. I am always amused by their advertisements in front of the shops. It is surprising to see Mary Pickford wearing a big smile with a large gold tooth in the center.

Often after a death in a Chinese family, the coffin is not buried for a while until some favorable date comes along. Consequently the funeral "party" may last quite a long time. Some time ago, on a small side street of very poor shops, I saw a large black and gilt coffin that had been laid in state in a shop so tiny there was no room for anything else. The funeral party, consisting of six adults and three youngsters, was seated around a table extending out into the right of way. The store would not hold the table and the coffin too, so there they sat, all dressed in white, playing cards and having a glorious time—practically in the middle of the road!

I tried to fire one of my chair coolies at the end of last month. When I came out of the office the other day I found him sleeping in the chair. It wasn't because he was asleep—they always sleep when they aren't carrying me—but the day or so earlier I caught a mess of fleas from my chair. I had warned them there would be trouble if I caught one of them sitting in it. When I made the No. 1 chair coolie come up to the office where I had a translator tell him that the other chap was through, he didn't say much. But when I arrived home, he and the others gave me fifty reasons why I shouldn't fire the fellow and said how sorry the man was and that it wouldn't happen again. Finally, to save face all around, I decided the chair coolie should be suspended for the whole month of July and that the No. 1 was to get a substitute. This was satisfactory to everybody except the chair coolie. It is remarkable how a staff of servants sticks together when one of them is in danger of losing his job.

July 24

I often wonder what I would be doing if I had not sailed away on the SS *California* two years ago. I wanted to go around the world and see the Orient. Now I am the manager of a Szechuan office. One never knows what the future will be once a decision is taken. I have had to serve notice on six members of my office staff. They will be released with three months' extra pay at the end of this month. D.D. Yang will continue to receive his present pay, but the others will have a 25 percent salary cut. I have been fighting to keep C.H. Lo, who studied in the States for five years and is a well-trained businessman. He has a good record with the company and has been with us for eight years. If the company is firing people like this, it means they are extremely pessimistic about the future and no one's job is safe.

It is unfair, in my opinion, to try to do so much economizing at the expense of Chinese staff. We operate of course on a U.S. dollar budget, and with the present drop in the Chinese dollar, the company is already saving money on the Chinese payroll. This is hard on a man like C.H., who feels quite correctly that he is just as valuable and necessary as many a foreigner who has all along been making two or three times as much money. The white men get all the breaks compared with the Chinese.

The day before yesterday Japanese planes came up the river beyond Ichang almost to Wanhsien, where we have a godown. Hankow is getting panicky. According to reliable reports, the ministry of foreign affairs as well as the remaining Chinese officials will leave for Chungking by the end of this month.

The English news service states that the American and other embassies will also come here directly. Tokyo is claiming that all foreigners in Hankow will leave within one week, but that is definitely not true. What is true is that the Chinese air force is no longer able to keep the Japanese away and that a big land push up from Kiukiang is now imminent. The moment that Hankow falls or the moment that the railroad between Hankow and Hong Kong is cut, Chungking is entirely isolated from the rest of the world. That is with the exception of C.N.A.C. planes and the primitive overland routes to Yunnan and thence out either by way of Indochina or Burma.

In a city bursting with refugees, rents have gone up enormously. It is not at all uncommon to pay $900 per month for an ordinary house. Food prices are on their way up, but so far not in any alarming speed. It is hot. I play tennis. I try to find things to do at the office besides keeping cool. I dine with the British navy people and play quite a bit of harmless poker. I cannot say I like Chungking, but it is only temporary. I can stand another six months.

July 27

There was a big tennis tea today starting at noon with tiffin on the gunboat and then a match at the B.&S. house. We have been having a series of tournaments with a Chinese team collected by General Fan, a wealthy retired warrior who goes in for sports and spends a lot of money bringing good players to Chungking for the matches. We took a bad beating today in all the matches, but it was fun to see some of the chaps play and to play against them. One of the men on the opposing team today was a nephew of the Generalissimo and a member of the aviation school here. Two of the others were semi-pros from Shanghai. Next Wednesday we go to the general's house for tiffin and a return match. Guests at Fan's house can gauge

Tennis at the home of General Fan: From left, a friend of the general, General Fan, Mrs. Tibbitts, and Lieut. Nigel Tibbitts of the British gunboat HMS Gannet.

their welcome and the respect he holds them in by the number of concubines he allows them to meet. I have heard they are real beauties.

This last week the river rose to a level of eighty feet, but in three days time has fallen back to forty. One never tires of watching the change in shoreline and wondering how high it will get before it starts falling. The record in recent years is something over a hundred feet.

Our community has been hard hit by misfortune in the last several months. First, it was Smith, the C.N.A.C. pilot who died of typhus; then young Delbrook got infantile paralysis. Now Mrs. Boehnert's son, who was working as an engineer somewhere between Kiukiang and Hankow, has been brought here out of his mind from shell shock after a bombing raid. Mrs. Boehnert flew to Hankow to get him and found him in a wretched Chinese police hospital. And Dr. Campbell, the American missionary doctor who relieved "Doc" Gentry, is sick with amoebic dysentery.

The heat is insufferable, and the mosquitoes and little midges won't leave me alone. Perspiration trickles down my face then falls from my chin. I must try to sleep and catch up on last night, when it was too hot to rest let alone sleep. Sometimes I wish I were home where things are clean and you don't see dead bodies on the streets almost every day on your way to the office and where the people don't use the streets as a bathroom. The beggars are a true horror and must be seen to be believed. On a five-minute chair ride through the streets of Chungking, one sees unimaginable sights. I saw a small boy lying on the street too weak to brush away the flies that were gathering on his practically naked body. He was lying alone and untended on the stone steps at Tai-ping-men not ten feet from housewives gossiping on their doorsteps and not even bothering to look at him.

The child was there for two days and two nights without moving. He evidently died some time last night and was carried away or tossed into the river. People were afraid they would have to bury him if they lifted a finger to his aid, so they left him like that at their doorsteps. They could at least have moved him into the shade and sponged him off. And yet it is not their fault. There are so many people dying all over in the most horrible conditions, and the ones who feel they cannot aid are but one jump ahead of them. If the fortunate forget their own self-interest for even an instant, they themselves will be lost.

I do not know how a missionary can keep his faith when he comes to Szechuan. Most of the missionaries, with the exception of doctors, are away for the worst months of the heat and misery in their cool bungalows in the mountains. I would certainly raise the salaries of the medical missionaries and the teachers who preach hygiene; the others I would send back home.

August 1

The river, which has fallen fifty feet in the past ten days, can be expected to stage another rise any day now. It is so amazing. The heat is deadening and is making me feel sick. If I thought I would have to spend two more summers in a Yangtze River port, I believe I would quit right away. A British chap employed by the Marconi outfit recently arrived to do some work on the new shortwave transmitting station. He has worked in India, Egypt and Portuguese East Africa, and thinks they were not nearly as bad as Chungking. He said he had never seen so many people with diseases walking the streets.

August 7

Another hot Sunday that takes every speck of vitality out of a person and makes me wish I were back in Tsingtao, where it was reasonably comfortable

The Qutang Gorge, the first of the Three Gorges encountered by the eastbound traveler on the Yangtze. The author always wanted to visit the gorges but never did.

The view of Hong Kong Harbor from the top of Victoria Peak, much changed since the time the author saw it in 1938.

The canal between Shameen (the English and French Concession), right, and the city of Canton, left.

and where I could go to the beach and swim. There is nothing here except tennis and it is too hot most of the time for that. My weight is lower than at any time since I left New Haven because the heat has taken away my appetite.

With all the government offices moving up here from Hankow, George Fitch, our man there, will probably be coming soon. One of us will stay and the other will go either to Kweichu or Yunnanfu. Plans are now definitely under way to ship gasoline overland by truck to Chungking. Fitch and I will probably have to spread out to handle it. I hope that I am the one to leave and go to Yunnanfu, which is over 6,000 feet high and has a fine climate. I think I would refuse Kweichu (Kweiyang). The weather there is only slightly better than here and there are no foreigners at all. Therefore there is nothing in the way of comfort: no foreign-built houses, no proper beds, etc.

I have a strong urge to go to Peking and concentrate on my health and writing. It is not that I am sick, but I just don't feel fit, and Chungking wears on one physically and mentally in an oppressive fashion. Three or four of our company men have left and gone home; I am beginning to understand why.

We can look forward to a short spell of decent weather at the end of September and in October, but then we must expect to go from November until March or April with no more than eight or ten glimpses of the sun. There is never any snow but just week after week of dreary, damp chill and fog.

It has been almost half a year since I left Tsingtao and just about one full year since I was evacuated from Tsinanfu on John Allison's orders. It has seemed a long year because so much has happened not only to China but also to me. Yet in some ways time has flown, and I feel much older for the first time in my life.

August 21

On the tenth the *Luzon* and *Tutuila*[1] came into port, and two of the embassy chaps moved in with me the following day. The *Luzon* came in first, early in the morning, as I was eating breakfast, and anchored just below my porch. For

---

1. On Aug. 3, 1938, the USS *Luzon,* flagship of the Yangtze River Patrol, followed by the USS *Tutuila,* left Hankow to take the American ambassador, Nelson T. Johnson, and his staff upriver to Chungking. Hankow, at the time the provisional capital after the fall of Nanking, would fall to the Japanese two months later.

these parts it is a snappy-looking craft. I had a real thrill as they blew their bugle call and raised the American flag at their stern, while I joined them at the same instant in hauling up my ragged Stars and Stripes. It was good to see so many Americans in port later in the same day. Counting the officers on the two gunboats and the embassy, we put twenty-four new names on the Chungking Club book that afternoon, which must be a record for Chungking.

The next several days were hectic with many parties. I also had to make my extra rooms livable. There was another party at General Fan's, to which we took five of the navy officers and two of them took a licking from the Chinese. There were tiffins on board the *Luzon* and on the *Gannet*. We saw movies on the *Gannet* and went to a tea party at the Joneses' up in the hills. Ambassador Johnson and Admiral LeBreton[2] were much taken with a couple of my Tibetan scrolls; the admiral commissioned us to find similar ones and send them down-river to him. After the *Luzon* sailed Sunday morning things became a little more normal, but even so our permanent guests, the embassy staff and the *Tutuila* people are so numerous that the port seems quite different.

During this time a wretched mosquito must have bitten me because I came down with chills and a high fever accompanied by awful aches and pains in all my bones and joints. The next day, I felt worse and could not get up on time. I finally made myself get across the river about ten o'clock and went straight to the hospital. Dr. Campbell diagnosed me as a malaria case and put me to bed there. My temperature was over 102 degrees and I felt rotten. After taking my blood count three times, the medical staff could not find the actual parasite in the blood. The white corpuscle count was very low, which, with the fever and the aching bones, seemed to indicate malaria. Finally they decided that I had dengue fever, a tropical disease from mosquito bites. There is no specific cure for it as quinine is for malaria. I left the hospital still feeling awful. I am sorely tempted to ask the company to find a relief for me. I am getting fed up with this town, the living conditions and never feeling well.

September 5

Last Thursday the river started rising from a forty-foot level and at midnight

---

2. Rear Admiral David McD. LeBreton, commander of the Yangtze River Patrol.

HMS Gannet, *river gunboat, and the British Navy canteen on the Yangtze.*

on Saturday had reached ninety feet! That meant that the stone paths leading along the shore on this side were under water and to get to Butterfield & Swire's Taikoo house or to the gunboats, one had to hire a sampan or to climb up the hillside and walk over the back paths. On Sunday the water started to fall and is now back to fifty feet. At the high level, the ships tied up at the B&S pontoon below my house were practically level with my first floor, and the noise of loading and unloading was terrific.

I keep thinking how much I would enjoy getting into a nice new car at home and going and going on fine roads through healthy green country; in fact, anything to get away from the daily view of misery, sickness and dirt that eats into your mind in Chungking. I find it hard to write as I do not have any of the enthusiasm that I had in Peking. This setting is China at its worst.

September 19

I'm feeling much better than the other day when I thought I would be glad to leave. Although I seem to go out a lot, life here can be lonely. It is partly because I am the only foreigner in the office. And now that the office has been closing at noon, the weekdays seem long. There is no more tennis because of the rain, and many people have moved up to the hills. When I come back to this large house and eat my meals alone, I lose my appetite as soon as I sit down. And then there are the mosquitoes.[3]

Mark Hodjash's wedding was a great success. The bachelor party we gave for him at the club the night before was a properly wild affair and the envy of all the married men, who were not admitted. I had been asked the day before to attend the ceremony at the British consulate as a witness. As the weather was comparatively cool, I put on my new dark striped suit. We all enjoyed laughing at the different outfits. Mark and his bride were in ordinary summer clothes, as were Mr. and Mrs. Hughes and Ding (British American Tobacco No. 2, Mark's assistant). The B.A.T. distributor, the only Chinese there, wore a dark silk gown; Aldington, the British vice-consul, and I were in dark suits. That completed the party except for Captain Orpen of the *Gannet*, who arrived in his chair at the consulate resplendent in morning coat, striped trousers and a gray top hat. He cut a remarkable figure as he came along through the narrow dirty alley in his four-coolie chair in that outfit. After the ceremony, which was simple, we went over to the Aldington house for champagne. The party broke up about eleven o'clock, then I went back to the office to sign my mail.

Mark had invited the whole community to dinner at the club over on this side, and it turned out to be a wonderful evening to start off the club season. About sixty people were present, the largest group of foreigners I have seen in over six months. The dinner was on the night when the news from Europe was at its worst.[4] Although there was a certain amount of veiled tension among the national groups, it wasn't as bad as might have been expected with Germans, French, Belgians and British under one roof on a night when everyone was thinking that war would be declared at any minute. In these times of scarcity it is a marvel how Mark managed such a grand party. People didn't stop dancing till about three in the morning. And then a group of diehards played poker until 5:30.

---

3. At one point in the fall of 1938 Jim had an extensive visit from Lily Lee, whom he must have informed about his illness. She would remain in Chungking until Nov. 13, when she was arrested on suspicion of being a spy for the Japanese.

4. Several days later, on Sept. 29, Britain, France and Italy allowed Hitler to occupy the Sudetenland of Czechoslovakia (Munich Pact).

The following night, I gave a dinner party for the three officers of the *Gannet* and Cumming and Hill (Marconi man), after which we went down to movies on the *Tutuila* and saw *Way Down East*. The next day, Saturday, the officers of the *Tutuila* gave a dandy tiffin party at their canteen and had all the business community and a few of the diplomatic people. In the evening, there was more poker at the club. Sunday, Jones of S.V.C. had the American Embassy staff and myself at his house for tiffin, and the day ended with an informal little party at Hodjash's. The port is waking up after the summer daze; it's hard to keep up with all that's happening.

I'm beginning to like our ambassador a lot as I get to know him better. A career man and not simply a political appointee, Johnson has been in China since 1907 except for a few years in Washington as assistant secretary of state. Raised on a farm in Oklahoma, he keeps the common touch and is easy to get along with.

October 1

My boy, Tien, is getting married today, and I am going to attend the ceremony. As is the usual thing, he will spend his whole savings and all he can borrow on putting on a big show. He is having the wedding and the tiffin party in the most expensive restaurant in town and will undoubtedly hire a band for the occasion. I am going to see the ceremony at noon and then stay for tiffin. I gave him a month's salary for a present and loaned him forty more dollars, which I will take out of future payrolls. His bride came up from Ichang several months ago in preparation for the wedding; when the embassy fellows came to stay at the house and we needed another amah, I gave her the job and let her stay at the house. I suspect there has been a little laxness in the young couple's behavior, but it won't spoil the pleasure of the wedding.

October 5

We had our first real air raid yesterday morning during a particularly bad fog. When I crossed the river at eight in my sampan, it was like thick soup and gave me the weirdest feeling imaginable. There was no visibility whatsoever, just a small circle of the river on which we floated without sensible progress in a world of white. It was hot and sultry, however, so the sun must have been out above us. That was most likely the case, for the Japanese could never have reached us otherwise.

The first alarm went off about eleven o'clock, followed within ten minutes by the ringing of bells indicating an urgent warning. It was still so foggy that I could hardly see the ground clearly from my fourth-story windows. The second alarm was still sounding when off in the distance we could hear the steady "booms" as about thirty or forty bombs were dropped on the airfield. Shortly afterward, we heard more explosions from a different direction, this time on the city side of the river. I didn't see any planes, however, even though they came right over and dropped pamphlets on the city after they had used up their bombs. Several people were killed at the airport and on the edge of town but no great amount of damage was done. The Chinese did not send up any of their planes in defense. It would probably have been futile in that fog.

A few antiaircraft batteries fired away without scoring a hit. The foreigner down at A.P.C.'s installations was out of the fog area and had a good look at the planes and their progress around the city. There was another alarm this morning, but the planes must have turned back or else switched to another destination. The bad feature of all this is the lack of a good communications system to warn the city before the Japanese are right on top of us. Yesterday, they arrived just fifteen minutes after the first warning. When I returned home in the afternoon, my boy told me that the USS *Tutuila* had fired on the Japanese. That may not have been true.

Tien's wedding on Saturday afternoon was a bit of a circus, but I'm awfully glad I went. My presence gave him a lot of "face" and I had one of the best times I have had in a long time. D.D. Yang and I went over to the hotel from the office and found my cook and house coolie and about twenty "boys" from other residences around here as well as some other people. The bride and bridegroom had not arrived yet from the other hotel, which was the starting place for their chair ride to the wedding. Finally, when word came that they were arriving, we all went out on the street to greet them as they came along in their flower-decked chairs. The bride's chair was entirely enclosed with curtains of flowers. While Tien's mother and a few other relatives haggled with the chair coolies about the fare, the bride and bridegroom went into another room in the hotel where the wedding paper was drawn up and all the witnesses signed. The retired steward of the Chungking Club was a sort of master of ceremonies and carried in his hand a printed instruction book to which he referred every minute or so. All the others also had ideas about procedure, but there never appeared to be any agreement as to how things should be done.

After all had signed, the party moved into a large room specially decorated in red for the wedding. There all the guests sat along two sides of the room with a decorated table across the space between them at one end. Tien and his bride came in and stood before the table facing the old steward, who was standing behind the table. The steward made a short speech and then called up several witnesses and introduced them formally to the couple to be married. Then he read through the paper they had just written and asked each witness if he agreed. After that, he came out in front of the table and supervised the changing of rings between the bride and the groom.

All this was done with constant reference to the book of instructions and an incredible amount of chatter in which everybody joined in, including Tien. After several short speeches Tien also made a speech. Then came the wedding dinner and we all fell to heartily. There were five tables of eight including one table for my chair coolies and a few others who were there in their bare feet. At my table were Yuan (my cook), D.D. Yang (my stenographer), the ambassador's boy, the local shoemaker who fixes shoes around the foreigners' houses and one or two others I don't recall.

The food was excellent and we all ate a lot. Things were a little quiet and restrained at first. But soon the married couple came to each guest in turn at his or her place at the tables; then the bride poured three drinks of wine for each, which the guest had to *gambei* (bottoms up) to her happiness. This took forever, and once the wine was started, it began to flow in a continual stream from dozens of small heated metal containers. I initiated a round of finger games at my table and had a great time. We heard that the cameraman was ready to take the wedding photograph, so we left the table and trooped downstairs to the courtyard.

We finally got back upstairs and resumed the meal staying on until four o'clock. When the party finally broke up, Tien came up to me sheepishly and asked me to lend him fifteen more dollars, as he did not have enough to pay the bill! I found out later that the whole thing had cost him $150 or eight months' salary. It was a fine party all in all and I can't remember ever laughing so much or being in such unusual company.

October 19

Modern times have certainly reached Chungking. Yesterday on the street, I saw a sidewalk shoe-shining establishment. No chairs, of course, but the regular little boxes for placing the customer's shoe while he stands on one foot. A crowd of fifty or so coolies milled around watching the new wonder.

For the very few miles of motor road in Chungking there must be almost as many cars and trucks as there are in New York. The increase has been tremendous. Although this advance of civilization may be a good thing, it makes sedan chair and rickshaw travel a precarious adventure. The drivers of cars and trucks drive just as fast and furiously as they possibly can, as this gives them face and makes them seem important. The military truck drivers are the worst and charge down the streets like juggernauts for no apparent reason, as their vehicles are usually empty. The Chinese can be the most maddening people on earth, but fortunately so many of the things they do are comic. I saw a funeral procession with a uniformed band playing "Sidewalks of New York," followed by professional mourners all in white carrying paper replicas of the deceased one's house and concubines. They all gaped and giggled when they saw me.

C.F. Lo often says it is the returned students from America who dislike the foreigners more than the Chinese who have never been abroad. This is because the students have seen that most of the foreigners are not well off in their own country and resent the foreigners' attitude when they are here. In a similar way, the Americans who have seen and know China are not as convinced of the greatness of the country as the Americans who have never been here.

By leaning out of my window, I can talk to Lester Jones of S.V.C. (Socony-Vacuum), who has the office right below mine. He says it is better to keep the windows wide open to prevent their being smashed inward if a bomb should be dropped nearby. That seems like good advice.

18

Chungking to Hong Kong
via Hanoi

Hong Kong, Nov. 23, 1938

GEORGE FITCH[1] was able to get out of Hankow two days before the Japanese entered the city and arrived, much to my surprise, in Chungking on November 3 to relieve me. The following day, I received a wire from Shanghai telling me to proceed to Hong Kong.

Leaving Chungking by plane on November 12[2] I had a nerve-racking ride through a blinding snowstorm at 17,000 feet, but I don't think I was quite as worried as a bearded Frenchman who recited his prayers aloud for the whole time. Everyone was glad when we finally found the field after circling over Kunming for almost an hour.

I had a stayover in Kunming of five days, waiting for a seat on the *Michelin,* the famous special train that runs down to the border, and stayed in

---

1. George's father, George Fitch, Sr., was the secretary of the YMCA in Nanking when the Japanese forces entered the city. He was able to send information to the outside world at great personal risk.

2. Lily Lee was arrested one day later, on November 13, and would be held five months without a trial before being released.

a French hotel. Butt, who relieved me in Tsingtao last February, is there now on a sort of survey visit.

We have no regular office in Kunming (better known as Yunnanfu), which is quite interesting in an old, slow moving way. The people are extremely lazy for Chinese and life moves at a snail's pace. Even the rickshaw men don't care much about making money. If they happen to have a few coppers on them at the moment, they refuse to pull you. It is very different from the rest of China. The city is over 6,000 feet high, so the climate is rather like Denver at this time of year. Most of the foreigners are French merchants who have favored positions because of France's special interest in Yunnan Province.

The railway line[3] to Hanoi in Indochina is certainly one of the most marvelous engineering projects I have seen, surpassing even the Panama Canal in the imagination and skill used to overcome obstacles. The route is entirely mountainous as far as the border, and there are well over a hundred tunnels and about a hundred bridges. The train races along the side of a terrific cliff, swoops into a tunnel at full speed, and then you suddenly find yourself hurtling across a thousand-foot chasm, and there you are on the face of the opposite cliff. It's breathtaking for the full twelve hours it takes to reach the border at Laokay. There you leave the *Michelin*, eat a poor dinner washed down with vin rouge in a poky little French restaurant, board the sleeper for Hanoi and arrive in a new world at seven in the morning.

The warm, balmy atmosphere, the shaded paved streets, the attractive shops and cafes and the tropical feel of Hanoi are a sudden and great blessing to the traveler from ramshackle, helter-skelter China.

It was disappointing to learn from one of our staff there that met me at the station that I had a stateroom already reserved on the SS *Tai Sang* leaving for Hong Kong that afternoon. I would like to have had several days in Hanoi and Haiphong, but maybe I'll have better luck next time. I took the train down to Haiphong, arrived at noon and boarded my ship at five.

I had an enjoyable, sunshiny trip up to Hong Kong on the *Tai Sang*, a brand

---

3. Built by the French at considerable expense, the Haiphong-Kunming line was begun in 1898 and completed in 1910. According to Chinese reports, more than 40,000 coolies died during construction of the line in formidable and malaria-infested terrain. The rail link was used by the Chinese to aid the Vietnamese in their war against the French and later against the Americans. Only at the end of the 1990's was limited international service resumed.

new ship belonging to the British firm of Jardine, Matheson. I arrived three days later, after stops at Pakhoi on the mainland and Hoichow on Hainan Island. Once or twice we sighted Japanese cruisers, which flashed their searchlights on us one night but did not bother us.

On arrival in Hong Kong on the twenty-first, I put up at the swank Peninsula Hotel (H.K. $14 per day) and called at our large office to receive the not too pleasant news that I am destined for Canton. The Japanese took the city a month ago and now the Chinese are putting on a big push to recapture it. There is absolutely no means of communication or transportation between Hong Kong and Canton except by British and American gunboats.

The gunboat USS Mindanao.

I'm leaving early next week on the USS *Mindanao*. My job will be to protect our property from interference on the part of the Japanese and possibly, in a short time, from the ravages of a Chinese army. In any case, there will be no actual business for some months, but we have valuable property that can be protected, if at all, by a foreigner. I'll be the only one in Canton for the company and one of the very few for *any* company. I will certainly see some excitement as right now, I understand that in Canton City the sounds of the battle raging outside can be heard. As the Japanese are rushing reinforcements as rapidly as possible, it is my personal opinion that they will succeed in lifting the siege and in driving the Chinese off, but a lot of people think differently.

I don't like the idea of going back into Japanese-occupied area—I had enough of it in Tsingtao for the six months after they came in. Also now that I am in Hong Kong after so long in the interior, I hate to have such a short time to enjoy the fine living here.

Hong Kong, November 24

This being a British colony, there is no knowing that today is Thanksgiving Day, except for the red mark on the office calendar. We don't have a holiday. It should be exciting but not dangerous going to Canton. All the foreigners there live on a small island near the Bund called Shameen, which is a British and French concession. I'll go up on an American gunboat and land right on the island. To go out into the city later, I'll have to get passes from the Japanese. I'm hoping, in a way, that the Chinese will retake the city. If they do, it will be a sight worth seeing. They are close now and the sound of shelling reaches into the city.

I spoke too soon about not having any way to know it was Thanksgiving Day yesterday. The boss here, Lawrence, had invited me to tiffin at the American Club, and it turned out to be a turkey dinner with all the fixings. Lawrence's mother was with us, too.

We had a blackout last night between 9:15 and 11:15 P.M., followed by the booming of the antiaircraft guns in practice. Hong Kong is in a decided state of preparedness. The news is full of volunteer activities, notices of anti-gas lectures, and navy movements.

I am staying at the Peninsula Hotel on the Kowloon side and find it satisfactory. I have a huge room with a little hall, a good bathroom and a closet about the size of a small bedroom. I have it on the American plan, eating my breakfast there and usually dinner. Tiffin I eat on the Hong Kong side to get a change. The company is paying for my hotel, so I am fairly well off, though everything is expensive here. A real meal outside costs about $3 or $6 Mex. Sometimes I wish I were back in a cheap-money place! A clipper letter from China proper costs about seventy Hong Kong cents, but here it costs $2.80, which is ridiculous as all the mail from any place in China must come through Hong Kong.

I had a Chinese farewell party every day for a week before I left. Each agent insisted on giving one, and then my staff did the same. The house servants and the chair coolies had bought about five thousand firecrackers in great rolls, which they carry at the ends of poles and turn around as they go off. It was quite a rumpus but nice though.

Hong Kong, November 28

Hong Kong has been aroused the last few days because of the fighting taking place right on the colony's border to the north. The Japanese are "mopping up" small bands of Chinese along the Kowloon-Canton Railroad and have now about finished their work. There have been blackouts, a dreadful nuisance, for three nights in a row. The other night I had the venetian blinds down and the heavy cloth curtains drawn across the windows and was in the middle of reading a detective story in bed by the meager light of the bedside lamp, when someone at the front desk phoned and asked me to put out the light.

I had tiffin at the Hong Kong Hotel with David Erskine of B.&S., whom I knew in Tsingtao. Stationed in Chungking two years ago, he knew many of the people up there and was glad to get the latest news from me.

Tonight I am going to have a Chinese dinner with Chuck Sharp, the C.N.A.C. pilot who brings the "blockade runner" through from Chungking. The Chinese food is one of the best things in this city. Mrs. Wilkie, the wife of one of the C.N.A.C. fellows I knew very well in Chungking, is going with us.

VI

CANTON
AND RETURN
TO PEKING

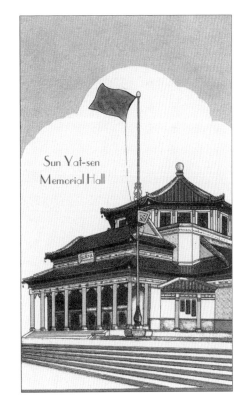

Sun Yat-sen
Memorial Hall

19

In Occupied Canton

CANTON WAS SUBJECTED for a whole year to what was probably the most intensive bombing of the war. The attacks reached their culmination in June, when the planes came in relays of fifteen or twenty at a time every two hours. Moonlit nights were simply a hell for the Cantonese and stormy days their only blessing.

The raids diminished in July, August and September, but renewed in October. On October 12 the Japanese landed two or three divisions at Bias Bay (above Hong Kong and the old notorious pirate den) and in nine days were in Canton. It takes seven days by ordinary walking to reach Canton from Bias Bay so their speed was surprising. Canton had been spending millions on what was supposed to be the best defense works in China, preparing them for two years. When the Japanese tanks and advance units paraded into the city on October 21, the city was almost empty, the population having fled to the interior. It was a mystery as to what had happened to the troops and patriotic militia. The real burning and looting occurred after the arrival of the Japanese.

Yesterday, I walked across the English Bridge to see what had happened. The destruction was devastating. Mile after mile in a city somewhat comparable in buildings and streets and modernness to Philadelphia, every single struc-

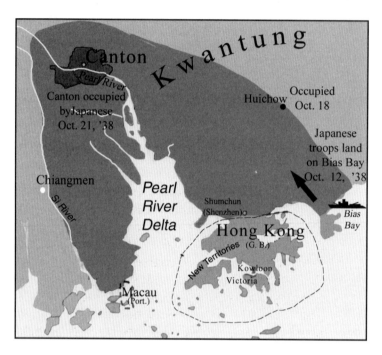

The Japanese occupied Canton on Oct. 21, 1938. Hong Kong,
a British colony, was not taken until December 25, 1941.

ture has been gutted by bombs and fires. It was once crowded and colorful, but now it is a silent hulk. Deserted streets, wrecked buildings, smoldering fires were all that was left.

I crossed over from Shameen[2] yesterday with Rosario, my Portuguese accountant, and went around the city in a rickshaw, one of the few available. For blocks and blocks the only living souls were Japanese sentries, ready to be obnoxious about our official passes. We passed by a score of streets with noth-

---

2. The Anglo-French concession

Postcard of Canton Bund on the Pearl River, in early 1930's.
Customs House is visible at left, with dome.

ABOVE: *Boat people on Pearl River, off Shameen.* BELOW: *View of Canton Bund, from Japanese-military-issue postcard of 1939. Notice Japanese flag, left foreground.*

廣東憲兵隊許可濟　　　ン バ ン サ 物 名 東 廣 （東 廣）

昭和十四年七月三日
廣東憲兵隊檢閲濟（S）
飛行機より見た沙面英佛租界と廣東市内の一部

ABOVE: *Aerial view of Canton, Pearl River and island of Shameen, the Anglo-French Concession, from a Japanese-issued postcard of 1939.* BELOW: *Texaco office (also known as the Andersen, Meyer Building) and right, the U.S. Consulate, formerly Yokohama Specie Bank, on Shameen.*

廣東憲兵隊許可済　　司公燈電とンパンサの江珠（東廣）

ABOVE: *View of Canton Bund, from Japan-issued postcard of 1939.* BELOW: *English Park on Shameen waterfront promenade and boat people, or* tanmin, *about half a million of whom used to live on the Pearl River. They have long since gone.*

ing but hulks of stone buildings left standing, and then turning left from the waterfront, we went to the New China Hotel, miraculously saved from the flames and in fairly good condition. A little farther on, we turned right and came upon the most incongruous sight. In a section of about four blocks by four blocks is the strangest market in the world. For here in the heart of a ruined city is the "looters market." Up and down both sides of the streets and piled in the roadway itself are the gatherings from thousands of ransacked shops, rich homes and government buildings.

Not one of the articles actually belongs to the grinning salesman. The looter looted from the looter and all buy and sell in a spirit of devil-may-care. One street was lined with Blackwood furniture selling for a song. In another, the curb was taken up from end to end with overstuffed chairs and sofas. There were small booths selling anything from safety pins to bronze jars. One old woman with a piece of sheeting spread on the sidewalk had the grandest collection, surpassing even the Thieves' Market in Peking. She had the taillight of a motorcar, two old Yale locks, a stack of old stationery and foreign books.

Everywhere people were gambling. The almost fanatical gambling spirit of the Chinese had been subdued for the past two years. The laws in Canton prohibited all forms of jollity from the gambling table to the public dance hall. They are now free to gamble and the old spirit is back. I saw people playing fan-tan, mah-jongg and poker and even the old army game. I saw many of these "looter merchants" make a sale and immediately rush to a gambling table with the proceeds.

December 9

We are virtually prisoners here, and I feel bound up and choked by the situation after just one week. This "island" of Shameen is about five blocks long by three blocks wide, with sandbags and barbed wire all about and armed guards at the two small bridges to the mainland. To cross over to the city (mainland) you must sign a register and then check in when you return.

As soon as you set foot in the city, you must have your Japanese pass ready to show every minute. Japanese, on the other hand, must have passes to cross into Shameen. Chinese are not allowed in unless they have armbands (good for one day only) to show they have business with a foreign firm on the island. The

The Texaco office (the Andersen, Meyer building) with company flat on top floor, on Shameen; photo was taken by the author when he returned to Canton in 1947.

rule is that only foreigners can live on the island, but in this time of emergency, the Chinese staffs of many of the firms, including ours, have been camping in the office. Not very pleasant for them after a couple of months!

No motors or rickshaws are allowed—or ever have been allowed on Shameen. There are few bicycles, but most persons just walk. With no traffic of any sort, no streets are needed, so we have nothing but sidewalks with wide boulevards of grass and trees and flowers in between. It is really quite a lovely, restful-looking spot.

The weather is marvelous at this time of year. It is getting on for the middle of December, and the trees are in leaf, the grass is green, the flowers are beautiful, and of course, the mosquitoes are plentiful. I went for a stroll at 10:30 last night before going to bed, and I noticed that the thermometer on the porch read 69 degrees.

The weather is practically the only thing about the place I am enjoying. The hotel is miserable: the food, the service, the atmosphere and everything. My work is a thankless sort of task of taking this and that up with the American consul general and the Japanese vice-consul and getting nowhere. Our curb pumps and filling stations over in the city are in the worst possible mess; our agents have run away.

Before the trouble, there was a daily express train that made the trip to Hong Kong in two hours and fifty-five minutes, besides a daily and nightly steamer. Living on Shameen was like living in a suburb of Hong Kong, but now I might as well be a thousand miles in the interior. Also, before the trouble there was life and gaiety in Canton—fine Chinese restaurants and movies, etc. Now there is no electricity and you could walk for miles without seeing anyone except Japanese sentries.

I have just returned from my twice-daily inspection trip to our godown down the river. I have a motorboat from Socony for the trip as ours disappeared into the hinterland on October 20.

I am certainly a big shot at the godown. Just before we get there, the coxswain of the motorboat gives a toot or two on his whistle, and by the time I step off onto our pier, there is quite a delegation to greet me. The young Russian watchman steps forward and makes a kind of half-bow, and the two burly Sikhs behind him snap into a military salute.

They have uniforms after a fashion and cut a grand picture with their full beards and their colored turbans. Well over six feet tall, they must weigh about 280 pounds apiece. Behind them scattered about are the godown staff of five, headed by Mr. Loo, the godown keeper. Also out to greet, bow and salute me are our six Chinese ex-policemen. In addition to all these, we have five extra-labor coolies and a No. 1 who help swell the ranks of the "Texaco Army." It is quite an outfit.

The godown is about three miles downriver from the city proper, lying on the riverbank in a rather lonely sector. Across the river, however, there are godowns belonging to the Salt Gabelle Administration, and there have been some pretty active battles between pirate-bandits and the Japanese in this area

The Texaco godown on the Pearl River. The U.S. flag at center of building was probably a precautionary measure in wartime.

during the past month. The front and one side of our godown are spattered with bullet marks. It is fairly quiet there now, the last "battle" having taken place a couple of days before I arrived. I've heard faint sounds of shelling from outside the city several times, but it is now evident that the much-advertised Chinese recapture of Canton was nothing but a dream and a newspaper headline. There is increasing talk in Shanghai from semiofficial sources of the new Japanese-managed Chinese government that soon all foreign concessions, armed forces and extraterritoriality will be cleared out, so we may have to leave at any time.

Hong Kong, December 16

I am in Hong Kong for four days on a special trip to buy some guns to take back to Canton for the protection of our godown. We had a raid three nights ago, and it looks as if we might be in for more trouble. The United States Navy commander fixed it up for me to make the trip down and back on HMS *Moth*.

It is a great responsibility protecting almost a million dollars' worth of gas, kerosene and lubricating oils. There aren't enough Japanese soldiers to keep order effectively with Chinese bandits successfully raiding place after place.

Canton, December 22

We have had a violent and sudden change in the weather. The day before yesterday I was sweltering in my light suit; today I am wearing a heavy suit and topcoat and blowing on my hands to keep them warm. There is no heat in the office and none in the hotel, except a grate fire in the dingy lobby downstairs. That is one of the chief faults with living conditions in China: not enough provision is made in buildings or homes for the cold weather.

This job is one headache after another,[3] and all without results. I spend from early in the morning until dark going between the godown, the American consulate, the Japanese consulate and the USS *Mindanao*. When the guns at the godown get out of order, I have to get the Navy to go down and fix them. My Indian guards want to quit and go back to Hong Kong because their work is "too dangerous."

The British concession authorities refuse to let a small gasoline shipment cross the concession, and I had to bribe the French police with a case of beer to let them go through *their* concession. The Japanese hold up permission for our motorboat to resume service between the godown and Shameen. As the junk we use now is chased off by a Japanese water patrol, I have to make arrangements to paint small American flags on a hundred pieces of loaned equipment that are scattered all over Canton. I am trying to open an agency in the city, and have to get permission from Hayasaki, the Japanese vice-consul, for every move I make. There are a thousand and one small errands I have to do every day. I am getting nowhere from a sales point of view.

---

3. The author decided to resign about this time, presumably because of the war news in Europe as well as China. He decided to make one more trip to Peking before going home. He and Lily Lee, who would not be released from prison until April, intended to get married. She met up with Jim in Europe in the summer of '39, where they would spend several weeks visiting Paris, the Riviera and Venice.

Chuck and Rosario both sailed for Hong Kong on the *Mindanao* today, so I have to rely on the young inexperienced clerks to handle matters in the office. A whole raft of stuff is left pending in the way of reports and records that must be handled.

Building on Shameen in the verandah style popular in warm climates.

Canton, January 31, 1939

We are having beautiful weather again. It is just like June at home, with the temperature hovering between 60 and 70 most days for the past two weeks. The air even smells like spring. We all complain, however, about the mosquitoes, which are out in force.

And the war situation remains unchanged. Japanese bombers start off in squadrons almost every morning shortly after dawn and hit surrounding towns and Chinese troop concentrations. Sometimes the points they raid are near enough for the explosions to be heard. Not a day passes without clearly audible machine-gun fire and sometimes heavy shelling. It's all rather a mystery and no one knows just what is happening.

Armed bands of Chinese looters, who often range between Shameen and our godown, continue to keep the whole area in a state of dangerous anarchy. As I cannot feel any reasonable safety yet about the security of our stocks, I go down almost daily on the company's private launch to keep a close watch on the place. I am getting another Sikh guard tomorrow via the *Mindanao*, as well as two new rifles and a few hundred rounds of ammunition. I am beginning to feel like an army commander.

Business is in awful shape, with Japanese-smuggled kerosene entering the market. I've been busy and have had more knotty, difficult problems to figure out since I resigned than before. The company will never be able to say I started neglecting their interests while waiting for relief.

20

Back to Peking and the Voyage Home

SS Tai Sang, *March 8, 1939*

WE ARRIVED in Swatow the day before yesterday at 6 A.M. but were in such a heavy fog that we couldn't get in till two in the afternoon. Swatow city itself is small and flat, but across the harbor is a large green and rocky island where there are a few good foreign homes and a mission or two. Around the whole section is a rim of hills about eight or ten miles from the harbor.

As soon as we docked I went ashore to the Jardine office, where I telephoned the Socony installation. Bill Watson is out there now, just having been transferred from Canton. The Jardine manager arranged a rickshaw for me, and I made the trip out to the installation in about fifteen minutes.

Back in China again! And perhaps for the last time. There are Chinese policemen instead of Sikhs or Japanese and the familiar Kuomintang signs are written over the government compounds. The streets are well paved and cleanly kept, and the houses that line them are fairly attractive with gardens. In this respect, the place reminds me somewhat of Tsingtao. The most striking thing to be noted in a quick ride through the town is the number of American flags flying over the houses. I counted at least twenty during my fifteen-minute ride. The reason is that from Swatow come almost all the fine handkerchiefs and drawn linen work sold in the States. The business is almost entirely in the hands of Syrian and American Jews from New York, who make periodic trips out here. On the basis of these connections, the Chinese who own the shops fly American flags not only on the places of business but also over their homes. A strict consul would probably raise a fuss, but the present one seems to be lenient, probably because of the war.

When I arrived at the Socony place, I found a fine compound on the harbor edge in a beautiful location. Five bulk storage tanks and three or four godowns and the manager's office and residence, all placed on a five-acre lawn overlooking the water.

The people Watson and his mother are relieving were still there but were busy packing and expected to leave in a day or two. They are a young couple just shortly returned from home leave, and the girl turned out to be the daughter of a woman my mother met in Amityville several months ago, which was a strange coincidence. Wat, as he is called, showed me around the compound, and then we all had a pleasant tea together. It seemed like going back in time over a year, for there in Swatow[1] they are in the same position of waiting for the Japanese to come that I knew so well in Tsingtao in 1937. The Japanese can evidently come in any time they wish as the Chinese seem to have given up any idea of defending the place. The army, such as it is, is entrenched in the hills outside the town, leaving only the mines in the harbor to delay a Japanese landing. An American destroyer lies just off the Socony installation, and an English destroyer is in and out most of the time.

The town was subjected to a small bombing two weeks ago, but only a few planes came and they dropped small bombs, one landing fifty yards from the American consulate. Last Thursday the Chinese government ordered the complete evacuation of all Chinese girls and women from Swatow.

At five o'clock Wat took me back to the *Tai Sang* in the company launch just in time for sailing. Just before we cast off, a little group of kids gathered on the dock below our decks and begged for *cumshaw* (tips). One boy of about ten, stone blind with a film covering both eyes, was led around by his small brother of not more than five, one of whose eyes was already starting to go. Barefoot and clad in the most miserable rags, with the sad look of neglected old men on their faces, they were as pitiful a pair as I have ever seen. Some of

1. Swatow, now Shantou, was occupied by the Japanese on June 21, 1939.

the other ragamuffins kept teasing the blind boy by throwing dirty bits of paper at him. The little brother paid no attention to them but kept looking up at us and calling *cumshaw*. Not a coin dropped. The scene was wretched enough without having to see a coin intended for the blind ones being snatched away by the others.

Off to the sea again, and a spanking sea it was—we have been pitching heavily ever since leaving Swatow the night before last, although today is somewhat better. The ship is expected to make Shanghai about eleven tonight but we probably won't be allowed to debark until morning. There are twelve first-class passengers on board, a fairly jolly group. The skipper is young, handsome and rather fancies himself but has the knack of keeping things going.

Among the passengers are two good-looking girls returning to Shanghai from a vacation; a British consul; a wealthy veterinarian returning after the Hong Kong races last week; a Mrs. Pasco of Hong Kong and her daughter; and a British Navy wife. As it is Mrs. Pasco's birthday today we have planned a tea dance in the lounge this afternoon. A group of us have been playing mild poker games each night with a twenty-cent limit and have had fun at it.

Shanghai, March 10

We arrived about 1 A.M. and were allowed ashore. After passing customs, five of us went ashore dancing and then returned to the ship at four in the morning. I left the ship about noon yesterday and am now settled in town at the Palace Hotel.[2] Expensive but not more so than the other hotels, the Palace is on the Bund at the corner of Nanking Road, the famous corner where the large bomb dropped during the trouble a year and a half ago. Although over thirty years old, the hotel is fashionable and popular—the place to see everyone you've ever known.

March 17

I spent last Saturday with the Henkels, who joined me for dinner at the Palace

---

2. Opposite the Cathay Hotel on Nanking Road.

and then took me to the Russian Ballet and afterward to the French Club. A few nights ago we had dinner at Mr. Le Fevre's flat and saw *Young Dr. Kildare* at the Nanking. We then went to the Park Hotel for dancing.

Shanghai is full of places to go dancing but they are all crowded every night. People go and go and go in this town with many spending half their salary or more for entertainment. Another evening I spent with an Italian girl who was on the *Tai Sang* and turned out to be the best dancer I've ever gone out with—and a bit close to balmy. We absolutely danced our legs off at the Park, Farren's, Arcadia and Del Monte's.

Yesterday was the day poor Czechoslovakia was turned over to Hitler.

Last night we went over to Farren's[3] *(the* spot this year) to the small place they have upstairs—very attractive, a small floor and swell music. A couple of Austrian refugees play the accordion and violin and sing Austrian songs in between the dance numbers. Today being St. Patrick's Day we had a special tiffin party at the Palace and had the hotel orchestra play all the Irish songs.

Shanghai to Tientsin on the SS Shengking,
March 19

I sailed from Shanghai yesterday noon and now (Sunday 5 P.M.) we are sailing past the Shantung Promontory and will soon be turning west toward Chefoo. The mountainous Shantung coast, clearly visible, puts my mind back over two and a half years ago when these same mountains were my first view of China. That was from the deck of the *Chojo Maru.* And now I am back here again. So much has happened to China in the meantime. So much has happened to me too. I never expected to travel by mule litter and bus through this very range of mountains that looked so otherworldly to me that day in 1936.

I was mistaken about this ship passing through Tsingtao this trip. The captain, disgusted with the conditions at Tsingtao harbor, never calls there if he can help it. That is precisely what the Japanese are after: their ships now monopolize all the trade as well as the passenger traffic.

---

3. Joe Farren, the Austrian-born owner of Farren's nightclub, is said to have been beaten to death by the Japanese in the infamous Bridge House prison in Shanghai after the outbreak of the Pacific War in 1941. He had refused to share his gambling business with the Japanese.

We should arrive off the breakwater at Chefoo about ten tonight, but the Japanese doctor won't come on board until seven or eight tomorrow morning. All passengers, even the through ones to Tientsin, as almost all of us are, must be up, fully dressed and ready for inspection at 7 A.M. sharp. If he comes on board at that time and finds one passenger not ready, he will stamp off the ship and keep us waiting until late afternoon. On the other hand he may not turn up until nine or ten in the morning, in which case we must wait patiently from seven on until his arrival; that is just one of their little tricks to discourage British shipping. There are many of them.

Peking, March 23

I arrived in Tientsin Tuesday afternoon and saw Harold and Audrey Dennis and their new baby. Dennis was with us in Tsingtao when I first went up there. I stayed overnight at the Astor House, and then caught the train yesterday for Peking. The train was packed with Japanese officers, and the two-and-a-half-hour trip wasn't much fun. Each officer carries swords, pistols, big dispatch cases, field glasses, canteens and other odds and ends in such number that he should have an entire compartment to himself.

The country is so flat and ordinary between Tientsin and Peking that one could almost imagine to be riding across our Midwest plains. The sudden appearance of the great walls of Peking comes as a startling experience, even when they are expected. The hotels in town are crowded to capacity, to a great extent with Japanese, this being the first indication I had of the change here. Two and a half years ago, a Japanese in the Wagons-Lits or Hôtel de Pékin was somewhat of a rarity. I managed to get a room at the Wagons-Lits and will keep it until I can make a better arrangement.

This morning I went to the Language School to deliver a parcel for the captain of the *Shengking*. Hatamen Street was a great disappointment for it has been paved. Streetcars, buses and motorcars whiz along where there used to be a dusty but romantic thoroughfare with plodding camels and donkey carts.

It is very cold and I shiver even in my heavy coat. Without it I would be in an awful fix for I'm not yet used to cold weather. It snowed in Tientsin yesterday, and except for the blizzard during my Chungking-Kunming plane ride, it's the first snow I have seen in over a year.

The home of Ed Martin, manager of the Texaco office in Peking, and his wife, Louise. "The compound is made [u]p of six buildings and two courtyards." The curved tile roofs had brightly painted eaves.

A Peking picnic, April 1939: TOP, *the author, with wineglass at right, with Louise Martin, second from left,
friends;* CENTER RIGHT, *picnic antics;* CENTER LEFT, *the author with Louise and a servant of the Martins.* ̶A̶B̶O̶V̶E̶
RIGHT, *the Martins relaxing in the courtyard of their Peking home;* ABOVE LEFT, *Louise monitoring the dog's b*

Photographs taken by the author in 1939 at the temple complex of Angkor in Cambodia. BOTTOM RIGHT: *The author's traveling companion takes a break while the driver of the hired car fixes a flat on the way to Angkor.*

The main approach to Angkor Wat, built in the 13th century, in the temple region of Angkor, Cambodia. The complex of temples was essentially unknown in the West until the 19th century.

I had great pleasure yesterday afternoon in walking in on Ed Martin, who was in Chungking before me, in the office. He was very surprised to see me because he thought I was in Canton. Yesterday, being Wednesday, was the day for Mrs. Calhoun's weekly salon in her beautiful Chinese home. Ed, his wife, Louise, and I went along there for an hour or so and had a very pleasant time. Then I went back to the Martins for dinner. They have a peach of a Chinese house on a little *hutung*.

Peking, April 1

I have just been up with Ed to the Lung Fu-Ssu Temple Fair, which is held three times a month for three days at a time and features acrobats, musicians, wrestlers and storytellers.

From my window over the desk where I write, I can see a considerable length of the wall dividing the Tartar City from the Chinese one. The Grand Hôtel des Wagons-Lits is in the Legation Quarter, just at the Water Gate, where the relieving Allied troops came through in 1900 when the Boxers were on the rampage. It seems a shame to have these magnificent embassies without a single ambassador in them; they are used, of course, by junior people stationed here. It is a far cry from the "good old days" before the capital was moved to Nanking.[4] If the Japanese should win this war, they might bring the Emperor Pu-yi back from his smaller throne in Manchuria and reinstate him here as the Son of Heaven. Even if they have occupied the major cities, it is doubtful if they can win in the end.

33 Tai Yuan Fu Hutung, April 13

I left the hotel a week ago at the Martins' kind invitation and have been living with them ever since. I wish so much my parents could see this lovely place. Ed and I agreed that I should pay them the regular company rate for visiting— $5 Mex. per day or about $25 per month. I have the temporary No. 2 boy and

---

4. Nanking was capital of a united China from 1928 to 1937, and again from 1946 until 1949, at which time the Communist government restored Peking as the capital.

my own rickshaw coolie, so I am getting a lot of practice speaking Chinese.

This compound is made up of six buildings and two courtyards with a red wall on either side. They are all one-story structures of brick and clay with a great amount of red wooden doorways and red-latticed windows. The curved tile roofs with brightly painted eaves complete the Chinese effect. In one corner of the inner courtyard is a sunken stone fountain with a rock garden behind it. The yard itself is about fifty feet square. The building on my left is an attractively furnished study. There is also a guest room with a bath. The smaller building in front of me is taken up by the master bedroom. Toward the street is the front courtyard, which contains the living room and dining room. I haven't described it very well but I can't imagine a nicer way to live.

I've had several fine days out at the Summer Palace and in the nearer part of the Western Hills, picnics, etc. Because it is supposed to be dangerous there many people (including Louise Martin) are afraid to go. But during the daytime, I think it's about as safe as most things. I wouldn't care to stay out at one of the cottages overnight, nor would anyone in Peking, but it is so beautiful there that anyone fearful of daytime trips is missing a lot.

I am having a few people over for dinner tonight, a farewell party really. After cocktails I will take them to the Hôtel du Nord, a German place with draught beer and a sort of beer-hall atmosphere. We had steak tartare, a kind of glorified hamburger, but the meat is very good. The staff brings in the meat rare, and everyone puts in his selection of condiments. You beat it all together and then tell the boy how you want it cooked. It comes to you later with French-fried potatoes and vegetables.

It will be very hard leaving Peking, but I must get away and be on the move before the end of another week.

Hong Kong, May 11

I am leaving Hong Kong on the *Président Doumer* of the Messageries Maritimes Line on May 25. I will arrive in Saigon on May 28, where I will meet Stephen Cumming (my good friend from Butterfield & Swire in Chungking, now on leave) and travel with him overland by car through the jungle to Angkor via Phnom Penh. From Angkor we will go to Aranya on the Siam-Indochina border, where we will catch a train for Bangkok. At Bangkok

Southeast Asia in 1930's showing British, French and Dutch colonies.

Postcard of the Hôtel Majestic in Saigon in the mid-1930's.

we separate, Stephen going by plane to Calcutta and I by ship to Singapore. On June 15, I sail from Singapore on the *Aramis*, the crack new ship of the French Line. I'm taking a stopover between ships and will have nineteen days for Indochina, Siam and the Straits.

Hôtel Majestic, Saigon
May 29

This is the tropics and no mistake. The rain is simply pounding down outside my window shutters, and I am dripping wet from perspiration in here under my ceiling fan. At 2:30 in the afternoon, the town is practically bottled up, not because of the rain but for the regular after-tiffin siesta. The Majestic is one of the two main hotels here, the other being the Continental Palace. Neither of them has running hot water, and I have to fight for soap and towels. On top of this, they speak only French or Annamite. I find my temper rising in this awful heat.

On our way to the Zoological Gardens we saw a little of the city, which is beautifully laid out with broad avenues, modern buildings and especially fine trees. In the main section there are shops, cinemas and scores of sidewalk cafes. The population (the foreign part, that is) being 95 percent French, getting by is tough for the handful of Americans who do not speak the language.

Stephen met me at the ship yesterday morning, having arrived an hour earlier himself by train from Hue. We are planning to start off to the interior by car tomorrow at 5 A.M. in the cool of the day and when rain is least likely. We should be in Phnom Penh before 9 A.M. with good luck and will see the King's Palace with the silver tiled room, the solid gold Buddha and whatever else there is in town. The following morning or possibly the next, we will be off for Angkor, a long day's ride through real jungle. I am not sure how many days we need for Angkor or how much time we need to save for Bangkok. I must leave the latter place on June 10 to make my connections on the fifteenth in Singapore, so that allows me twelve days starting tomorrow.

On the street yesterday evening I met my old Tsingtao friend George McLaughlin, now an accountant with the Texas Company here. He is taking Stephen and me to Le Cercle Sportif for a swim this afternoon. We watched a pair of magnificent tigers at the zoo yesterday. I wonder what animals we shall see on the way to Angkor.

Penang, June 11

By repute the prettiest place in the Far East, Penang is no disappointment. It's on a green, hilly island about a mile off the mainland. I crossed over on a

Postcard of Eastern and Oriental Hotel on Penang, off the Malayan coast.

launch in the midst of a beautiful sunset. The hotel is right on the water and couldn't be finer in any way. My room, which consists of a well-furnished lounge, a little hallway, a large bedroom and a bath, is fit for a king.

The *Aramis* leaves on June 15 from Singapore. After Port Said and Suez, we shall be in the Mediterranean in July, and then I will spend two nights in Marseille. How strange it will be to be back in the Western world.

It has been such a wrench to leave the East.[5]

---

5. Jim returned to New York from Europe in August on the *Ile de France* after a six-week vacation on the French Riviera and in Paris (where he met up with Lily Lee) and Venice.

APPENDIX

Lily Lee 李麗

*L*ITTLE IS KNOWN *about Lily Lee from G.H.T.'s letters home because he was reluctant to tell his parents about his affair. When he did inform them, in November 1937 from Tsingtao, they were not supportive. Jim never discussed her again, that is, until the summer of 1939, when he returned to New York, with Lily arriving shortly thereafter. Jim possibly thought that by introducing her to his parents, he might succeed in swaying them to think differently about the relationship. But Lily's arrest, mentioned briefly in the* New York Times, *could only have complicated matters.*

The affair and Lily's arrest on suspicion of being a spy for the Japanese are mentioned briefly in the book China to Me, *an autobiographical account by Emily Hahn of her years in China, published in 1944. And an interview in the* Hong Kong Sunday Herald, *of Sept. 22, 1940, describes in some detail Lily's visit to Jim in Chungking, her arrest by Chinese nationalists and her subsequent trip to Europe and New York, where she and Jim hoped to get married.*

According to the Hong Kong Film Archive, Lily Lee, an accomplished actress in the Chinese theater and movies, was born in 1910. She had already appeared in several films when she met Jim in 1937. In 1939 she made a film in Hong Kong called The Perfect Woman, *a romance in Mandarin. When Hong Kong fell to the Japanese in 1941, it is believed she moved to Chungking to continue her film career. She returned to Hong Kong after the war where she made several more films. She retired after appearing in a stage show in Taipei in 1958.*

From *China to Me,* by Emily Hahn
(1944, Blakiston, Philadelphia; 2002 reprint by E-Reads)

SHANGHAI IS A WONDERFUL CITY for the theater. I have heard some of the best plays produced in Shanghai. Have you heard any of the famous girl performers? Have you heard Lily Lee? She is really good."

Lily Lee! I remembered suddenly a girl Sinmay had brought to my house one afternoon, with a story of squandered fortunes. I had seen Lily again in Hong Kong. I told Ping-chia about it. "We had dinner at Lily's house," I explained. "She's improved wonderfully in her English, hasn't she?" He looked mysterious. "There was a reason for that," he said .

"Oh, I know." It was a romantic story that Lily had told me at the dinner table that night, while Sinmay drank rice wine and chattered with friends. She had fallen in love with an American she met in Hankow.[1]

After the latest exodus she had gone up to Chungking to see him. Followed a few weeks of loving bliss, and then she started back to Hong Kong, her plane ticket in her pocket, going in a sedan chair down to the riverbank, as befitted a great lady and famous artiste.

Lily Lee had never reached the plane. Chinese plain-clothes men took command of her chair coolies before she entered the airfield, and Lily was whisked off to prison for "questioning." She stayed in jail for five months without trial, while the young American made frantic endeavors to get her out. The government was very suspicious of Lily, and accused her outright of being a spy. As to what sort of spy, they were rather vague. I suppose they thought she had been planted by the Japs, and then her fondness for the foreigner was not so good, either.

"I was not uncomfortable," Lily admitted. "But one bad old official, he pretended to set me free, and when I realized what it was all about, I was living in his house. He wanted me to live with him, to be his concubine, and when I would not they put me back into the jail. I was never tried at all. My boyfriend was very good about it. After I got out of jail, after I came to Hong Kong, he lost his job. I am going to America to marry him."

———

1. Emily Hahn is possibly mistaken here. It was more likely in Tsingtao.

An Interview With Lily Lee

A year after her trip to New York in September 1939, Lily is once again settled in Hong Kong. The following are excerpts from an interview with the actress by the Hong Kong Sunday Herald, *September 22, 1940. The city was not occupied by the Japanese until December 1941.* [2]

ONE OF CHINA'S most highly paid film stars . . . and . . . one of the most attractive, Lily Lee, or Peiping Lily as she is sometimes called, is at present completing a picture in Hong Kong. . . . Apart from the novelty of interviewing a leading Chinese film actress, we were particularly interested in getting from her the first full account of her arrest in Chungking some time back as a "Japanese spy!"

She was rather reticent about this at first and suggested it was past history, but we persuaded her that a frank statement would give the lie to one or two false rumors flying around, and she agreed. We'll go into this later but for the moment it may be mentioned that she convinced the Chinese Government that she was anything but a spy . . . in token of which is the fact that she was released.

Few Europeans go to see Chinese films, so you'll have to take our word for it that she is an accomplished actress even by Occidental standards. Young, slim and rather quiet, she is in reality a bundle of energy and in between films has found time to develop a number of other accomplishments. She rides daily at Shatin, she swims, she drives even the largest car skillfully, and she's pretty hot at billiards. In addition, she is thinking of taking up flying. . . .

We interviewed here without the benefit of an interpreter and had no difficulty in understanding her. In another three months she should be speaking English fluently.

She actually comes of a wealthy Chinese family which for generations has been definitely in the upper crust. . . . Unlike most Chinese stars, she is a traveled woman, and has been around the world twice. The present World War, incidentally, interfered with her second trip, and due to a series of circumstances, she ended up spending a weekend at Ellis Island, off New York. "So

---

2. Interview with Lily Lee, courtesy of the Hong Kong Film Archive, Bede Cheng, program assistant; collection of Mr. Law Kar.

Conte di Savoia of the Italian Line, which from the outbreak of war in Europe in September 1939 until June 1940 was the only steamship company making the transatlantic crossing. The vessel was bombed and sunk by Allied aircraft near Venice in 1943.

for the second time I was in jail," she smiled.

She has relatives dotted about the place in Europe and intended to look them up on her tour. She took a ship as far as Italy and then proceeded overland to Paris.

After visits to London and so on, she was to have caught the *Normandie*[3] for the transatlantic journey to New York, but war broke out and the giant French liner canceled its sailing. So she returned to Italy to book a passage on the *Conte di Savoia*, and the company officials insisted she pay gold for her ticket.

Fortunately, she had enough "loose change" on her to oblige, and this did not worry her unduly as she could draw on her account with a New York bank when she got across. But when the ship arrived at New York, the immigration officials refused to allow her ashore, as she did not have the required sum of money required of all visitors. She had a bank account, she told them. They politely scoffed. On the wharf was an American friend who would vouch for her, she told them. They were skeptical and refused to allow her to see the friend. This was on a Saturday morning. Pending inquiries, therefore, she was sent to Ellis Island, and there she spent the weekend. Monday morning, of course, she was released, with apologies!

---

3. Because of the war, the *Normandie* was held up at Pier 88 in New York, where it would stay until destroyed by a fire in February 1942.

This seems an appropriate moment to bring up the "spy story," which dates back to 1938 and before the fall of Hankow. The tale begins in Tsingtao, where normally she has her home. A very dear friend of hers was transferred to Chungking, and when later, the friend fell ill, she decided to go there on a visit. She got as far as Hankow all right, but then found that all airplane bookings to Chungking were taken up, and she would have to wait a few weeks before she could continue the journey. . . .

Eventually she got to Chungking. . . . She was young, attractive and an excellent dancer, and she soon had a wide circle of friends. Now the trouble with being popular and having a wide circle of friends is that one's acquaintances tend to be of all sorts and types. Once or twice, a close friend would warn her to be a bit more "choosy" and that rumors were beginning to get about that she was really a China "Mata Hari." She laughed at this for her conscience was quite clear. Had she not worked hard for China war relief and other praiseworthy charities whilst in Shanghai? To call her a spy was ridiculous!

Then one day she decided to fly down to Hong Kong.[4] She was on her way to the airport and indeed, could actually see the plane on the field, when she was stopped by a body of men who said, "Come with us." Startled, she said, "Why, what am I supposed to have done?" "You know very well," was the reply. She protested she didn't know what it was all about and pointed out that the plane was about to take off and if she missed it she would have to forfeit her ticket, in addition to the inconvenience of last-minute changes in her program. The men were obdurate, and she was forced to accompany them on foot a long distance to what appeared to be a run-down hotel. . . .

She then found herself in prison charged with being a "Japanese spy"! Protestations of her innocence got her nowhere, and the next thing that happened was that she was appearing before a military tribunal, surrounded by a "bodyguard" of 50 armed soldiers.

She caused some amusement in the court when she sarcastically asked if an army that size was required to guard one lone woman. The court was not amused; the court did not believe that she was a Chinese patriot and had worked for China's cause; the court condemned her to be shot as a spy.

---

4. According to an account of her arrest in the *New York Times* on Nov. 21, 1938, Lily Lee was detained by Chinese secret service agents "for observation" in Chungking, on Nov. 13. Jim had left for Hong Kong on Nov. 12.

Fortunately, friends in Chungking and Hong Kong[5] were hard at work getting in touch with responsible officials and vouching for her innocence. Five minutes before she was due to be shot and she had given up all hope, a temporary reprieve arrived, ordering her to be held "pending investigations." This enabled her friends to collect the evidence necessary to prove her innocence, and after a total of six months in prison she was released.

She can look back now and smile at the chain of circumstances which led to her arrest as a "Japanese spy," but she admits that those few minutes before the reprieve arrived were the most nerve-racking she had ever undergone.

Correspondence between China and the United States in the late 1930's was often subject to long delays. On March 31, 1938, in Chungking, Jim received a letter from his parents in reply to one he sent them from Tsingtao in November telling them about meeting Lily. Here is the reply to their letter (sent from New York in late January), which was critical of the relationship and his and Lily's future plans.

WE ARE TOO FAR APART for any real discussion of an issue. I raise a question late in November, and receive your reaction with April practically in the sky. I must say that it was not at all necessary for you to give reasons and arguments against a mixed marriage. I know them all, and living in China as I do, where the prejudice is strongest, I'm more deeply aware of them than you could be. I was just anxious to get your impression, and I see that it was that of shock. Not that I blame you in the least. It was quite a bombshell to drop on the folks back home, wasn't it?

Now I'm going to talk straight from the shoulder and ask a favor of you both. The chances now look practically nil that anything will ever come of it. If the prospects should change, I promise faithfully that you will know long in advance. The favor I ask is that we disregard the matter entirely in future letters unless and until I mention it myself, which I very much doubt will happen.

---

5. The author, at this time stationed in Canton, is believed to have flown from Hong Kong back to Chungking in an effort to release Lily.

I hope you will understand my request. You see, you can't possibly grasp from the little you know about it, anything of what we have been through, what we had hoped, and all the ramifications and intricacies of such a situation. I would fail utterly in an attempt to lay the whole thing out, so correspondence on the subject would consist mainly of misunderstandings and unintentional hurts. Please try to believe that I am sincere in trying to do my best and that I believe this request of mine is right.

Brief Chronology
From 1644 to Present

CHING DYNASTY

1644-1912   Fall of Ming Dynasty and beginning of Ching Dynasty (Manchu). Warlike tribes from Manchuria invade China. Native Chinese are forced to wear the queue hairstyle and are forbidden to enter Manchuria until the 18th century.

1699   British East India Company establishes trading post in Canton.

1830-42   The First Opium War. China is defeated by the British and in 1842 is forced to open five treaty ports (Shanghai, Canton, Foochow, Amoy and Ningpo) and lease Hong Kong.

1850   Tai Ping Rebellion, a religious antigovernment movement, causes great havoc until suppressed by the government.

1856-59   The Second Opium War. Further concessions are forced on China by the British and other powers. The extraterritoriality, foreign privileges and free movement of missionaries are greatly resented by the Chinese.

1894-95   The First Sino-Japanese War. Japan wins a decisive victory and gains the island of Taiwan along with other concessions. Foreign powers scramble for more concessions.

1897   Germany occupies Tsingtao and Kiaochou area in Shantung.

1899-1900	United States commercial Open Door policy, stating that there should be equal privileges among nations trading with China and that China's territorial and administrative rights should be respected, was issued to the various powers.
1900	Boxer Rebellion. An anti-Christian, anti-foreign rebellion which was later supported by the Empress Tz'u-hsi. The foreign legations were besieged for eight weeks until a large international force was sent from Tientsin.
1904–05	Russo-Japanese War. Japan and Russia struggle for control of Manchuria. Russia loses and cedes rights to Japan.
1908	The Empress Tz'u-hsi dies, apparently having had the emperor poisoned the day before her death. She names the 3-year-old Pu Yi to succeed her.
1911	A revolution is started by Hupeh army officers.

CHINESE REPUBLIC

1912	The Ching court abdicates and Sun Yat-sen becomes the first President of the Chinese Republic and Chairman of the Nationalist Party.
1913–16	This title is relinquished to the autocratic Yuan Shih-kai, considered the right person to bring unity. Continuing struggle for power among the revolutionaries.
1917	Sun Yat-sen tries to organize a rival government in Canton.
1914–18	World War I. Japan fights on the same side as the allies and gains further privileges in China. Patriotic students protest the Versailles Peace Conference, which gives Japan Germany's rights in Shantung province. There are large-scale riots.

1920   A new revolution led by the Nationalist Party (Kuomintang) and the Communist Party (Kungch'antang).

1921–22   Washington Conference. Nine powers agree to respect China's sovereignty and give her tariff autonomy.

1925   Sun Yat-sen dies and Chiang Kai-shek is made commander of the Nationalist Army.

1927   Chiang reorganizes the party and expels the Communists.

1931   Japan seizes Manchuria and sets up the state of Manchukuo with Pu Yi as the puppet emperor (1934-45).

1934–35   The Long March. The Communists are forced to retreat to an impoverished area in northern Shensi known as Yenan.

1937   A clash between Japanese and Chinese soldiers outside Peking starts a full-scale Sino-Japanese War. Peking, Tientsin and Shanghai are taken. The Rape of Nanking.

1938   The Chinese Government first moves to Hankow (Wuhan) and then Chungking, further up the Yangtze.

WORLD WAR II AND CIVIL WAR

1941   December 7. The Japanese attack Pearl Harbor; the U.S. enters the war. Hong Kong falls on December 25 and free China is virtually blockaded. Supplies have to be brought in by the dangerous "Hump," the air route from Assam in India to Kunming.

1942   Singapore falls. Gen. Joseph Stilwell is sent out as chief of staff to try to check the Japanese advance into Burma but runs into difficulties with Chiang Kai-shek and is replaced by Gen. Albert Wedemeyer.

1944   Communists and Nationalists are poised for civil war. President Roosevelt sends out Patrick Hurley to negotiate.

1945   President Truman sends Gen. George Marshall to try to avert the civil war but without success.

1945–49   Civil war. The Nationalists are defeated and Chiang retreats to Taiwan with his forces to set up his government.

PEOPLE'S REPUBLIC OF CHINA

1949   Mao Zedong establishes the People's Republic of China.

1950–70   Much suffering as Mao launches reforms, including the Great Leap Forward in 1958 and the Cultural Revolution in 1966.

1969–71   U.S. restrictions of trade and travel are eased. China takes over the seat in United Nations held by Taiwan.

1972   President Nixon visits China.

1976   Mao dies.

1977–97   Deng Xiaoping is president of China. Introduces market oriented reforms.

1979   U.S. transfers diplomatic recognition from Taipei to Peking.

1981   Demonstrations in Tiananmen Square; hundreds of people are killed.

1997   Jiang Jemin becomes president. Hong Kong reverts to China.

1998   Presidents Clinton and Jiang Jemin exchange visits.

2003   Hu Jintao becomes president.

Illustration Credits

Front of book:
Title page, *Chinese Doorway*, ca. 1930's, by Bertha Lum. Woodblock print, collection of Beverley M. Thomas; photograph Contents page: *Clouds White, Mountains Blue* by Wu Li, 1668, detail of handscroll. Courtesy of National Palace Museum, Taipei, Taiwan, Republic of China.

Part I
Page 1: Postcard of SS *California*. Page 4: "Entering Havana Harbor," postcard of SS *California*. Page 5: postcard of Havana Cathedral. All from "My Trip Through the Panama Canal" (1932, International Mercantile Marine Company), a brochure given to Panama-Pacific Line passengers: map, page 8; cover of brochure, page 10; photograph of Old Panama ruins, page 11; and photograph of Gaillard Cut, Panama Canal, page 11. Page 9: photograph of Panama Canal by Adia Tenaglia, 2000. Page 21: *Satta Pass, Yui,* from the series *Fifty-three stages on the Tokkaido Highway,* by Ando Hiroshige.

Part II
Page 23: *Nakamura Sen-ya I* by Torii Kiyomasu, gift of James A. Michener, 1988 (20,487), courtesy of Honolulu Academy of Arts. Page 29: *Evening Scene, Saruwaka Street,* from the series *One Hundred Views of Famous Places in Edo,* 1856, courtesy of the Freer Gallery of Art, Smithsonian Institution, Washington, D.C. Pages 39 and 42: end decorations from *Japanese Design Motifs* (Dover Publications, New York, 1972), pages 39 and 49.

Part III
Page 51: *Forbidden City* by Bertha Lum, 1933, collection of University of Oregon Museum of Art; reprinted from *Bertha Lum,* p. 48, by Mary Evans O'Keefe Gravalos and Carol Pulin, from the series *American Printmakers* (Smithsonian Institution Press, 1991). Page 55: postcard of Chien Men, Peking. Page 56: drawing of Peking wall from Grand Hôtel de Pékin brochure, Albert Nachbaur, editor. Page 57: postcard of Legation Quarter, Peking. Page 63: end drawing from *Traditional Chinese Designs,* edited by Stanley Applebaum, Dover Publications, New York, 1987. Page 65: drawing of design for Yale-in-China, 1916, courtesy of Yale-China Archive. Page 66: American Consulate, photograph by Deke Ehr, reprinted from *The Last Colonies: Western Architecture in China's Southern Treaty Ports,* by Tess Johnson and Deke Erh, Old China Hand Press, Hong Kong, 1997. Page 72:Texaco sign from 1930's, courtesy of Texaco.

Part IV
Page 75: *Junks, Weihaiwei,* by Bertha Lum, private collection. 1922; reprinted from *Bertha Lum,* by Gravalos and Pulin, (Smithsonian Institution Press, 1991). Page 79: postcard of Tsingtao Club, 1930's. Page 84: photograph of Tsingtao in 1914, from *Tsingtau, Deutsche Stadt am Gelben Meer, 1897–1914,* compiled by Dieter Linke, Herzberg. Page 86: postcard of Christ Church, Tsingtao, late 1930's, from Japanese occupation. Page 86: drawing from *Traditional Chinese Designs,* edited by Stanley Appelbaum, Dover Publications, 1987. Pages 94 and 95: postcards of Dairen, ca. 1934. Page 104: studio photograph of Lily Lee, ca. 1937, photographer unknown. Page 113: royal insignia, from Coronation of George VI program, 1937. Page 118, USS *Canopus,* National Archives. Page 119: photograph of Edgewater Mansions, by Deke Ehr, reprinted from *Far From Home: Western Architecture in China's Northern Treaty Ports*, by Tess Johnston and Deke Ehr, Old China Hand Press, 1996. Page 134: press photograph of bombing outside Cathay Hotel, Shanghai, 1937. Page 134: *Idzumo,* off the Bund, courtesy of Peter Kengelbacher. Page 138: press photograph of *Augusta, 1937.* Page 140: press photograph of Sincere Department Store bombing, 1937. Page 144: USS *Marblehead,* from Web site *United States Navy Yangze Patrol and South China Patrol*, prepared by Philip R. Abbey, 1999-2000. Page 146: press photograph of Chapei burning, 1937. Page 153: press photograph of Japanese soldiers. Page 157, USS *Panay,* from Web site, *U.S. Navy Yangtze Patrol.* Page 166: headline from the *New York Times,* Jan. 11, 1938, reprinted with permission from the *New York Times.* Page 167: Japanese marines, Tsingtao, 1938, Nohara, from the magazine *Die Woche,* March, Berlin, 1938. Page 174: postcard of Park Hotel, 1930's. Page 177: *Junks, Hong Kong Harbor,* 1952, by Werner Bischof/Magnum Photos. Page 181: 1930's poster of DC-3's of the C.N.A.C. from San Diego Aerospace Museum.

PART V
Page 183: *Bamboo,* detail, by Wu Chen, ca. 1350. Courtesy of National Palace Museum, Taipei, Republic of China.

PART VI
Page 223: Dr. Sun Yat-sen Memorial, from 1920's Canton brochure, China Travel Service. Page 232: USS *Mindanao,* from Web site, *U.S. Navy Yangtze Patrol.* Page 242: Postcard of Majestic Hotel, Saigon, 1930's. Page 243: Postcard of Eastern & Oriental Hotel, Penang, 1930's. Page 244: Illustration from Grand Hôtel de Pékin brochure, 1930's.

APPENDIX
Page 250: *Conte di Savoia,* from Internet, *Mike Starborg's Ocean Liner Page.*

Japan color insert
Plate I: *Mount Fuji and Lake Shoji;* by Suzo Mitsui/Pacific Press Service. Plate II: *Imperial Palace,* Tokyo, by Steve Vidler/Pacific Press Service. Plate III: Imperial Hotel, courtesy of Imperial Hotel, Tokyo, Japan. Plate IV: *Iris Garden,* Heian-Jingu Shrine, Kyoto; by Shigenobu Hayashi/Pacific Press Service.

China color inserts
Plate V: *Summer Palace,* by Jiang Chao/Imaginechina. Plate VI: *Great Wall,* by Li Shaobai/Imaginechina. Plate VII, Edgewater Mansions Hotel, Tsingtao, late 1930's hand-colored photograph from Japanese occupation. Plate VIII: *Qutang Gorge,* courtesy of the National Tourism Administration of the People's Republic of China, New York. Plate IX: Hong Kong Harbor from Victoria Peak, courtesy of Information Services, Department of the Hong Kong Special Administrative Region Government. Plate X: View of Shameen from English Bridge, circa 1947, Canton, photograph by G.H. Thomas; hand-colored 2003.

On the Calligrapher

Charles Lu is a computer scientist at Yale University. Mr. Lu, who was born and grew up in China, began to learn Chinese calligraphy when he was 9. He continues to practice as a hobby.

Pinyin Equivalents

Amoy	Xiamen	Mukden	Shenyang
Anhwei	Anhui		
		Nanking	Nanjing
Canton	Guangzhou		
Changtien	Changdian	Pakhoi	Beihai
Chefoo	Yantai	Peitaiho	Beidaihe
Chengtu	Chengdu	Peking, Peiping	Beijing
Chowtsun	Zhoucun	Poshan	Boshan
Chungking	Chongqing		
		Shameen	Shamian
Dairen	Dalian	Shansi	Shanxi
Fukien	Fujian	Shantung	Shandong
		Shensi	Shaanxi
Haichow	Haizhou	Shikiuso	Shijiusuo
Hankow	(now part of	Shitao	Shidao
	Wuhan)	Soochow	Suzhou
Honan	Henan	Swatow	Shantou
Hopeh	Hebei	Szechwan	Sichuan
Hsuchow	Xuzhou		
		Taku	Dagu
Ichang	Yichang	Tangku	Tanggu
		Tehchow	Dezhou
Kalgan	Zhangjiakou	Tientsin	Tianjin
Kialing Kiang	Jialing Jiang	Tsangchow	Cangzhou
Kiangsi	Jiangxi	Tsinan	Jinan
Kiangsu	Jiangsu	Tsingtao	Qingdao
Kiaochow	Jiaozhou	Tsimo	Jimo
Kueiyang	Guiyang		
Kwangsi	Guangxi	Wanhsien	Wanxian
Kwangtung	Guangdong	Weihaiwei	Weihai
Kweichow	Guizhou	Weihsien	Weixian
Kweilin	Guilin	Wuchow	Wuzhou
Lienyunkang	Lianyungang	Yangtze Kiang	Chiang Jiang

INDEX

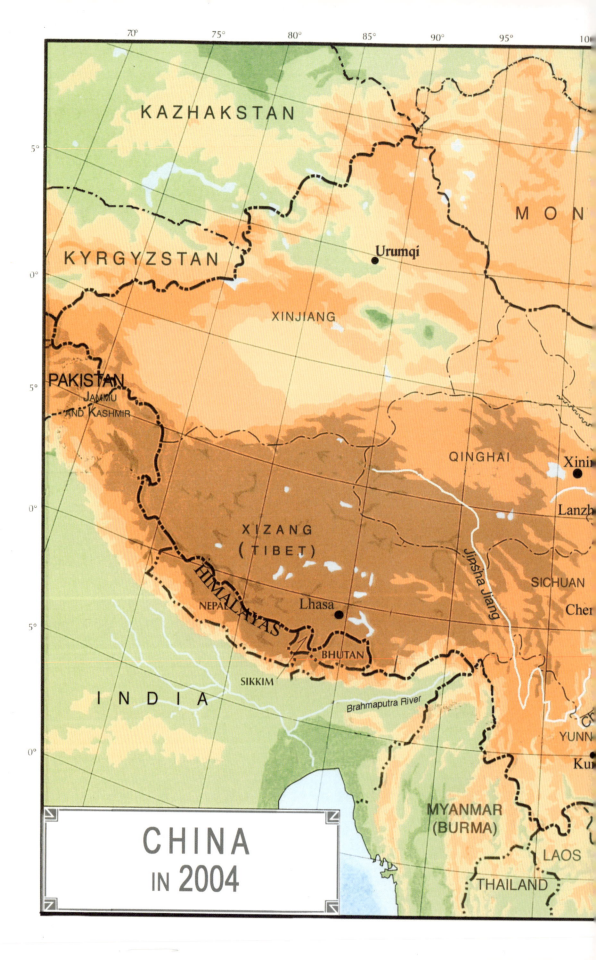

CHINA

IN 2004